Patricia Godwin-Dunleavy

LANDSCAPE LESSONS

*A Practical and Inspirational Primer
for the Southern Soil and Soul*

Patricia Godwin Dunleavy

TerraType Press, LLC
Ila, Georgia, USA

Published by
TerraType Press, LLC
Post Office Box 390
Ila, GA 30647
www.TerraTypePress.com

Printed in the United States
ISBN 978-0-9823801-0-9

Cover Design and Graphics: Catherine A. Dunleavy
Book Design and Production: Patricia G. Dunleavy

To obtain copies, visit your local bookstore or Pinebush Farm and
Nurseries, Inc. (www.PinebushNursery.com). Or buy direct from
the publisher by visiting www.TerraTypePress.com for ordering
information. Quantity discounts available.

FOR MY MOTHER, SARA MOAK GODWIN
AND TO THE MEMORY OF MY FATHER, JOHN T. GODWIN, MD

WITH GRATITUDE FOR PROVIDING ME
THE FOUNDATION FOR MY LANDSCAPE

We are the children of our landscape . . .

—*Lawrence George Durrell*
(1912–1990)

TABLE OF CONTENTS

SPRING • 169

ILLUSTRATIONS

PHOTOGRAPHS

Photographs *(continued)*

Tables

PREFACE

My journey to this publication finds its conception in 1981 when my husband, John, and I started a nursery without specifically intending to. We had recently been inspired to grow Christmas trees while at a fair in Massachusetts. At the same time, we had decided to move south. We ended up obtaining a portion of a farm that my family had owned since 1957 in Walton County, Georgia. And, in our naiveté, we planted Virginia pines that we planned to cultivate as Christmas trees. But we quickly realized that we weren't going to have the handsome holiday trees that grow in the cooler climates. So John, who was working part time with a nursery and landscaping company, started bringing home trees, shrubs, and perennials that were a "good deal," and he set up some overhead irrigation for them. One thing led to another, and before long our twenty-by-twenty-foot plot of container plants grew tenfold and more, and our field of pines branched into fields of shade and ornamental trees and shrubs. Within a few years we expanded to a second farm, and today Pinebush Farm and Nurseries has seventy-five acres of containerized and field-grown stock in Madison County, Georgia, near Ila.

Over the years, our customers, friends, and casual acquaintances have sought advice and insight on various plants and ornamental horticultural techniques, and we've found that the same questions arise over and over again. The vast majority of queries are quite basic: How do I plant a tree or shrub? How often do I water? What's that tree I'm seeing in bloom right now—you know the one with big, round white flowers? When do I prune my crapemyrtles? Why won't my Leyland cypress, which is planted in the woods, grow?

To address some of these questions and to educate folks, I first started writing about many of these issues in *The Leaflet*, a seasonal publication I have produced since 1994 for our customers, both real and potential. In the latter part of the 1990s, I expanded my audience by writing a weekly gardening column I called "Landscape Lessons" for a local newspaper. Then I got the notion to write a book incorporating many of the subjects I had already written about, as well as many more.

I started writing the book ten years ago, and it has evolved in fits and spurts with many dormant years interrupting its course. But its evolution has complemented its messages, I believe, and has, in fact, helped me define and refine its themes as I too have evolved. And, as has been its character in gestation, the book changed dramatically at the very end with the addition of pictures. That augmentation gave me a completely new avenue for conveying to you one of the themes of the book: the influence of my Southern heritage, family, and upbringing on my landscape. It also gave me more opportunity to give you a better glimpse at the workings of a nursery, another component of my landscape and an interesting element to an understanding of the world of ornamental horticulture.

So with that brief explanation of the genesis of this book, I would like to start by thanking all of the horticulture professionals who I have come to know throughout the years. In one fashion or another, they have all contributed to this book. What a wonderful group of folks to be associated with. I especially give thanks to the horticultural gurus at the University of Georgia as well as those in the Cooperative Extension Service who provide so much information to and work closely with the green industry.

One such professional who deserves special thanks is Paul A. Thomas, Professor of Floriculture at the University of Georgia, for his kind remarks and suggestions on a manuscript I was determined was complete at last. It was at his behest that I added pictures—and for that I am truly grateful. My gratitude also goes out to all those who have encouraged me in my endeavor at some point or other through the years, most particularly Mike Sikes, Ann Cabaniss, and Susan Russell. And loving thanks to Melanie

Howington for graciously listening to my moans for well over a year and reminding me that I was engaged in an activity that is most enjoyable to me, that failure to finish would not be acceptable to me, and that bumps in the road cannot stop the journey but only make it more interesting.

As is often the case with any enterprise, a single person or core group lends support, encouragement, and love that keeps the fires alive in times of despair or failure. In my case, that would be my husband, John, and children, James and Cat. They have endured me talking about "my book" for ten long years. When I have been totally absorbed with the project, they have understood, and their patience with me and silent show of faith has been enough to keep me moving, ultimately, to completion. Thank you for that and for the wonderful times we have had over the years that are portrayed in small part here.

I give special thanks to Cat for her participation in the production of this book. I cherish her opinions about design and appreciate her taking the time to look at a page layout, or two, or ten (and for accepting my creative and space limitations in that department and my need to just move on). I also thank her for working with me at the last minute, and on a holiday, to improve the quality of many of the photographs. But I most proudly thank her for her design of the book cover, with its Tree of Four Seasons, as well as the season graphics, which she has generously created while carrying a demanding course load in college this semester. Not only do I admire her artistic talent, I am also grateful for her perfectionist ways and concern for my satisfaction with the product. Awesome, girl!

Finally, but certainly not least, I thank John. This book would not have been possible without his help. In fact, it would not have been possible had he not, over the years, been consistent and persistent in developing and maintaining the nursery and our life on the farms. For without those elements, this story would not be. But most importantly, without his teaching me, answering my questions, and reviewing my manuscript, I would have been lost in many of the details.

I close by mentioning all the other characters in my story, whether specifically identified or not, who have been a part of my life, thus contributing to my landscape. Most particularly, there are my parents and grandparents, whose influences—on me, the lessons I have learned, some of the paths I have taken, and the quality of my landscape—are palpable. My thanks to them especially for their insistence on a good education and work ethic and for opportunities that have brought me to this point. Thanks to them for contributing to my landscape.

Notwithstanding the assistance I have received from those mentioned here and others, I do not always heed advice given, nor do I always get things right, despite direction given. Therefore, I take sole responsibility for any misstatements and mistakes herein and beg forgiveness of anyone offended thereby.

Patricia Godwin Dunleavy
Ila, Georgia • April, 2009

INTRODUCTION

THIS BOOK IS A PRIMER on how to know, manage, and manipulate your physical landscape and the materials that make it, while paying attention to your spiritual one. The two are inseparable, each affecting the other. It is a practical and inspirational guide with ecological ramblings, infusions of Southern culture, glimpses into life and work at a nursery, and reminiscences of growing up in the landscape that shaped me. It is, in fact, a book of lessons that reach beyond the horticultural landscape and into the soulful one, using my landscape—the one deeply rooted in family, the South, and a nursery business—for reflection. It seeks to encourage a holistic approach to gardening.

It's been ten years since I wrote the first draft of this book, which I completed, I thought, in 2002. Then matters intervened and it lay dormant for four years. When I resurrected it, I realized how much had changed in that short time. There were new cultivars, new taxonomy, better favorites, new ideas, better information, more information, more issues needing attention—and a writer with four more years of growth, change, experience, and input from reading, asking, listening, and observing. *My* climate had changed a bit, and I had to adjust accordingly.

Then the book lay dormant again for two years with another flurry of activity in 2006 and yet another rest until 2008. During each suspension, change continued rapidly, forcing me upon resurrection to update some subjects and reevaluate my opinion on others. So the book evolved, reflecting its landscape and its new relationship to the events of my life—and the rapidity of change in our environment, attitudes, and horticulture. Despite all of the change, our customers' and acquaintances' questions, misconceptions, and misunderstandings remain essentially the same. So I proceed with my attempt to help you learn and understand the essentials of ones landscape while peeking at mine.

First, I'd like to acknowledge that I know just how overwhelming it can be to try to understand all there is to know about plants—to learn their names and place in the landscape, their proper care, and the myriad other issues we face as gardeners. When I became certified as a Master Gardener many years back, I thought the process would solidify my horticultural knowledge. It did not. The more I learned, the more I was aware of how little I knew. I certainly can't identify every plant I see. And I am the world's worst with the names of those I've rattled off umpteen times before—memory lapses I've more recently been able to justify as senior moments. But I know that I don't have to retain all of this information. I just need the general idea so I can formulate my questions and seek resources for reference.

With that concept in mind, and knowing that many folks of different persuasions seek the same information, I have written this book for several people: the novice gardener; the new home- and yardowner; the gardener transplanted to the South; the seasoned gardener who just can't get enough; the environmentalist who is looking for yet another approach to understanding, explaining, or considering our place in this landscape we call Earth; and anyone who is searching for greater meaning—trying to fill the void created by a lost connection to the natural world.

For all readers, this book is a journey toward an understanding of some basics about the manipulation of your landscape. For that's what you do in your yard or garden—you change and ornament the natural landscape to suit your needs and desires. That understanding involves an appreciation for the value of your landscape to your soul (your interior landscape) and your soul's influence upon your physical landscape (the one you exhibit to others)? In fact, it's this synchronous relationship that compels me to write this practical book with spiritual overtones and ecological threads weaving throughout, urging you to use your surroundings as classroom and cathedral—meant to teach and inspire.

With these dual purposes—practical and inspirational—this book is arranged into fifty-two weekly lessons, starting with the week of the autumnal equinox, the fourth week of September. I begin the yearlong journey at this juncture since I believe it is the true time of beginning—the time when life is engulfed in the process of death for the purpose of renewed life. It is a starting point, of sorts, in the never-ending cyclical state of nature in which we find ourselves.

The lessons—on issues such as plant selection, planting and pruning techniques, soil conditioning, bed preparation, activity timings, creative gardening, and so forth—are tuned and timed to the rhythms of the Northeast Georgia area of the Southern Piedmont region, which is in USDA Plant Hardiness Zone 7. And, because I am unable to separate my discussions of the horticulture from my upbringing and experiences—*my* landscape—they are seasoned with the flavorings of my Southern childhood and heritage as well as my life at the nursery with my family. But no matter where *you* are, where you're from, or your background or experiences, you can extrapolate from these lessons, using them to understand the landscape in your area. You can change the timing of your gardening activities from those presented here to coincide with your climate, or alter your plant selection to similar, but more suitable plants for your gardening zone.

Although the reasons for the placement of particular lessons during certain weeks is this timing with the rhythms of nature, be aware that the pendulum is not swinging smoothly these days, and the clock strikes at odd times. Daffodils, forsythia, Japanese magnolias, star magnolias, and cherry trees blooming during January have been an burgeoning spectacle over the past ten years. I have seen many supposed-to-be spring-flowering azaleas blooming in early December. And I've nervously enjoyed the sight of oakleaf hydrangeas, crapemyrtles, and a host of typically summer-flowering perennials blooming in mid-May. It's a scary but increasingly common phenomenon we're experiencing as our climate and the behavior of our plants are changing. Whether this portends a long-term or short-term shift of nature remains to be seen. But scientists, so we are told, seem to have reached a consensus that we are in fact experiencing "global warming," although not all agree on the causes, and that we are on a path leading us to uncomfortable and, perhaps, frightening consequences. Despite this unsettling situation, I've timed the lessons in this book according to what is still considered the normal rhythm of nature in this Piedmont area. Just be aware that that timing may be off by a little or a lot in any given year.

In discussing various plants, I have stuck primarily with the basics, at the risk of perpetuating the tendency toward sameness in our landscape in the midst of limitless chances for diversity. There have been far too many plant introductions over the past several years—seemingly exponentially—to attempt much discussion beyond the bread and butter. My goal, then, is not to give you a treatise on all, or even the best varieties as there are numerous books serving that purpose. Rather, I want simply to make you aware that there are many choices of plants that can serve you and your landscape needs in many different ways.

Similarly, my goal is not to detail how to accomplish various landscaping tasks, whether it be laying a path or picking a color scheme for a perennial bed. Rather, I want simply to make you aware of the choices and possibilities. I want to lay the foundation that enables you to ask the right questions and seek out more, detailed information from nursery professionals, Cooperative Extension agents, other books, magazines, the Internet, and any of the numerous resources available. I'm interested in helping you to enjoy what I hope to be a refreshing approach to ornamental landscaping inspired by the plants themselves, your natural surroundings, and your authentic tastes—with a soulful foundation. And I'm interested in making it possible for you to enjoy a lifelong evolution with your *entire* landscape—within as well as without.

So follow me through the seasons for a spattering of this and a smidgen of that. Since each lesson stands alone, you can start at any point during the year. Several of the first lessons in the fall touch upon some of the most essential facts about and ingredients to your landscape—botany, soil preparation, and bed preparation. Learn those lessons well and the rest will be immensely more fun and profitable in the undertaking. Throughout the remainder of the year the lessons evoke more creative and soulful relationships with your surroundings as you are instructed more specifically about the plants themselves and artistry in the landscape.

Because I have written this book to be read a week at a time over the course of a year, in some instances I have repeated information or provided a reminder of what or who something is. If you do in fact take just a small interval of time each week and read the lesson for that week, perhaps in a year's time you will learn enough to give you the foundation you need to have the landscape you want. Perhaps you will gain a glimmer of and a feel for the simplicity in nature that appears so complex and sense its order, rhythm, and rhyme. Perhaps those of you who are new to the South will gain a sense of some of our culture—an ingredient in creating our landscapes. And perhaps you will come to love our landscape as much as I do, if you don't already, without judging your skill in manipulating it.

For what a glorious home we have, this Earth, and what a magnificent opportunity we have to make it even greater. With some creative thought, loving work, and a bit of knowledge, you can enhance your landscape.

Joyful journey to you!

This is my family; they are critical elements to my landscape. You will hear quite a bit about them in this book. John is our cook (and has kept me well fed during the busiest and most trying times of this trek of mine). From left to right: James, me, John, and Cat. Christmas holidays, 2008, at our home, with the extended family joining, as is tradition.

AUTUMN

As THE DAYS GROW SHORTER and the shadows longer, I walk through the woods and envelop myself with the excitement of life. My lungs swell with pleasure as I inhale the sweetness of wild muscadines strewn about. My eyes twinkle in time with the twittering leaves, flipped and tossed about by the breeze, their stems barely clinging to the rapidly denuding trees. My arms flinch with the stickiness of a spider web in harm's way. My ankle winces with the brush of a yawning yellow jacket. My ears pulse with the crackling of fallen leaves beneath my feet, the caws of crows perched overhead, the incessant shrill of crickets and grasshoppers, the occasional punctuation of the saw of a katydid. My nose tickles with the fragrant bouquet of the decaying bounty drifting through the crisp, dry air. And I smile.

I rejoice with the fate of those leaves—their vitality will renew the soil. I sing with the songs of those insects—their fruitful summer anticipates next spring. I soar with the flights of those birds—their journeys find new horizons.

Autumn—the beginning, the middle, and the beginning again of life.

LESSON 1 ⤳ September 17–23
The Autumnal Equinox

The sky is round, and I have heard that the earth is round like a ball, and
so are all the stars. The wind, in its greatest power, whirls. Birds make their
nests in circles, for theirs is the same religion as ours. . . . Even
the seasons form a great circle in their changing, and always come back
again to where they were.

—Black Elk (1863–1950)
Oglala Lakota Sioux Holy Man

The Circle of Life Uninterrupted

EACH YEAR THE SUN GLIDES across the equator during the fourth week of September, making its illusory journey from the lands of the midnight sun, through the lands of cruises and winter vacations, to the lands down under. As it edges over our southern horizon, the torturous summer heat wanes. The sky sharpens. The sunlight sparkles. Sunrise and sunset ignite the freshened air. And the stars twinkle, once again.

This autumnal equinox is the calendar call for fall—dew-fed, misty mornings erased by crystal-blue skies and billowing white clouds, cool breezes, and dramatically changing landscapes. In my estimation, it's the most glorious season of the year. It's a season of maturity and incipient decay. It's a time of color, and of darkening; of activity, and of retirement; of death, and of renewal. It's harvest time—a time to gather the fruits of our labors. And it's commencement time—a time to assess, regroup, renew, and leap forward with new activities.

There's much to do in the landscape during the fall months. Harvesting fruits, vegetables, and flowers immediately comes to mind, as does preparation for protection from winter's impending cold to assure the continuation of life. Preparing for the renewal of life also demands our attention. Fall is the time to plant spring-flowering bulbs, cool-season annuals, trees, shrubs, and perennials; it is, in fact, the best time to plant in the Southeast. It's also the time to prepare beds, nourish soils, and encourage composts with the rot of spent flora. Fall is an arc in the perpetual circle of life, an interval in its continuum.

In your role as planter, caretaker, and sometimes harvester of your landscape plants, a bit of knowledge about plant structure, growth, and life will serve you well in your quest for earthly paradise. Although perhaps a bit simplistic for some of you, the following basic explanation of plant growth in relation to the supporting environment is essential to an understanding of the interrelatedness of plants to all of nature. And, if you understand plants in their context, you will be better equipped to work your landscape with positive rather than negative impact on them and the environment. You and your landscape will be healthier and happier as a result. So here's a little Botany 101.

IT'S A MATTER OF FACT

United States Department of Agriculture (USDA) hardiness zones progress in ten-degree increments (with five-degree subdivisions denoted "a" and "b") and indicate the lowest temperatures a plant will tolerate. Zone numbers go up as temperatures go up. Zone 1, for example, has the lowest temperatures at less than -50°F. The lowest temperatures in Zone 11 are more than 40°F. Perhaps more important than these absolute temperature tolerances is a plant's ability to acclimate or develop cold hardiness early in the fall to survive early freezes and to maintain cold hardiness until the late-spring freezes end.

Plants are the most self-sufficient living organisms on Earth. In fact, they are said to be autotrophic, which means self-nourishment. They manufacture their own food from the earth, air, and water, and the sun is the fuel that starts the photosynthetic process that results in the formation of sugars, which equate to energy. That energy, stored in the plants' cells, becomes the fuel for their own growth as well as for other organisms like cows and human beings that eat plants and their fruits. As Brian Capon says in his book *Botany for Gardeners*, "Autotrophic plants hold the key to life on Earth; they alone are the intermediaries between the sun and all other creatures."

So how do plants manufacture food and grow? Essentially, they use sun, air, soil, water, and a variety of chemical elements, using the following described sources and processes. The basis for plant sustenance, **soil**, provides support, water, and nutrients. It receives water and oxygen from the air to support soil organisms and plant roots. The soil's texture (compact or loose), water-holding capacity or porousness, ability to release needed nutrients to a plant, and population of beneficial soil organisms (primarily bacteria) help determine the health of a plant.

Roots are the conveyors of water and nutrients for a plant's nourishment. Hairs at the root tips draw water (through the process of osmosis wherein the water molecules are seeking equalization of concentration within and outside the root cells) and nutrients from the soil while larger main roots transport the food and, in some instances, act as storage bins for winter survival. The large roots also hold a plant upright so it doesn't fall to gravity or yield to the wind. Root pressure pushes water and soluble nutritional minerals (xylem sap) up from the roots to the stems and leaves, but needs their assistance in plants that are too large for the force of root pressure alone to move the nutrients throughout.

So **stems** of a plant also act as conveyors, and anchors. They pull water and nutrients from the roots and transport them to the leaves. They also support the leaves and flowers, keeping these appendages from drooping and breaking off of their umbilical cord to Mother Earth.

Similarly, the **leaves** of a plant use transpirational pull, another osmotic process, to get their necessary nutrients. It is in the leaves, by use of their chlorophyll, that photosynthesis takes place. They capture the sun's light and use that energy to remove hydrogen from the water in the plant and carbon dioxide from the air. When the atoms of these two elements combine, sugar is made, to serve as the food for growth and survival. Leaves are the factories that manufacture life itself.

A plant's carbon dioxide intake and oxygen exhalation is through its leaf pores, or stomata. The result of the gaseous exchange is the circular, symbiotic relationship between plants and animals whereby we animals breathe in the oxygen given by the plants, and they breathe in the carbon dioxide given by us. A similar circular motion of water occurs through leaves by transpiration, like our perspiration. The amount of water evaporated from the leaves depends upon the plant's size, as well as environmental factors such as temperature, humidity, wind speed, and light intensity.

Transpiration through leaves is just one segment in a water cycle that functions uninterruptedly through Earth's systems, because water molecules move in unbroken chains. When each molecule of water that evaporates from a leaf goes into the air, it is replaced with water from below by transpirational pull. And as those water molecules are pulled from the roots, the roots absorb more water from the soil by osmosis. That water from the soil is replaced with water from the air—rain, snow, and other forms of precipitation. And that water from the air comes from evaporation of waters on the Earth as well as water transpired from plants, through their leaves, as well as their stems, flowers, and roots, in some instances. It's an eternal cycle, one that functions because of the constant demand for equalization between all elements.

The interrelatedness of plants and animals involves more than just their sharing of air and water. Animals eat plants for nourishment. They also leave their waste on the ground to decay, nourish the soil, and provide nutrients for more plants to grow. Furthermore, with the help of microorganisms, plant waste that falls to the ground decomposes to become compost that serves as a bed for seedlings to sprout in. The new plants become food for animals, which provide waste that nourishes the soil in which new plants grow, and so on—another unbroken chain.

A segment of this grand circle of life includes the reproduction of plants. Animals eat and transport plant seeds, the wind blows them, and gravity pulls them down. Some seeds then receive protection from the mulch of other plant waste and nourishment for growth from the compost. Earth's nursery awaits new life.

And so, you see, a plant takes from the Earth, and gives back to it the very elements it consumed or converted. It does not create waste; it only creates energy and matter for further growth. A plant is positioned in the circle of life like all others, interrelated and interdependent. There is no better time than fall to witness this life as it really is—eternal, like the circle itself.

Surrounded by annuals that will still be blooming in early fall, John and I pose for an advertising piece in the spring of 1996.

ARE YOU IN THE ZONE?

WHEN SELECTING THE PLANTS you plan to plant this fall, pay attention to the likelihood of their surviving where you live, both because of their cold hardiness *and* their ability to withstand heat, humidity, and moisture. This book is written from my perspective in the Athens, Georgia, area, which is in USDA Zone 7 and the Southern Piedmont. More specifically, my area is in what some people call the Middle South and others call Zone 7b. But I am only a one-hour drive from Zone 8 in the Lower South and less than two hours from portions of Zone 6 in the Upper South. According to the USDA, the average annual minimum temperature here is 5–10°F (based on the lowest temperatures recorded in the years 1974 to 1986.) The blue spruces I see and love that grow healthily within a short distance north of my home will not survive here. My fatsia and pittosporum, which I see frequently to the south of

Macon, are touchy—at least they were until things started warming up. Tropical plants won't survive my winters. But my azaleas burst with blooms, and crapemyrtles thrive.

The first and most obvious thing you can do to determine survivability is check for the recommended planting zones for the plants you want. Nursery tags often provide this information; so do nursery catalogs. Gardening books and the Web are other good sources. Realize, however, that the "hardiness" referred to often relates only to cold hardiness. A plant that is marked for Zone 5 will survive the typical winters in Zone 5 as well as those in Zones 6, 7, etc.; however, it may not survive the heat and humidity of a Southern Zone 7 summer. So, in addition to checking the hardiness zones for plants, inquire also about their heat tolerance.

Even if your zone *should* be suitable for a particular plant according to the information you've gathered, your specific microclimate might not be. Prevailing winds, sun exposure, soil pH, elevation, humidity, proximity to water, and topography are all factors that can affect a plant's survival. So if you are close to a large body of water, high on a hill, low in a valley, or exposed to heavy winds, some plants otherwise suitable to your planting zone may be unable to handle these environments.

Reading, asking, and sharing information with other gardeners can help you determine whether a particular plant is likely to survive in your landscape. Sometimes trial and error is the only way to find out what works and what doesn't. But if your chosen plant just wasn't meant for your area, don't fret. You will most likely be able to come up with a similar alternative by sorting through the many new cultivars that are being produced specifically to suit different regions. If you can't find a closely related alternative, well—not all plants were meant for all places on this Earth. You can't force something that wasn't meant to be.

A footnote: When I first started writing this book in the late 1990s, there was a great deal of argument about the reality of global warming. In the intervening years, that phenomenon has taken on new meaning as evidence of its effects has rapidly progressed to the point of alarm and common parlance, and experts for the most part now agree that global warming does in fact exist. Many experts and laypeople choose to call the trend climate change, perhaps a more accurate moniker for the new temperature averages and consequent weather events. Either way, I have never doubted the relentless course toward an altered environment since I have witnessed changes in plant behavior and survival and have noted that the average annual minimum temperatures of 1974–1986 officially used by the USDA are quite different from the temperatures of recent years. I am curious how long or short it will be before we see a shift in the demarcation lines of the official plant zones.

My willingness to try a fatsia in the corner of my patio garden lies in my awareness that we are not nearly as likely to have a killing winter now as we were when I was a child growing up in North Georgia. Although I was prepared for my fatsia's doom during its first several winters, I no longer anticipate a corner vacancy come spring. In fact, I'm becoming anxious about its overgrown state and, in a perverse way, wish for a killing winter—I'll regain some control over the relentlessly growing giant; I'll be given a sign, or renewed hope, that all is not completely out of whack with our environment; and I'll be thankful for a proper discipline of the insect population.

It's always worth trying marginal plants; you never know how long they may last—perhaps for your lifetime, if the climate change continues on its course.

This fatsia is tucked in a corner of our patio against the house for protection from weather extremes. The flower globes remain for quite some time, adding interest against the huge leaves in the winter months.

LESSON 2 ✎ September 24–30
Fall Flowers

Earth laughs in flowers.

—Ralph Waldo Emerson
Hamatreya

Fall Is Full of Flowers

AS THE AIR COOLS AND THINS, the morning dews form, and the atmosphere promises change in the offing, I look forward to the reinvigoration fall always brings. My thoughts turn to new beginnings, and my mind-set is colored with golds, rusts, oranges, and yellows. My reprobate sentiment for summer's end—with its horrid heat and flourishing flora, engrossing to the point of exhaustion—takes over.

But I have to remind myself, year after year, that the early-fall transition does not herald the end of flowers. Rather, fall is full of flowers. They come in all colors, shapes, and sizes and in all forms—trees, shrubs, perennials, annuals, and vines. Some extend the highlights of summer, some shyly suggest the coming of winter, and some are fall, pure and simple.

Many annuals (plants with life spans of one year or one season) are summer saviors, preserving that season into this one. Zinnias, for instance, bloom until frost in our area; they come in all colors except blue. To insure **zinnias** in the fall garden, do a second planting in late summer, and to increase blooming, deadhead the flowers (that is, pinch off faded flowers to prevent seed production and promote reblooming). Better yet, plant some of the improved Star series Mexican zinnias (*Zinnia angustifolia* 'Star Orange', for example) that persist until frost, do not require deadheading, are drought tolerant, and are resistant to mildew and bacterial leaf spot.

Other annuals that are summer stretchers include petunias, begonias, marigolds, and lantanas. By this time of year, **petunias** (*Petunia × hybrida*), particularly the newer Wave® varieties, should have grown into large mounds with their masses of color—whether the lighter pinks and whites or darker purples—adding tremendous effect to the traditional fall colors. All of the Wave® petunias are spreading, but some grow taller (the Tidal Wave® group) and some have double flowers (the Double Wave® group).

Many **begonias** appear bedraggled as summer dwindles, but dragon wing begonia (*Begonia × hybrida* 'Dragon Wing') persists beautifully until frost; then you can cut it back, pot it up, and enjoy it indoors all winter. And **marigolds** are good ole standbys with their yellows and golds, creating a tremendous amount of color, especially when colors and sizes are mixed and massed together.

Lantanas lend perkiness to the landscape; there are several varieties, some of which can be overwintered by using a straw or light mulch covering. 'New Gold' is vibrant and, because butterflies love it, attracts even more color to the fall landscape. Another lantana, 'Miss Huff', is particularly interesting with its spots of varying, bright colors and has served well as a perennial in Zone 7 since it is hardy enough for the winters. And watch for the newly introduced 'Chapel Hill Yellow' that has lovely, calming, medium-yellow flowers and leathery, dark green foliage.

There are numerous cultivars of all of these annuals, with varying habits and colors. Mix and match for the most interest, and add perennials. To start, there's **sedum**, or stonecrop, a remarkable succulent that bears large heads of tiny flowers in late summer and fall. *Sedum × 'Autumn Joy'* and *S. spectabile* 'Brilliant' are particularly pretty varieties with their purplish heads that are decorated with visiting bees and butterflies galore. They make terrific dried flowers for your inside pleasure as the chilly air nudges you there. John and I have always used a blue ceramic vase, which he made, just for our dried sedum; its wide body and narrow top are perfect for holding one tall stem, which we enjoy for months. There are numerous sedums, some upright like those mentioned above, and some low growing; most need full sun.

The list of fall-flowering perennials (herbaceous plants that live for more than two years) is long. The popular **purple coneflower**

(*Echinacea purpurea*), has large seed heads that poke into the air, skirted by the nearly bright purple, daisy-like petals. They complement the still-flowering butterfly bushes, particularly the white varieties. Another group of perennials, *Asters*, come in white, pink, blue, and purple and look very similar to mums.

One of my most favorite fall bloomers is **swamp sunflower** (*Helianthus angustifolius*), a 4- to 7-foot-tall, rapidly growing perennial with relatively small, 2-inch-wide, profusely blooming, bright yellow flowers. The 1-inch-wide, deep green leaves run the entire length of the stems. The new cultivar *H. salicifolius* 'First Light' grows to a more manageable height (up to 4 feet) and has an even greater profusion of flowers. These sunflowers, like their cousins in the *Helianthus* genus that is composed of sixty-seven species, have inspired countless artists with their complement to the deepest fall-blue sky.

In addition to the herbaceous fall-flowering perennials, there are many woody ornamentals that display as the days cool. **Autumnalis cherry** (*Prunus subhirtella* 'Autumnalis') is a 25-foot-tall and 25-foot-wide tree that bears semi-double pink flowers in spring and fall (and now in our global-warming winters). And **sweet autumn clematis** (*Clematis ternifolia*), a vigorously growing vine that blooms in clouds of star-shaped white flowers in fall, has a deliciously sweet vanilla aroma, but it will take over, reseed, and continue to invade relentlessly. So beware, and see Lesson 38; or at least prune it back severely in early spring.

Reblooming azaleas (like the Bloom 'N Again® varieties), **continuous-blooming hydrangeas** (such as the Endless Summer® collection), and **roses** (like the Knock Out® varieties) also add color to the fading fall landscape. And Heaven Scent™ **gardenia**, with its tight growth habit, dark green foliage, and single white flowers, reblooms from April until frost, lending incredible color *and* fragrance to the fall landscape.

I don't quite know how I feel about all of these reblooming plants that merge the seasons and dull the lines of distinction. But I do know that I often cringe at the colors of spring and summer in fall. Perhaps I'm stuck in a mindset created by the literature of my youth that portrayed fall in the New England sense—gold, orange, yellow, red, russet, and brown—failing to speak of the Southern season. Or perhaps I just can't get used to all of the new color being introduced into our fall landscapes because we did not have it for so very long, and it doesn't yet compute for me. I do have to say: I am becoming more accustomed to the ever-presence of color and am becoming more appreciative of the spice it maintains in the darkening, cool days. But, again, I question whether we really need to have all that splash when, in my way of thinking, it tends to overshadow the traditional beauty of the changing landscape. I don't yet know; my jury is still deliberating the issue.

While I continue to ponder those newcomers, let me tell you a story. One October afternoon many years ago, while sitting in Atlanta traffic, I had my windows down and music up, capturing the confusing tangle of summer turned to autumn—warmth

It's a Matter of Fact

Chrysanthemum gets its name from the Greek for "golden flower." It is sacred in Japan and China, the subject of legends, rituals, religious motifs, and celebrations. Chinese medicine uses the tea of the flower to clear the head before prolonged meditation since it is a flower of contemplation. American churches used to add the flower to arrangements to help keep congregations attentive during sermons.

brushed with a cool breeze; fresh and decaying aromas intertwined; and long, dark shadows underscoring bright skies. To this day I vividly recall looking at the bushes lining the edge of the hot pavement and noticing the frantic flight of bees among the flowers, pouncing around as if agitated by the sexual innuendoes of my tunes. I was struck by the incessant movement but also by the intermingling of the seasons—the tiny trumpet flowers held the remnants of summer's sweetness while the changing leaves displayed the reddish-bronze beginnings of fall.

Those bushes were **glossy abelias** (*Abelia* × *grandiflora*). Having been pruned for the purpose, they made an impenetrable hedge about 6–7 feet tall. A multi-stemmed, medium- to fast-growing shrub with arching branches, glossy abelia is a spreading, dense, rounded shrub that can become loose and leggy without adequate pruning. It generally grows 3–6 feet tall and wide and often up to 8 feet in this area.

Flowering begins in May or June, becomes quite intense by mid-July, and persists until as late as November or December, depending upon the severity of frost. Although there are several cultivars with varying characteristics, in general the flowers are whitish-pink, clumped in leafy panicles, and slightly fragrant.

Glossy abelia stems are reddish purple when young. The leaves are lustrous dark green in summer, turning to bronze-green to bronze-red and bronze-purple in late fall; in our area, they remain on the plant throughout the winter, although some may yield and fall during a markedly cold winter, giving the plant a semievergreen appearance. With its fine stems and small leaves, glossy abelia provides a textural effect and contrast in the landscape. And the constant presence of butterflies and bees adds delightful movement.

Three abelias deserve special mention. *Abelia* × *grandiflora* 'Little Richard' is more compact than the norm of the species and has prolific white flowering. Industry experts state that the plant grows 2–3 feet, and possibly 4–6 feet, high and wide. You can easily maintain it at the shorter heights, and pruning requirements are minimal to keep the dense form.

The hybrid *Abelia* × 'Rose Creek' is another cultivar with a low-mounding, compact habit, growing 2–3 feet. Some experts anticipate growth up to 5 feet, but with easy maintenance at the lower height. This plant is rapidly becoming a favorite in the landscape, with its crimson stems and white flowers that cluster profusely. I especially like the rusty-pink winter calyxes (modified leaves) that hold onto the plant after the flowers fade, giving the appearance of a dried flower arrangement with a foliage background. Another new cultivar, 'Canyon Creek', is similar to 'Rose Creek' but grows 4–6 feet high and wide and has slightly different leaf and flower coloration. Both are from the breeding program of Michael A. Dirr, retired professor of horticulture at the University of Georgia, and were placed on the Georgia Gold Medal Winners list for 2006.

Because of their compact habits, these new abelia varieties are easier to maintain than the leggier, older ones. They have a medium growth rate that slows as they mature, again making maintenance easier. They also provide more opportunities in the landscape because of their smaller size, as does *Abelia* × 'Edward Goucher', a medium-sized, lavender-pink to purple-pink flowering hybrid. 'Rose Creek' and other compact abelias make nice walkway borders and mass plantings.

Abelias perform best in acidic, well-drained, moist soils. They prefer full sun, which helps produce the best floral display, but they will tolerate partial shade. Because they bloom on new wood, you can prune your bushes anytime, but not within 3–4 weeks of frost. Heavy pruning is best done in late winter before the spring flush.

You will enjoy the transition from summer to winter with these fall flowers, as well as the many others that are available. Try an assortment of the newer varieties of annuals, perennials, and shrubs to augment and prolong the mixture of color, texture, and movement in your landscape in the fall and year-round.

Mum's the Word

THE MOST TRADITIONAL OF the herbaceous fall flowers is chrysanthemum. My earliest memories include going to the Georgia Tech football games, negotiating the crowded sidewalks, and admiring—actually, coveting—the huge yellow chrysanthemum corsages draped with yellow and white ribbons and tacked to boards by vendor tables. I've been wishing for several years now that my son, James—a Yellow Jacket—would surprise me with an invitation to a game and a similar floral gift. Finally, this fall of 2008, he did give me such an invite. But I became ill, could not attend, missed the exciting defeat of Florida State (although I did witness it on TV), and still don't have a corsage to dry and keep for sentimental reasons—yes, I know the corsage thing is highly unlikely, but it's okay to have fun with memories and to dream. I'm now promised a game or two next year, so I'll look forward to then.

Those monstrous floral mums have a short life, just like the potted mums that are available year-round. And neither is the same as the hardy garden mums, which are perennials. There are two kinds: Cushion types grow low, bushy, and compact; cutting types grow taller and are ideal for cutting gardens. Mums come in a multitude of colors: bronze, white, pink, yellow, orange, red, and lavender. Some have petals of one color with a differing center color. Mum flowers also differ in petal arrangement and shape. Some have single petals spread around a center eye; some have globular, pompon shapes. Spoon-shaped petals and long, tubular, spider-like petals with hooked ends grace some mums, while others have petals that look more like quills. There are also decorative flowers with petals that curve loosely or tightly toward the center, and anemone types, which are daisy-like with a rounded crest of petals in the center.

The inexpensive mums often surrounding the doorways of grocery stores, hardware stores, and big-box stores in early fall are good for one-season enjoyment but are often not worth the effort of planting for long-term use. They just don't seem to have the fullness of life needed to sustain themselves through multiple seasons. Furthermore, their colors are not as striking as the colors of varieties such as *Chrysanthemum coccineum* 'Brenda'. But bright color isn't everything. With its plain ole yellow center and white petals, my favorite garden mum remains Shasta daisy (*Chrysanthemum* × *superbum*). Although it may not last for years and years, it nevertheless provides the love-me, love-me-not playfulness so endearing to us ladies.

Planted in a sunny, well-drained spot in the yard, many mums will in fact perform year after year. Pinch them back in May and July to prevent them from becoming leggy and to encourage more buds. Every other year or so, divide the plants, preferably during the spring (since they are fall flowering).

LESSON 3 Ꮗ October 1–7
The Planting Season

If you stand in a meadow, at the edge of a hillside, and look around
carefully, almost everything you can catch sight of is in the process of dying,
and most things will be dead long before you are. If it were not for the
constant renewal and replacement going on before your eyes, the whole
place would turn to stone and sand under your feet.

—Lewis Thomas (1913–1993)
Lives of a Cell: Notes of a Biology Watcher (Death in the Open)

Fall Is for Planting

"FALL IS FOR PLANTING." Surely you've been notified—perhaps by
your local garden center's radio jingle or by banner flapping across
some storefront. This advertising is no gimmick; it's not just a
slogan for promoting sales at the opposite end of the spring shopping shower. It's a fact, in this part of the world, because plants,
like people, have the best chance of developing a strong foundation, establishing themselves, and attaining and maintaining good
health when they are allowed to grow with minimal stress for a
prolonged period. And in our Southern climate, cooler temperatures and damper soils that last from fall well into spring give trees,
shrubs, and perennials the most ideal nursery for early growth, for
the longest stretch of time we can muster.

We all know that plant growth (at least the part we see) slows
to a crawl in late fall and winter. During that resting time, plants
need fewer nutrients than usual. But in early fall, before the cold
sets in, the soil is still warm, encouraging nutrient uptake before
dormancy. This additional nutrition, combined with the more tol-
erable, cooler air temperatures, gives many plants a fall boost; they
thrive until the days become shorter and colder. Then top growth

virtually stops, but the roots continue to slowly develop, using the plant's stored food through the winter. In early spring, the roots experience a vigorous expansion in the still cold soil. By late spring, when the air and soil have warmed, the deeply rooted, fall-planted material has a growth surge. Larger root systems developed over the winter months easily transport lots of nutrients to the maturing adolescents.

Because plants given a start in the fall develop a good foundation with strong roots, they are prepared for the attack of our cruel, sizzling summer months. Spring plantings, on the other hand, have little or no time to adequately establish themselves, to grow the all-important roots that will reach deep into the soil away from the drying summer sun.

Not only is fall planting easier on your plants, it's also easier on *you* since the critical caretaking chores required for new plantings are greatly reduced. Because the fall soil is relatively moist (unless summer drought conditions persist), it's easier for you to work it. Furthermore, because winter rains generally provide more than adequate water for plants, you won't be burdened with the extra watering that is necessary to a new planting's survival. And because weeds don't grow as aggressively through the winter, you don't have to worry about their soaking up the nutrients that new plants need—the very reason you should be vigilant about pulling weeds when they grow in the warmer months.

IT'S A MATTER OF FACT

Fall isn't fall without fall festivals and autumnal rites. The festivals are a market for the fruits of labor and a place for games, food, and community. The rites are a reflection of the abundance of the fall harvest amid the ever-encroaching leanness and darkness of winter. The giving spirits are glorified while the spirits of darkness are placated.

Although relieved of some work by planting in the fall, you nevertheless should fertilize if you plant in September, October, or November, using a 3- to 4-week-feeding fertilizer (not a slow-release type) with low nitrogen and high phosphorus, to encourage root growth but not new leaf growth, since the danger of frost is present. But if you plant during December and January (which you can do if the ground is not frozen), do not fertilize until spring.

For the health of your plants and yourself, don't wait for spring to plant. Go ahead and participate in the cycle of decay and renewal—plant when the leaves color and fall, the air turns chill, and the lure of the hearth beckons you in. Resist the temptation to stay in, however. Remind yourself that you are, in your participation outdoors, a part of the grand scheme.

PURCHASING CONTAINER PLANTS VS. FIELD-GROWN PLANTS

WHEN PLANTING THIS FALL, consider whether it's better to buy containerized or field-grown plants. There are advantages and disadvantages to each, so knowing the differences will help you best choose for your needs.

Plants grown in a nursery start as liners, which, in the nursery industry, are plants that are going to be replanted to grow to a larger size before sale. Liners may be seedlings (plants started from seed), rooted cuttings (plants started by rooting a cutting from a known parent plant), divisions (plants started by dividing roots or other parts of larger plants), grafts (plants started by budding new growth of one plant onto the root stock of another), or tissue culture (plants started from a very small piece of another plant in a laboratory).

Liners for containerized plants are usually grown out in plastic nursery pots (although there are also metal, clay, and wood containers) to sizes that vary from small cell packs in flats to 200 gallon and larger pots. Liners for field-grown plants are sometimes started in a container, grown until a healthy root system is formed, removed from the container, and planted in the field. Sometimes field-grown plants are started from large bare-root stock that is placed directly into the ground.

The main advantage to containerized plants is that when one is transplanted, 100 percent of the root system goes with it, optimizing nutrient and water uptake. Unfortunately, some plants don't grow well in containers because of excessive aboveground heat. And some plants have such fast-growing roots that they outgrow the container in a short period. But, if not too large, container plants are easy to handle and, once in the ground, pose none of these problems.

To match the effectiveness of container growing, field-grown plants are produced using methods designed to achieve a full root system at harvest time. Proper soil preparation, irrigation, fertilization, and pruning techniques produce a tree or shrub that can be dug up and balled and burlapped (B&B); the size of the plant determines the appropriate size of the root-ball. Furthermore, for larger plants, field-grown ones are more cost-effective to produce and harvest, translating into less cost to you. They grow to a large size in less time than container-grown ones due, in part, to cooler root temperatures. And they cost less in labor, equipment, and overhead since they do not need winter protection or continued transplanting to larger pots.

There is one disadvantage to field-grown plants. Since they are rather large, they are quite heavy, ranging from 80 to 2,500 pounds or more. Handling them becomes a problem. Except for the smallest sizes, you will probably have to hire help or rent machinery if you are doing your own planting—adding to your cost. But before rejecting the notion of purchasing a B&B plant, keep in mind that large containerized plants are also heavy and often more cumbersome. It may be that you will have to reconsider your desire to start large, and let patience become a valuable ally.

John digs a tree with spades, the first step in harvesting a balled-and-burlapped (B&B) plant.

If you do start small, it's usually more cost-effective to buy a

Wholesale customers (landscapers, garden centers, and rewholesalers) often need big quantities of large trees and shrubs. The plants are dug with spades on a skid-steered loader (see photo on opposite page) and then lowered into a wire basket that has been lined with burlap. The burlap is then tied around the base of the trunk, and strapping is criss-crossed over the top, securing the wire basket that is then crimped to tighten it around the root-ball. Here, our children, James and Cat, watch this process of creating balled and burlapped (B&B) stock.

container-grown plant. As you start to reach the 15-gallon and larger sizes, you should think about buying field-grown plants. Either way, do your best to buy during the fall into winter. At this time, many containerized plants will have just reached their maximum root development in the container, and they are big and healthy and just waiting to be bumped up into a larger pot by the nursery. But it's better that, instead, *you* bump them up into *your* huge pot of soil, otherwise known as your yard. Also, it's best to take advantage of the fall harvesting of field-grown plants. Although nursery digging continues for nearly all of the year, most occurs when the plants are dormant, so the likelihood of your purchasing freshly dug B&B plants is best just at the time you should be planting them. The just-out-of-the-ground plants won't endure the stress of much time away from their accustomed habitat if you purchase and plant them when they are harvested.

LESSON 4 ⚛ October 8–14
Preparing for Winter

The earth is not a mere fragment of dead history, stratum upon stratum
like the leaves of a book, to be studied by geologists and antiquarians
chiefly, but living poetry like the leaves of a tree, which precede flowers and
fruit—not a fossil earth, but a living earth.

—Henry David Thoreau (1817–1862)
Walden (Spring)

Cool-Season Annuals for Those Winter Blues

FALL IS HERE, HERALDING the onset of winter—that dreary, cold, and wet time of the year. Fall is here, begging us to plant cool-season annuals—those eye-stopping winter wonders that lift our spirits.

The ever-popular pansies are blooming now and will continue until May. Although they shrivel in freezing temperatures, they bounce right back with a little sunshine and warmth. Snapdragons bloom through late fall and again in very early spring. They'll survive the coldest periods but will not show color. Ornamental cabbage and kale, on the other hand, will maintain their striking textural display throughout the season.

Pansies come in a multitude of colors and range in size from the Majestic Giants with 4½-inch-faced blooms to the Crystal Bowl varieties with 1½-inch, solid-color blooms. Violas and Johnny-jump-ups, cousins to pansies, have even smaller flowers, as well as smaller leaves and stems. For the best display, pinch off the flower buds and plant pansies in beds or in pots, spacing them 6–10 inches apart. To produce a mound of solid or mixed color, plant a group of two pansies of the same color 4–6 inches apart, and then plant another group 12 inches away. In the vacant spaces, plant tulips or other spring-flowering bulbs, for a surprising burst of spring color.

A fantastic companion to pansies, **snapdragons** provide a taller display of color. The 6- to 10-inch dwarf varieties are good fillers, edge plants, and potted accents, while the tallest varieties grow up to 24 inches and work best as backdrops, borders, and cut flowers. To keep snaps blooming longer and fuller, pinch off the first spike of the non-dwarf types so smaller side spikes can take hold. Also, remove spent flowers.

Dianthus is nothing new in gardens; your grandmother probably had some in her yard. But the new Amazon series (*Dianthus barbatus* 'Amazon' series) is giving the cool season a profusion of color that lasts into spring. 'Neon Duo', 'Neon Purple', 'Neon Cherry', 'Rose Magic', and 'Bouquet Purple' all have a profusion of varying flower color. Sometimes there are multiple colors on the same plant; a single flower cluster of rose, pink, cherry, and white hues fill 'Rose Magic', for instance. The flowers also have a sweet fragrance and attract hummingbirds and butterflies. The plant height of 24 inches on strong stems makes dianthus a great complement to the lower-growing pansies, as well as a good cut-flower.

IT'S A MATTER OF FACT

As soon as leaves fall to the ground, scores of organisms begin consuming them. Bacteria, mildew, and fungi break down the tissue with digestive enzymes. Earthworms, mites, centipedes, fleas, and other tiny animals then eat the decomposed leaves, reducing them to a fine dust. Bacteria and fungi, in turn, eat the tiny animals' excrement and leaf dust. Ultimately, the organic matter is reduced to mostly proteins and minerals that are reabsorbed by living plants. Under normal conditions, this saprophytic chain takes about one year to complete in our temperate forests.

If all that color keeps you from enjoying what you might think is deserved winter melancholia, don't plant **ornamental cabbage** and **kale** since it's just as energizing. The large rosettes of leaves of these annuals may be curly, smooth, or fringed and green with white to purplish pink to red centers. Growing 6–10 inches during the cool months, they have small yellow flowers that stalk up in the spring, adding even more height to your beds. Plant mature, one-gallon cabbages with heads touching, or set smaller, 4-inch potted plants about a foot apart to allow for outward growth. Use these ornamentals for borders, potted eye-catchers, or in your vacant vegetable garden to be cut for indoor arrangements and garnishes.

To prevent root rot, plant cool-season annuals after the hot, humid days of summer are over. A good rule of thumb in our area is to wait until after October 15. Be sure to place them in a spot that's sunny for at least six hours to promote more prolific flowering and healthier greenery. Most important, take time to properly prepare annual beds by turning, tilling, or otherwise pulverizing the soil and mixing in an amendment to create a loose, rich medium.

Preparing for winter in the nursery comes around Thanksgiving time. For our container stock, it means jamming the plants together into greenhouses, properly called coldframes because of their use—serving as protection from the cold but without heaters. The ends, which are yet to be covered in this photo, will also have doors that are opened and closed throughout the winter, depending upon the temperatures. These same structures serve as shade houses for those plants needing protection from the direct sun; a shade cloth is fitted over the plastic. These houses at our Loganville, Walton County, farm, which are in the construction phase in this 1986 photo, were the first of many erected there and at the Madison County nursery over the years.

Mushroom compost or other organic composts with manure have proven to be the best supplement for annuals and will feed them for the entire growing season with little other fertilizer needed. In the absence of this or other similarly rich amendments, fertilize annuals throughout the season.

Cool-season annuals like to stay moist but well drained. Use mulch to help retain moisture and protect against undue cold, and be sure to water during dry spells, especially if the beds are raised or the annuals are in pots.

Prepare for winter now and plant cool-season annuals. The vibrant palette of the violas, pansies, snapdragons, and dianthus and the lively effect of the cabbages and kale all give your landscape life in the dead of winter. There's no need to despair winter's gloom, when pansies and snaps, their flowers bloom.

LEAVE THOSE LEAVES

FALL BRINGS A FLURRY of leaves. They can be gold in your landscape if you approach them as something to gather and use, not as something to be cleaned up and disposed of. To confront fall leaves:

- Keep them and eliminate the tedium of bagging, dragging, and otherwise messing with disposing them.
- Rake them first into piles for the kids to play in, being sure not to leave them for more than a few days since they will cause any underlying grass to rot.
- Add the leaves to your compost pile to create rich, dark humus by spring.
- If you don't have kids to enjoy the leaves, avoid the raking by mowing over the leaves and catching them with the mower bag.
- Or, rake them into small rows about 1-foot high by 2-feet wide and run a mower over them a few times. Put a tarp to the side to catch the shredded leaves, and transport them to your beds.
- Use the shredded leaves as mulch around your trees, shrubs, annuals, and perennials. And you may want to try overwintering or perennializing some of your annuals by covering them with about 6 inches of the natural blanket.

- Use your leaves—shredded or otherwise—under the pine straw or bark mulch in your beds. Their less-than-attractive appearance will be hidden, and they will reduce your mulching costs by extending the life of the cover.
- If you can't stand the idea of keeping your leaves, ask a neighbor if she wants them. Then rake them onto a large old sheet, pull the corners together, and laboriously (although lovingly) drag them next door (or down the street) and thank your neighbor for putting them to good use.

Seven of our coldframes were destroyed in a March 1, 2009, snowstorm in which the 7–8 inches of snow was exceptionally wet, producing 2 ½ times the normal amount of water—and extreme weight. I took this photo as I first discovered and surveyed the damage early the following morning. We usually move the non-shade-loving plants out of the coldframes around the first of April and hope for no more hard freezes, like the severely damaging one we got in April, 2007.

LESSON 5 ∽ October 15–21
Preparing the Planting Beds

The perpetuation of my matter in crocus, coal, or comet is all I need know
about the next act—that atoms continue in nature.

—Robert Michael Pyle (b. 1947)
"And the Coyotes Will Lift a Leg"
The Norton Book of Nature Writing, 1990

Bed Preparation Is Critical to Plants

SOIL IS THE BASIS of a growing landscape or garden. It is the physical home, protecting the roots of plants from frost, extreme heat, drought, predators, and diseases. It supports both roots and aerial shoots as they grow, and, of course, it provides nourishment for growth.

Think of soil just as you would the house and home you provide your spouse and children. It must be carefully built and prepared to provide protection and support. It must be continually enriched to provide nourishment for optimal growth. And it must occasionally be reviewed, repaired, and reworked to renew vitality.

The first, and most critical item for soil—building and preparation—involves the planting bed, which is the area of soil around plants. *All* plants, large and small, grouped or standing alone, need a bed in which to grow—it doesn't matter if they are hostas, hollies, or hickories.

But most folks don't prepare beds. Rather, the most common method of planting among do-it-yourselfers is to dig a hole, add soil amendment, and insert the plant. But in *this* area, where clay is king, the undisturbed native soil that surrounds the hole acts as a flowerpot. The plant is no better off, and perhaps is worse off than it was when living in the plastic nursery container because, rather than having room to branch out and reach for nourishment and establishment, the roots stop at the impervious sides of the hole or turn back on themselves. Furthermore, poor drainage in the concrete-like hole aggravates the unsuitable conditions and leads to root rot.

But you can prevent this retarded and strangled root growth by thoroughly working the soil in the area you intend to plant. The depth you go and the tools you need depend upon the type and size of plants you have. For instance, you can prepare a small bed for pansies with a shovel and rake, turning and chopping the soil again and again to a depth of about 8 inches, then raking the bed clean and smooth. On the other hand, a bed for large trees or a long screen planting should be worked to 36 inches deep, so a subsoil plow on a tractor is the best implement for the job. Medium-size jobs, like the foundation beds around a house, are best worked with a rotary tiller. You should cross-plow or till several times to a depth of 10–12 inches so that all clay clumps are broken up.

After you've pulverized the soil, add 3–6 inches of compost or soil conditioner to the top of the chopped area and mix it in as deep as you can, again using the tools you used for chopping and tilling. Also mix in fertilizer and lime to adjust for nutrient

One of John's first toys at our new home in Loganville was a rototiller. He was amazed at the hard clay soils and needed some help preparing planting beds around our house and our vegetable garden. March, 1982.

deficiencies or to correct pH levels in the bed. If a large bed has an area just for annuals, you may want to add other amendments to encourage continuous, prolific flowering.

When you have finished chopping, churning, and mixing, the bed will be several inches higher than when you started. You can lightly roll the bed, but simply walking and working in it usually packs it sufficiently.

With the bed properly prepared, you will now be able to plant—easily. If you have spent the time, energy, and money required, you should be able to plant with as little as a garden trowel or spade. Planting will be pain free, fun, and fast. (See Lesson 31 for proper planting techniques.)

By spending more time, money, and perspiration on the preparation of planting beds, you will have made the best investment possible in your yard or garden plot. You will be giving your plants the best chance to thrive to their potential, so don't hesitate to beg, borrow, or rent the implements you need to do the job right. And remember—the larger the plants, the deeper and wider your prepped area should be.

IT'S A MATTER OF FACT

The life of the soil is humus. In agriculture, humus is often thought of as the end result of composting; the organic matter has reached a point of stability and will not break down any further. It is dark and has a soft, cushiony feel to it. In nature, without human assistance, it takes about a century for one inch of humus to form in the forest.

COMPOSTING IS NOT COMPLEX

COMPOSTING IS CONVERTING ORGANIC matter for use in the landscape. Compost can be used as an organic amendment—improving the soil physically, chemically, and biologically. It can be used as mulch—reducing soil erosion, modifying soil temperatures, conserving soil moisture, and suppressing weeds. And it can be used as a component in potting mixes—enhancing the growth of small beds and container gardens in the landscape.

Decomposed material has several advantages in the landscape. Soil amended with compost improves its tilth (fitness to support growth), water-holding capacity, drainage, and infiltration. Humus is valuable to the soil because it increases the availability of essential minerals to growing plants and reduces the competition for nitrogen. And composted material, because it is fine and broken down, is easier to handle and mix with the soil.

Efficient decomposition requires the maintenance of certain levels of aeration, moisture, particle size, and nutrients. Odorless, faster decomposition requires that sufficient oxygen reach the microbes. Mixing a compost pile once or twice a month can dramatically speed up the decomposition process because of the oxygen enhancement. Also, placing coarser materials, like larger twigs, on the bottom of the pile creates a chimney-like effect, inviting oxygen in.

Proper moisture levels encourage the growth of microorganisms, which break down organic matter and produce carbon dioxide, water, heat, and ultimately, the sought after humus. Rainfall usually suffices. But if there is not enough, periodically watering a compost pile helps. Your goal should be a damp but not soggy pile.

The rate of decomposition also depends upon the size of the materials added to the compost pile. Smaller sized particles decompose more quickly, so using shredded leaves and chipped woody materials is preferable.

Warm temperatures also hasten decomposition. Ideally, a composting pile should reach between 110°F and 160°F. Microbes actively feeding on the organic material will produce these temperatures, which help destroy weed seeds and disease organisms that may be present.

Many organic materials that you might otherwise dump and send to the landfill can be used in a composting pile. Leaves, grass clippings, small twigs, vegetable scraps, tea bags, ground egg shells, spent herbaceous and vegetable garden plants, wood ashes, coffee grounds, black and white newspaper, livestock manure, fruit waste, straw, and sawdust are all candidates for the pile, in varying degrees. Human or pet feces, meat, bones, whole eggs, dairy products, grease, and weedy or diseased plants are not acceptable additions.

There are many books on how to create and maintain a composting pile. Get one. Try a pile. Recycle your waste and enjoy the benefits.

LESSON 6 ∽ October 22–28
Conditioning the Soil

The real strength of a farm is in the soil.
—Wendell Berry (b. 1934)
The Gift of Good Land: Further Essays Cultural and Agricultural

Conditioned Soil Enhances Plant Performance

WE ALL KNOW THAT if we don't get enough calcium our bones will be brittle, and if we don't get enough vitamin D we may develop rickets. Our diet and nasty habits affect our skin tone. Not enough oxygen makes us weak, light-headed, or lifeless. And insufficient water prevents the portage of nutrients and waste, causing all kinds of stress to our bodily functions.

These principles that make or break our health apply to plants as well. The soil in which plants are rooted is the basic medium for the elements needed for healthy growth. So its condition matters— more than any other aspect of a plant's environment. Soil texture and drainage, pH (acid-alkaline balance), and chemical content are key factors for plant health.

Texture & Drainage: Good drainage is essential to balance soil aeration and percolation. In my part of the South, we tend to have a problem with soil that is too dense due to the clay. Many amendments such as gypsum, pumice, vermiculite, compost, and humus can be used to help create air spaces and break up the compacted clay.

The most cost-effective solution for correcting poor drainage is to add *well-decayed* organic matter (bark, leaves, and composted material), trench it in, and turn it over so it constitutes 33–50 percent of the volume of the soil. These amendments should be used in the chopped-and-churned beds discussed in Lesson 5.

pH: The acidity of soil affects the availability of nutrients for plants. Because each plant has different nutrient needs, each has its own pH requirements; however, there are ranges within which you can count on most plants thriving.

A pH of 7 is neutral. Above 8 and below 4 indicates a severe imbalance, while a pH between 5.5 and 7.0 serves most plants well. Our area is naturally acidic; you can correct the imbalance by applying garden lime, and maintain a balance by continuing with periodic applications. Note, however, that many of our native plants thrive in the naturally acidic environment and do not require a change.

Chemical Content: Nitrogen (N), phosphorus (P), potassium (K), and numerous micronutrients constitute the chemicals found in soil and required for healthy plant growth. Nitrogen produces leaf growth and good chlorophyll (the green in leaves), phosphorus promotes root growth and stimulates flower and seed formation, and potassium helps a plant build strength and disease resistance. There are also many micronutrients that contribute to plant health and vitality.

Fertilizers contain various percentages of these nutrients, the percent weight represented by a series of three numbers. So, for instance, a fertilizer marked 10-10-10 means it is composed of 10 percent nitrogen, 10 percent phosphorus, and 10 percent potassium. The remainder 70 percent is filler and possibly some micronutrients. As an all-purpose fertilizer for trees, shrubs, and perennials, use one that has an approximate ratio of 3-1-2, a full micronutrient package, and a 3- to 4-month release (known as slow release). Apply it two to three times each year, but not immediately prior to or during dormancy. The longer the release, the higher the nitrogen ratio should be, so adjust accordingly. If you want to use more specific fertilizers for some plants, consult the label or a nursery professional.

Soil Testing: Soil testing is a smart investment. It's like taking your yard's body to the doctor for a checkup to see if it's healthy and, if not, to determine what nutrients might make it better. Testing several different areas of your yard is important since the condition and nutrition of the soils may vary from spot to spot. Pay particular attention to pavement runoff areas where fossil fuel pollutants flow. Note that the foundation area around your house may have excess lime that has leached from or was residue from building construction. Areas that previously have been worked and planted may be quite different in aeration and nutrient composition than those that have not. And rocky areas differ from those that are not. If you are wondering about your soil, test it. The easiest way is to contact your local Cooperative Extension Service and ask about testing procedures. It's simple, inexpensive, and well worth the effort.

Soil Amending: Review your test results and determine what you need to add to the soil to enrich it. There are many products on the market. I recommend organic amendments and a specially blended (commercial variety) fertilizer with micronutrients. Mushroom compost, which is the spent growing medium for commercial mushroom production, is an excellent organic product that also serves as fertilizer for some plants for as long as a year or more after planting.

Soil provides protection, support, and nourishment for plants. The healthier you make it, the healthier your plants will be. Start plantings with the best possible bed preparation and soil conditioning. Review the conditions periodically, preferably before signs of stress appear, and repair and rework the soil when necessary to renew vitality and assure continued healthy growth.

IT'S A MATTER OF FACT

Most soils in the South, east of the Mississippi River and the lime line—and particularly our red clay—are acidic. Calcium and magnesium quickly leach from the soil in the high rainfall areas, leading to acidity. Liming and fertilizing to raise the soil pH increase calcium and magnesium as much as 100 percent, resulting in sweeter, more fertile soil for healthy plant growth. Since the lime eventually leaches out also, it must be reapplied periodically to prevent a return to acidity.

Because we, in our manipulated landscapes, have disturbed the balance of nature and its processes of soil conditioning that occur from aerating insects and rodents and nutrient enriching, decaying matter, we must continually create conditions for healthy growth. We can, and should, do this by applying organic fertilizers and conditioners. Using these natural additives (as opposed to the fossil fuel–based fertilizers that have harmful environmental consequences), foregoing pesticides and herbicides, and encouraging native species growth will help restore a microcosm of balance that will be beneficial to our environment at large. Even if you fall short of reestablishing a balance, at least you will be giving a living thing a nourishing, healthy home and heightened chances for growing to its fullest potential. So remember, as the saying goes: don't treat your soil like dirt.

KNOW YOUR PLANT NUTRIENTS

PLANTS NEED MANY NUTRIENTS for growth. Carbon, hydrogen, and oxygen come from the air and water. The remainder—primary nutrients, secondary nutrients (macronutrients), and micronutrients—come from the soil.

- Most micronutrients are adequately available in the soil and are absorbed, especially in nonarid regions. Iron deficiency (chlorosis) is probably the most common microdeficiency and results in yellow leaves with green veins. To assure a broad-spectrum feeding for your plants, use fertilizers with micronutrients.
- The macronutrients—calcium, magnesium, and sulfur—are also usually present in the soil and are often imported in other products like lime, soil conditioner, and gypsum.
- The primary nutrients—nitrogen, phosphorus, and potassium—often need supplementation. Deficiencies may be apparent, and soil testing can confirm soil needs.
- Nitrogen comes mostly from organic material and is used by plants and the soil organisms that support plant growth. Deficiencies result in stunted growth and yellow leaves—starting at the tips, moving toward the stem,

and progressing from the bottom up. Nitrogen fertilizer comes in various forms, and your selection depends upon the time of year and type of plant needing it. Consult your local Cooperative Extension Service agent for advise.

- Phosphorus should be incorporated into the soil since it does not move readily through the soil to the roots. Purplish-tinged leaves, poor flower or fruit production, and stunted growth suggest a deficiency. Older growth is affected first.

- Potassium is abundant in the soil, but plants are unable to absorb it easily. Scorched or fringed leaf margins, mottled leaves, slow growth, poorly developed root systems, and weak canes suggest a deficiency. Incorporate available or soluble potash or water-soluble potash into the soil so it's in the path of root growth.

In 1993 when we started building the container area at our Madison County nursery, James helped move mums to their new growing spot. Although they are not woody ornamentals like the majority of our plants, their cultural requirements didn't differ too much, making their addition to the nursery suitable. But we did apply fertilizer more often than we did on the trees and shrubs since we wanted to push the mums' growth so we would have plenty of them for sale at the appropriate time.

LESSON 7 ☙ October 29–November 4
Fall Color

Culture springs from the actions of people in a landscape, and what we,
especially Southerners, are watching is a daily erosion of unique folkways as
our native ecosystems and all their inhabitants disappear.

—Janisse Ray (b. 1962)
Ecology of a Cracker Childhood

The Charm of Southern Fall Color

I REMEMBER THE FIRST TIME I commented about our colorful fall when I was about eight years old and my mother was driving me to school. We were on the last leg of the crosstown trip, approaching the Chattahoochee River and its one-lane steel bridge. There was a stretch of woods on the left, not yet raped for a homesite. The leaves on the trees were clinging, waiting for a sneeze of air to break them free from their lifeline. The sunlight danced through them, illuminating their colors, and I was at once filled with the beauty of the fantastic fall foliage. I recall saying to my mother that it was the best fall color I had ever seen.

Well, I don't think a year has gone by since that I haven't said the same thing each fall—*this* year, the dogwoods are spectacular. Their leaves are so red, accented with lots of bright red berries. It has to be the best year yet!—or did I say that last year, and the year before? And so it seems, year after year.

Now, I have lived in New England where the falls are unbelievable. In fact, most of our images and expectations of autumn reflect those of New England—pastoral landscapes soaking up the remaining warmth before winter sets in with its blanket of snow; misty mornings followed by bright blue, crisp skies with billowing white clouds; and vibrantly colored sugar maple leaves lining country lanes. Truth be told, I ended up in New England because I picked my college based upon the absolute beauty of its campus in the peak of fall, a pleasure I happened upon when visiting there during my high school senior year. I came to love everything about the Mount Holyoke College campus and its woods, where I walked daily and ran through countless rolls of film. And I discovered that the school and its Connecticut River Valley area were an excellent choice for me—not just because of the overwhelming allure of autumn.

Despite my sentiment for New England falls, upon returning to the South in 1981, I realized that Southern autumns are just as fine as those of our northern neighbors. Our native plants paint a pretty picture, filling the canvas with subdued yet lively color. And each year the image changes since the plant colors vary, depending upon the summer endured and the timing and temperature of fall onset.

But a lot has changed in ornamental horticulture since then, and our modern-day fall painting includes more than the native palette. Numerous cultivars add brilliance as well. These specially bred varieties of our native plants provide accent in unsuspecting places with their guaranteed and consistent color. For instance, the newer maple cultivars such as October Glory®, Red Sunset®, and 'Autumn Flame' that are becoming commonplace in our landscapes burst brilliantly into flame as the days grow cooler. Similarly, most Georgia Gold Medal plants have particular appeal in the fall, true to their award-winning status. Whether it's their leaf color, berries, or bark, they add interest to the browning and graying landscape. I have gone through the list of gold medal winners from the program's inception in 1994 through 2008 to find those winners with fall appeal and have listed them with brief descriptions of some of their prized fall attributes.

Dianthus 'Bath's Pink' (*Dianthus gratianopolitans* 'Bath's Pink'): This herbaceous perennial ground cover for sunny locations retains good 4- to 6-inch gray-green foliage through fall.

Mt. Airy Fothergilla (*Fothergilla major* 'Mt. Airy'): With brilliant orange, yellow, and red fall color, this deciduous 5- to 6-foot shrub is good for sun or partial shade locations.

Blue Anise Sage (*Salvia guaranitica*): The numerous deep blue tubular flowers of this perennial that grows 4- to 5-feet tall with a 2- to 4-foot spread persist into October and attract butterflies and hummingbirds.

Annabelle Hydrangea (*Hydrangea arborescens* 'Annabelle'): This deciduous, broad shrub for shady areas holds its 6- to 12-inch flower heads into early fall. It will bloom for a second time in September if pruned after its first June flowering.

Athena Elm (*Ulmus parvifolia* Athena®): In early fall, petite flowers appear intermixed with the small, lustrous dark green leaves of this deciduous shade tree that grows 35 feet tall and 50 feet wide.

Lipan, Sioux, Tonto, and Yuma Crapemyrtles (*Lagerstroemia indica* × *L. fauriei*): These flowering deciduous shrubs/small trees all bloom into early and late September, have great fall leaf color, and reveal their excellent stem color as they lose their leaves. Lipan has light orange to dull red fall color and mottled, near white to beige bark. Sioux has light maroon to bright red leaves for the season to complement its mottled, exfoliating, light to medium gray-brown bark (on mature specimens). Tonto is bright maroon in fall, with red-purple young branches that are cream to gray-brown in maturity. And Yuma displays light fall color with light gray exfoliating bark.

Pink Chinese Loropetalum (*Loropetalum chinense* var. *rubrum*): This 6- to 10-foot-tall evergreen shrub mixes the old with the new in fall. The older leaves turn yellow, orange, and red while the new leaves, emerging to replace the old, are maroon. Some pink flowering persists into fall.

Yoshino Japanese Cedar (*Cryptomeria japonica* 'Yoshino'): After frost, the tips of the needles of this full but loose evergreen, which grows 50–60 feet, become a bronzy color while the underlying needles remain green. The late fall and winter winds move the branches and ripple through the needles, creating a multicolored wave of motion.

Bottlebrush Buckeye (*Aesculus parviflora*): This Georgia native is a deciduous shrub that grows 8- to 12-feet high and wide and has a bright yellow fall color.

Trident Maple (*Acer buergeranum*): This deciduous tree grows 25–30 feet tall with an equal spread. In the fall its three-lobed leaves turn red, orange, and yellow, with multicoloration on some leaves. The more mature specimens have interesting exfoliating grayish brown bark that is revealed as the leaves fall.

Lenten Rose (*Helleborus orientalis*): This shade-loving evergreen perennial that blooms in midwinter, starts new growth in the fall as the cool weather creeps in, lending green to the browning fall floor.

Mohawk Viburnum (*Viburnum × burkwoodii* 'Mohawk'): The leaves of this deciduous 7- to 8-foot-high and -wide shrub with fragrant, early spring flowers turn from bright orange to wine red in fall.

Alice Oakleaf Hydrangea (*Hydrangea quercifolia* 'Alice'): A 12-by-12-foot-tall deciduous shrub with flowers persisting into fall, this shade-loving specimen has rich burgundy fall leaves and cinnamon-colored exfoliating bark.

Little Gem Magnolia (*Magnolia grandiflora* 'Little Gem'): A 20-foot-tall evergreen tree, this dwarf cultivar of the larger Southern magnolia species has dark, glossy green leaves with fuzzy brown undersides. It continues blooming in early fall.

Autumn Fern (*Cryopteris erythrosora*): This filtered-shade-loving herbaceous perennial, which has coppery red new growth in spring, provides continuing green interest on the ground amid the fallen leaves.

IT'S A MATTER OF FACT

Georgia Gold Medal Award winners are plants selected by a committee of nurserymen, flower growers, garden center retailers, landscape professionals, County Extension agents, and faculty from the University of Georgia, whose goal it is to promote the production, sale, and use of superior ornamental plants. Based upon consumer appeal, low-maintenance, survivability, ease of propagation and production, and seasonal interest, an annual, herbaceous perennial, shrub, and tree are picked each year. Other states have similar programs.

Inkberry (*Ilex glabra*): This Georgia native evergreen shrub, which is good for naturalized areas, has black, berry-like fruit in late fall through early spring that the birds love.

Chastetree (*Vitex agnus-castus*): A small deciduous tree, this plant is similar to crapemyrtle and has yellow fall color. The flowers persist into early fall, and the dried panicles remain an interesting element.

Blue Mist Bluebeard (*Caryopteris × clandonensis*): This perennial, with its clusters of sky-blue flowers, complements the yellow and orange flowers of early fall.

Purple Beautyberry (*Callicarpa dichotoma*): The shiny, dark lavender berries of this deciduous shrub form clusters along the stems, creating a truly magnificent display.

Miss Huff Lantana (*Lantana camara* 'Miss Huff'): A herbaceous perennial, this 5- to 6-foot-wide and 10-foot-high shrub-like plant bears a mixture of pink to orange and yellow flowers from spring until frost. Butterflies love to flit around this plant, adding even more color.

Anise Hyssop hybrids (*Agastache* spp.): Butterfly and humming-bird attractors, the cultivars 'Apricot Sunrise', 'Firebird', 'Tutti Frutti', and 'Blue Fortune' bloom until frost in a variety of colors depending upon the cultivar. Deer do not like them.

Summer Snowflake Viburnum (*Viburnum plicatum* var. *tomentosum* 'Summer Snowflake'): This compact deciduous shrub not only blooms from spring until fall, it has bright red fruit and wine-red leaves in the fall.

Bald Cypress (*Taxodium distichum*): A large, pyramidal conifer tree that thrives in swamps, bald cypress is handsome in the uplands too. It has bronze-orange needles in the fall.

Creeping Raspberry (*Rubus pentalobus* syn. *R. calycinoides*): This evergreen ground cover is fast growing but not invasive. Its coarse-textured leaves with deep veins turn burgundy in the fall.

Rose Creek/Canyon Creek Abelias (*Abelia* hybrids): Excellent shrubs for flowers from spring until frost, these plants dance with bees and butterflies in the fall while their leaves are turning rosy bronze.

Glowing Embers Japanese Maple (*Acer palmatum* 'Glowing Embers'): In its glory during the fall, the leaves of this elegant tree fade from green to purple and fluorescent orange or yellow. The sequence of change varies with each leaf, so the tree is multicolored and ever changing.

Perennial Plumbago, Leadwort (*Ceratostigma plumbaginoides*): This herbaceous perennial ground cover has shiny green leaves that turn bronze-red in the fall.

Overcup Oak (*Quercus lyrata*): Wildlife love this tree because of its nutritious acorns that fall to the ground while its leaves turn yellow.

Firespike (*Odontonema strictum*): The crimson-red flower spikes of this shrub-like annual bloom from late summer through fall, projecting upright. Their brilliance attracts hummingbirds and butterflies.

Swamp (Scarlet) Hibiscus (*Hibiscus coccineus*): A water lover that works well in poorly drained areas as well as around water gardens and pond edges, this native herbaceous perennial has blood-red flowers that are 3–5 inches across and bloom from late spring until frost.

Rozanne Cranesbill Hardy Geranium (*Geranium* 'Rozanne'): This patented hybrid herbaceous perennial has blue-violet flowers with pale centers. A light shearing will encourage continued flowering, complemented by the deeply lobed brownish red fall foliage.

Bowhall Maple (*Acer rubrum* 'Bowhall'): This narrowest of red maples has a symmetrical, columnar habit that makes it perfect for tight spaces. It has dependable red fall color.

Commemoration Maple (*Acer saccharum* 'Commemoration'): This sugar maple is fast growing and vigorous. It does well in our Zone 7b and appears like the sugar maples of New England with its yellow, orange, and red fall coloration.

Sugar Maple seedlings (*Acer saccharum*): Yes, we can have non-cultivar sugar maples in the South. But they are very slow growing (unless they have been improved like the cultivar Commemoration Maple mentioned above). Or, unless they have been watered and fertilized regularly, like the ones that have grown very rapidly in our backyard. Their autumn gold and yellow color is magnificent, especially when the leaves fall and blanket the ground.

Fall color includes the orange of pumpkins, harvested for Halloween carving and Thanksgiving pie. John and Cat play together to create a masterpiece in 1996.

Before concluding, I have to add some texture to our fall color by mentioning ornamental grasses. Their plumes are full in the fall and sway with the wind while shining with the sunlight. The native pink muhly grass (*Muhlenbergia capillaris*) is particularly appealing to me with its inflorescence that is a billowy mass of pink, airy flowers. In large groupings, the color is spectacular. (See Lesson 21 on ornamental grasses.)

With such a wealth of color, there's no wonder that I have never tired of our Southern fall landscape; it's far from boring with the old native standards and new cultivars of trees, shrubs, and perennials, and it rivals that of New England with a more demure, yet flashy display. People often say that Southerners are a unique breed; well, so are the Southern autumns: spiced just enough, but not too showy; interesting enough, but not overwhelming; down to earth, warm, and inviting, yet secretly alluring just the same. The wildness and authenticity is manifest.

The show changes year to year, and each year is the best run yet. By planting a wide range of native trees, shrubs, and perennials, as well as their improved cultivars, you will have variety and certainty, subtlety and flamboyancy—and color. The Georgia Forestry Commission sells native seedlings and remains one of the best sources for inexpensive, albeit small (requiring patience), trees. They usually announce their tree availability in the fall each year, with pickup during the winter planting season.

How Do They Change Color?

AS YOU WATCH THE LEAVES change color and fall to the ground each autumn, do you wonder why and how that happens? Like everything else in nature, the mechanism occurs as a necessary step in the cycle of life. The steps are orderly and tuned to the demands of the changing seasons.

It's a truly miraculous process that prepares deciduous plants with thin leaves (as compared to the thick-leaved evergreens) for the harsh winter. By dropping their leaves, the plants decrease the water loss that occurs through them. This operation is vital since root activity and water absorption decline during the colder months, so the plant needs some water retention. The dropped leaves also help the plant eliminate toxins and waste products that have accumulated over the summer.

In autumn, the shorter days and cooler temperatures trigger a decrease in the amount of transpiration (like our perspiration) of moisture from a tree's leaves into the air. Less water and fewer nutrients are sent up from the roots because of the decreased demand. Leaf activity slows, and the soft cells form a separation layer (abscission) across the base of the stalk of the leaf. As the layer grows, the enzyme pectin forms, decomposing the cell walls of the stalk. The leaf weakens its attachment to the tree and eventually falls off. A cork layer then forms, protecting the severed stem.

As the formation of the separation layer interrupts the flow of nutrients to the leaves, chlorophyll production declines and the green coloration fades. Leaves that contain masked carotene change to bright yellow as it becomes dominant. And in some plants the increased sugar in the leaves resulting from its arrested flow produces anthocyanin, the producer of reds, purples, and crimsons. All of these changes are influenced by the weather. Dry, sunny days followed by cool, dry nights generate the brightest fall colors.

LESSON 8 ∽ November 5–11
Bulbs for Spring Flowering

Like a bulb, the soul is planted.

In soil, its roots go deep into the earth.

Its only needs, light and love.

And given those, it surely will flower.

—Rosemary Altea
*Proud Spirit: Lessons, Insights & Healing from
"The Voice of the Spirit World"*

There's Beauty in Bulbs

It's hard to think about spring right now—I'm too enthralled with the fall fiesta—but we have to plan ahead to get the spring we want. If the plan is to include flowering bulb plants, such as daffodils and tulips, now is the time to plant them.

I don't believe I've ever witnessed a spring without daffodils—they are the epitome of the season. When I conjure up images of my childhood home, they always include the magnificent tall, large-cupped daffodils that dotted the liriope beds under the stately oak trees in our backyard. I'm not sure of the variety of those daffodils, but I suspect they were King Alfreds, an heirloom since 1899 that set the standard for trumpet daffodils.

As a child, I anxiously anticipated warm spring days as I watched the daffodil leaves emerge from the soil. The first signs usually peeked through in January, looking like green Popsicle sticks being forced up from down below. The more they rose, the closer the days of shorts and sneakers.

I always had to wait, however, to find the hidden treasures I most wanted to see. Mixed within the beds were a few—just a very few—daffodils that, to this day, I call scrambled eggs. The flowers were a mass of yellow and orange petals in a seemingly disorderly array. I thought these mixed-up flowers were really special—after all, there weren't many of them. So I would search the beds to find these favorites.

Today, I still look for these tantalizing treats. Although totally different in style, my home at the nursery was built in the same era as that of my childhood. Throughout the yard, remains of early plantings pop up, including what I call "country" daffodils with petite flowers and sugary-sweet smells. Dotted among them and their larger cousins, I find, on occasion, a scrambled egg. I rejoice, reminisce, and relive moments of youth as I give special attention to my perennial friend.

Tulips are more dignified darlings of spring than daffodils, but I learned at an early age that they aren't trusted friends in the South like daffodils. One year, my mother and I planted six of them in a narrow border next to our patio. The first rain plunged the petals and stripped the

IT'S A MATTER OF FACT

Get-rich-quick schemes have been around forever. Sometimes a fever strikes a few, sometimes a multitude. When first writing this book I mentioned our then recent witnessing of the dot-com craze, where fortunes were made and then lost. Today—fall 2008—I must extend the example to include the host of fast-fortune financial-market schemes that have ultimately caused an implosion in the economy and consequent losses of riches overnight. Such greed has always been around. It swept through Holland in the 1630s when the trading of tulip bulbs, which had become prized possessions and symbols of power and prestige among the aristocrats, turned into the selling of futures in them, an infection that ran rampant among the common folk. A seasonal market became a year-round market, and speculators sold all of their possessions to get in on the windfall. Prices soared—to as much as $44,000 in today's dollars for a handful of bulbs—but the laws of economics forced a market crash, ending tulipmania.

stems bare, leaving a deadly looking picture of failure. It was an exceptional rain, and I accepted the act. My real disappointment came in the succeeding years as the flowers increasingly failed to bloom. I then learned that tulips should be treated as annuals rather than perennials in the South since they don't get enough chill hours, especially now, with our milder winters. You need to plan to plant new tulips each year, or you can try planting them in raised beds since those soils will chill more easily and may promote better tulip performance.

In my younger days, I never thought much about the mysteries of the reliable daffodils. They just kept coming back, year after year. They graced our city yard and dotted the landscapes of country yards alike. Our urban ones were statelier than the homelier varieties in the country, but the effect was the same—bright yellow beacons of life from the soil, evidence of the bulbs below. Their wonder finally grabbed me when I realized that the bulbs are hiding places, caves, and cocoons—protecting the sleep of developing lives eager to burst forth at first opportunity. They are storehouses of creation and color, containers of complete plants that erupt from storage and rudimentary development. The embryonic leaves, stems, and flower buds are held inside the organ, which is filled with food for growth that begins in the fall. Roots start developing, leading to blooms in spring. The bulb becomes dormant in late spring; regeneration then begins. By late summer, well-developed buds exist inside the biosphere, just waiting for the proper moisture and temperatures to stimulate upward growth through the winter. The cycle continues.

You have to engage yourself in this cycle if you want to enjoy daffodils/narcissi, tulips, crocuses, hyacinths, alliums, irises, and other spring-flowering bulbs. To enjoy these jewels, you must plant the bulbs in mid- to late fall.

Here are a few hints that apply to all spring-flowering bulbs:
- Buy only pre-chilled bulbs since they require a certain amount of cold to produce blooms.
- Buy only firm, dry bulbs. Moist, mushy bulbs are signs of rotting to come.
- Buy top-sized bulbs—the largest size. Larger bulbs produce larger flowers and more vigorous plants. You get what you pay for; bigger *is* better in this instance.
- Plant when the ground temperature is at or below 60°F (late October or later in Zone 7). The soil must be cool enough to prevent the bulb from accelerating its growth cycle.

- Plant in full sun or under deciduous trees. The winter sun will warm the soil and promote emergence of new growth at the proper time.
- Plant in well-drained, fertile soil. Bulbs abhor wet feet and love organic matter. Proper drainage is critical, so proper bed preparation is essential.
- Read the label for your bulbs to determine proper depth for planting. Planting depths are measured from the base of the bulb and are generally two to three times the bulb size. Dig even deeper than required and add loosened soil back to the hole or bed along with bone meal.
- When planting, use bone meal or a specially blended bulb fertilizer. Follow label instructions and fertilize again after the plant emerges. Do not fertilize after the leaves die. In older, established beds, only fertilize during or soon after flowering in the spring.
- Mulch bulb beds to improve the soil and add protection from excess cold.
- Be patient after your festival of flowers. Do not remove the leaves until they have totally yellowed (8–10 weeks after bloom) since this is when the bulb is gathering nourishment before dormancy.

There are endless possibilities when designing with bulbs:

- Create a formal look by digging a wide trench and spacing bulbs according to the label.
- Create a naturalized look by putting your bulbs in a wide-topped container and tossing (as if throwing out water) to scatter them. Plant each bulb where it lands.
- Distance bulbs according to the effect you want—massed color or loose dots.
- Plant bulbs among cool-season annuals for a truly grand show when bloom times overlap.
- Plant bulbs among daylilies and other long-leafed, sun-loving perennials that emerge in the spring just in time to hide the yellowing bulb leaves. However, observe your results since the perennials may shade the soil too much, preventing the soil from becoming warm enough to

induce bud formation in the bulb. Some early-flowering bulbs can be planted under deciduous trees along with shade-loving hostas or liriope. The bulbs will bloom before the tree leaves create a shaded canopy.

- In the southern climate, at least, think of tulips as disposable annuals, not perennials, since they rarely rejuvenate for successive years in the warmer environment that doesn't provide enough chill hours.

Nature hides its beauty in bulbs. But with nourishment, the bulbs grow, reach light and warmth, and reveal the incredible creation within, just as our growth, encouraged by truth and love, reveals our hidden beauty.

WHAT KIND OF BULB DID YOU BURY?

THERE ARE FIVE KINDS OF BULBS. Daffodil and tulip bulbs are true bulbs. They have an embryonic plant that lies on top of a basal plate and is surrounded by fleshy leaves (scales) that have a dry, papery covering known as a tunic. True bulbs form offsets or bulblets that can be separated from the mother bulb and replanted. Some plants will only grow in subsequent seasons from the bulblets. But others, like daffodils, will grow from the bulblets as well as the original mother bulb.

Gladiolus is an example of a corm, which is a swollen, underground stem base. These are very similar to true bulbs in appearance, but an individual corm will last only one year. New corms (cormels) form on the top of the old ones; smaller cormels may take as much as three years to bloom while larger ones will bloom in the following year.

Rhizomes are thickened stems that grow entirely or partially below ground. Growth buds (eyes) usually emerge from the tip, opposite from the underside root area, and there may be additional growing points along the length of the rhizome. To divide plants, like irises and callas, you must cut the rhizome into sections, being sure each section has a visible eye.

Growth buds also occur on tubers, like those of a begonia. Tubers are swollen, underground stem bases, similar to corms. But roots of a tuber will grow from all sides, and there are multiple growth buds. Some tubers simply enlarge over time. Others, such

The entrance to our nursery in Madison County, Georgia, with spring daffodils smiling. We named Pinebush Farm and Nurseries, Inc. for the farm in Walton County where we started the business in 1981. When in their teens, our daughter, Cat, made the sign, and our son, James, built the fence. She's now a landscape architecture student at the University of Georgia, and he's a Georgia Tech civil engineer—both expanding upon their talents.

as caladiums, produce offsets, which can be removed and planted separately. When dividing tubers it's important that each section has a growth bud for replanting.

In contrast to the other bulbs, tuberous roots are actually roots rather than stems. A daylily is a prime example of the cluster-growing root that has swollen tuberous parts radiating from a central spot at the bottom of an old stem. The growth buds form at the bases of the old stems, and divisions for replanting should include one of these eyes along with some roots.

LESSON 9 ∽ November 12–18
Plant Reproduction

There is no death in mortal things, and no end in ruinous death. There is only mingling and interchange of parts, and it is this that we call "Nature."

—Empedocles (ca. 490–430 B.C.)

Cash In on Perennial Dividends Now

THEIR LEAVES HAVE FADED, yellowed and drooping like a beagle's ears. Their flowers are gone, scentless and withered, immune now from the ravages of the winter lying before us. But the perennials—plants that live more than two years, dying back seasonally but producing new growth from a persistent part, year after year—are not dead. They're quite alive, and some are ready for dividing.

In my childhood yard, we didn't have any perennials to speak of other than the all-too-common liriope (*Liriope muscari*). My mother divided the clumps every once in a while, but the daffodil bulbs that were strewn about in the beds made for a slightly tedious task since she wanted to be careful not to disturb them. Nevertheless, there was great satisfaction in "getting something for free," and the liriope babies always ended up somewhere else in our yard, usually creating a border for a new bed—frugality at its best, since in those post–World War II years with parents of the Depression era, parsimony was the standard by which we lived.

Although there are differing schools of thought about dividing perennials, in general, spring- and early-summer-flowering ones should be divided in the fall, and late summer- and fall-flowering plants in the spring. Perennials do not need division every year, but they will benefit from division every few years.

How do you decide if your perennials are ripe for division? Consider whether they are occupying a space greater than you had planned. Then divide and conquer the invaders. Are they becoming stunted or otherwise misshapen? Then divide and reform the miscreants. Do you want more of the same in other places in your garden? Then divide and spread the spoils.

To divide a perennial, start by digging around the plant and removing it from the ground. Then, with a sharp knife or spade, cut the root system as you would cut a slice of pie. Take as many wedge-shaped slices as you desire, and plant them elsewhere in your garden—or give them to a friend.

Plant the divisions in a properly prepared bed that has been amended with organic matter, which will significantly increase their productivity. Mushroom compost and other organic composts with manure are perhaps the best amendments for perennials as they are very long-term, slow-release fertilizers. Although you will be relieved of the time and expense of a regular fertilizer application, some plants may produce green growth better if you add some nitrogen to supplement the low-nitrogen content of these organic composts.

Water the new dividends every 3–4 days for several weeks to insure a successful root system. Or pray for rain. Either way, do not overwater, and be sure that the perennial bed is well drained.

Now, before you jump out of your chair, let me state that you don't *have* to divide your perennials now. You can wait until early spring to divide all of them (spring-, summer-, and fall-flowering). Some gardeners prefer spring dividing because they can work with the plant while seeing the new growth popping up through the ground. These gardeners find fall dividing somewhat harder because the dead foliage tangles with their hands and spade and masks the ground, making it difficult to find the plant outlines. Take note, however: You can cut back all of that dead foliage now, making your fall division easier and your landscape more attractive for the winter. But there are some exceptions to cutting back; for instance, you do not want to cut the canes of lantana now since the hollow stems will fill with water and freeze, causing damage or death to the plant.

I prefer to divide my perennials in the fall for three reasons. First, I am giving them a longer period to reestablish themselves and develop a stronger root system before next year's warm weather. Although this subterranean growth is rather small, it does make a difference. Second, I am giving myself one less thing to do in the spring when I inevitably have more than I care to handle in the yard. Third, and most important, I am giving myself some much needed time in the yard—relieving stress brought on by the hectic holiday season and allowing me time to meditate.

Do it now, or wait, but either way, what a great reward it is to divide your perennials. You give the members-of-the-clump more root room, allowing greater and better nutrient uptake, resulting in healthier plants. You create multiple clones to enhance your own garden or that of a friend. And you get down and dirty in the soil, manipulating life and beauty, participating in our earthly paradise.

SEX . . . AND OTHER MEANS OF REPRODUCTION

AS I'VE DISCUSSED, we can easily divide our perennials to create additional plants for our gardens, just as nurseries often divide their overgrown or root-bound perennials, planting the dividends in new pots and adding to their stock. But the plant world has numerous methods of reproduction, some natural and some man induced.

Reproduction from seed is sexual. It's the uniting of genetic material from a male and female of one species. It's the birds-and-bees metaphor. Asexual, or vegetative, reproduction is clonal, producing genetically identical offspring. Plants have overcome the limitations of sexual reproduction by increasing vegetatively from modified roots or stems. Man has taken this process a step further and learned to propagate plants not only by division of clump-forming plants but by rooted cutting, layering, grafting, budding, tissue culture, and division of bulbous plant organs as well.

Reproduction by seed enables plants to adapt over time to environmental changes and to colonize new areas that may have originally been unsuitable to the species. Reproduction by seed also enables plants to survive unfavorable conditions since seeds have the ability to lie dormant during drought, cold, or other hostile conditions, waiting for favorable conditions before growing.

Because of the mixing of genetic material of the parents, plants grown from seed may take on differing characteristics, creating botanical subspecies or varieties. The crossing of two species from the same genus produces natural hybrids, adding to the botanical diversity of the world.

Vegetative reproduction is nature's way of overcoming the limitations of sexual reproduction. Rather than relying upon the wind or animals to transport seed to favorable sites, most plants have the ability to multiply on-site and more rapidly than with seed dispersal. However, this type of reproduction, if it's the only means, poses a threat of widespread destruction by disease. Since genetically identical plants carry the same susceptibility to disease, all can be wiped out at the same time. So, in keeping with Mother Nature's infinite wisdom, most plants have sexual *and* asexual reproduction mechanisms, garnering the best of both worlds.

It's a Matter of Fact

"Though many flowers, like lilies, possess both male and female organs, they go to great lengths to avoid pollinating themselves. That would defeat the flora point, which is the mixing of genes that cross-pollination ensures. A flower can avoid self-pollination chemically (by making its ovule and pollen grain incompatible), architecturally (by arranging stamen and pistil in the flower so as to avoid contact), or temporally (by staggering the times when their stamens produce pollen and their pistils are receptive)," explains Michael Pollan in his book *The Botany of Desire*.

Enter man, who has always sought to improve conditions. In modern times, he has discovered that he can alter the offerings of nature—by manufacturing sweeter and more prolific corn, longer blooming annuals, shorter bushes, variegated foliaged perennials, hardier trees, and so forth. But Mother Nature will not allow perpetuation of human-altered species by seed alone, mainly because of cross-pollination that naturally occurs in uncontrolled environments. So, rather than rely on the unpredictable, man usually reproduces hybrid plants and cultivars by cuttings, budding, or tissue culture. A 'Red Sunset' red maple (grown for its superior red fall coloration) is vegetatively propagated to insure the breeding qualities. Similarly, vegetative methods are used to achieve uniform behavior and appearance in 'Claudia Wannamaker' magnolias since seedling (unimproved) magnolias grow at varying rates, first bloom at varying ages, and appear quite different from one another.

So, if you have a bunch of one kind of plant that's been cultivated and produced vegetatively and not by seed, you run the risk of losing all of them to disease or insect invasion. But it's generally a risk worth assuming when weighed against the benefits of whatever the man-induced attribute happens to be—larger flowers, more colorful foliage, or perhaps even increased disease resistance. Of course, variety is the spice of life, and the beauty of the plant world. Take advantage of the many choices you have, regardless of their reproductive genesis.

Plants reproduced in propagation nurseries are very, very small. In contrast, in nurseries like ours where we grow out those infant plants, we deal with very large plants that require much more equipment for harvesting. We use a skid-steered loader with various sizes of spades to dig large trees and shrubs. This October Glory red maple is 5 to 5½-inch caliper, the diameter of the trunk 12 inches from the ground. (The caliper of a tree that is 5 inches or more is measured 12 inches from the ground. Smaller caliper trees are measured 6 inches from the ground.) The root-ball is 48 inches in diameter. We used a short basket to reduce the root-ball weight, which if it were in a regular basket would be about 1,800 pounds. In the short basket the root-ball weight is about 1,400 pounds. The tree itself weighs, without leaves, 600–800 pounds. So this dug tree weighs 2,000–2,200 pound.

LESSON 10 ∽ November 19–25
Growing Plants Indoors

*Pity the poor houseplants in custody of neglectful owners . . . stuffed into
undersized pots. Kept in the dark . . . soil-bound hostages yearning to be
free—or at least moved to better light.*

—Griffin Miller
"Totally Self-Sufficient Plants?"
The New York Times, July 1, 1993

Bring the Outdoors In for Winter

I'VE ALWAYS HAD PLANTS inside my house and office; I couldn't live
without them. Through the years, I've carried them in their pots
from home to home, workplace to workplace. Sometimes they
have survived the move or the new environment, sometimes not.
Sometimes they have survived a period of neglect, sometimes not.
Some pots have broken. Some have changed patina. But most have
remained as special as the plants in them.

I can tell you stories about all of my plants. A peperomia that
was given to me while I was in college grew no more than an inch
in twenty years. But several years ago I gave it its own perch in my
new sunroom, right in the brightly lit, south window, and it took
off, sprouting new growth in all directions.

When she was two, my daughter Cat brought home from day-
care a Mother's Day gift—a pothos with three tiny leaves. After
being in my office for several years, that plant made its way to my
house where it thrived. I took cuttings. I grew its offspring and
took more cuttings. And for years, I have had pothos everywhere—
so much so that one fall I supplied enough cuttings for rooting
about seventy-five clumps of plants (just a drop in the bucket as
my cuttings go) for Cat's high school class to pot, grow, and give

to elderly folks. One of those classmates since took delight in my Web description of pothos: "The stems will grow on . . . and on . . . and on . . . There's one in my bedroom that grows noticeably each day—the stems are inching across the floor, coming closer and closer to my chair. One night the stems started shaking, shoving each other aside, competing for room for themselves as they branched out. IT'S ALIVE!!!!"

One of my greatest journeys involved the transportation of houseplants when my husband and I were moving from Massachusetts to Georgia. On the final moving-our-things trip, he was driving the big truck (that was to become our first nursery delivery truck) with the last load of our belongings, and I was driving our pickup truck with a truck-body camper on the back, filled to the brim with our houseplants. Most of them were in gorgeous ceramic pots thrown by our potter friends in Western Mass. I don't recall how we kept the pots from tipping or breaking, but I do recall the enormous weight on the truck.

We were on I-77, barreling down the steep incline from the top of the Blue Ridge Mountains of Virginia to the North Carolina valley below. With each sway of the truck, I laughed nervously as I envisioned me and my cargo exiting the road onto one of the many escape ramps, plants flying everywhere, our dreams of a new life dashed en route.

So much for fear. We didn't crash, and the plants made it. They survived, but didn't much thrive for many years—we were too busy building our new house, starting our nursery business, and planting our own feet. But even though our plants lost our attention, they retained their resilience. We still live with many of those that were transported, and they and their offspring are an integral part of our home.

Lots of plants make terrific indoor additions, many of which are those whose natural habitat is the warm, humid climate of the tropics or subtropics. Many grace the outdoor landscapes we see at the southern beach areas of the United States. But if these plants are north of their comfort zone, they need to be indoors in this area during the winter. They need to be your houseplants, and should be, as they do nothing but good in your house. They bring the outdoors in, giving your home a softening, a lushness, a glow of life and breath. They help filter the air in your home and provide a moist environment. They provide bugs and spiders a harbor, creating ground for their natural selection (better in your plants than elsewhere in your house). And they add immensely to the aesthetic pleasures of your home, creating a landscape that you can enjoy without braving the elements outdoors.

Just as variety is the spice of life in the outdoor landscape, the greater the variety of indoor plants in your house, the better. Each one will add texture, color, height, dimension, fragrance, or movement to the interior design. I use plants to soften corners and fill voids. Some—especially those in particularly handsome pots—stand alone as specimens, works of art, and decorative centerpieces. Others serve like knickknacks—hardly noticeable, but exceptional upon examination.

My sunroom is filled with plants. It's their special space, and they love it. I sit each morning during my meditation time and admire their beauty, watch their growth, feel their life. I water them as needed, turn them so they will grow more evenly, pinch off dead stems and leaves when they appear, and move them if they seem discontent with the light they are receiving, trying other spots until they're happy.

This care is not an onerous task. In fact, it's not a task at all because it doesn't require a green thumb or an extensive knowledge of the plants and their cultural requirements. It just requires attention.

I have often said that I wish the hospital had given me an instruction manual when I had my children. Then I would know exactly how to raise them, the precise answers to the many dilemmas that confound me in their upbringing, and when and what to say and do to assure their healthy, happy growth. Without such a manual, I have learned that I just have to pay attention, try new approaches, seek advice on occasion, and then pay attention some more. Agonizing, giving up, or remaining stagnant are not viable options.

Plants are the same as children. Although you may be able to get an instruction manual on your plants' cultural requirements, or some advice on their care (starting with the sticker that comes with your store-bought plant indicating its basic needs for light and water), ultimately you will learn that plants, like children, just require attention. I was reminded of this principle just this month when two of my oldest and largest jade plants, which have taken me over twenty years to grow and shape into elegant form, died. These slow-growing succulent gems showed some signs of stress a couple of months ago when they started losing leaves, but I was too busy to, you got it—pay attention. In fact, to make matters worse, I was on the go during the summer so much that I watered the jades each time I was to be gone for a while, just to be sure they didn't go thirsty. Well, I know better than to water a jade before the soil is completely dry. But it was easier to ignore that maxim and water them before I hit the road.

Well, the results of my neglect of plants and principle became apparent when all of the stems suddenly drooped and fell this fall. Mushy insides revealed the culprit: brown rot. I killed my prized plants with too much water and lack of attention. I do have to add this point: As if it were known that this tragedy would occur, earlier this year I started about twenty jade plants in trays and then 4-inch pots and have been growing them and pinching back the stems (to help with branching and stability). They have been happy in the windows of our mountain cabin. I'm grateful that I can bring some home to grow and enjoy—and I will try to pay better attention.

IT'S A MATTER OF FACT

The Romans developed the first hothouses to cultivate roses and exotic plants. The "houses" were actually heated pits covered with mica. During the sixteenth century when plant explorers returned to Europe with tropical plants and exotic cacti, the aristocracy constructed glasshouses to keep the plants through the winter, but they mistakenly thought that heat was more important than light. As knowledge and technology advanced, the greenhouse roofs became curved to allow more light in, and cast iron rather than wood was used, resulting is less light-inhibiting bulk. The construction also became more affordable at a time when urban life and time-saving technologies afforded folks leisure time for cultivating indoor plants. As a result, conservatories, atriums, and glass morning rooms graced many upper-middle-class Victorian homes.

So that's the lesson: pay attention and be aware of your plants' health. If things aren't going well and you've exhausted the basic care practices (see "It's a Matter of Culture" in this lesson), try something different. Water more, less, more often, or less often. Try a sunnier spot or a darker spot. Try a less drafty location or a livelier one. Fertilize during the growing season but not during the slow season. Make a change and try new things. But always, always, give it time. For plants, like children, need time to adjust.

I hear people berate themselves more about their inability to grow indoor plants than anything else in the gardening world, and I honestly believe they are trying too hard and do not have sight of the basics. Plants are living things that need proactive care, not just reaction to troubles. It does take some effort, but it doesn't take extensive knowledge, scientific experimentation, or expensive training. It just takes a willingness to apply your mind to your plants' lives.

So, as it starts getting chilly outside and your thoughts turn to warm firesides, cozy blankets, and weekend afternoons spent inside, make your transition as smooth as possible by bringing the landscape in. While you're continuing to enjoy the charm, character, and appeal of the outdoor winter landscape, extend its beauty and pleasures by creating an indoor landscape of sorts.

Treat your plants with love and respect, and be in awe of their individual and unique beauty. Talk to them, play music for them, and I guarantee they will respond with lively growth.

It's a Matter of Culture

A PLANT'S CULTURAL REQUIREMENTS include the environment in which it grows and how it is cultivated. The better its needs are met, the more flourishing growth it will have.

Light: Light is the energy source needed to manufacture food, and indoor plants are grouped according to their light needs:

- Low light—several feet from eastern windows or in northern windows
- Medium light—up to several feet from southern or western windows or in eastern windows

- High light—in or near southern or western windows

Natural light indoors is substantially dimmer than that of the outdoors and might be affected by roof overhangs, shade trees, wall colors, curtains, and the time of year and length of day. Artificial, fluorescent, or special incandescent lights can supplement sunlight, especially for low-height plants. Because plants grow in the direction of the strongest light (phototropism), turn them to prevent lopsidedness.

Temperature: Most indoor plants fair well in normal house and office temperatures, but avoid excessive or sudden changes in temperatures. Few indoor plants tolerate freezing temperatures, and some will sustain injury if the mercury drops below 50°F. Use only room temperature water on your plants.

Soil: Use a potting mix, not dirt from the yard (unless you're prepared to amend it and sterilize it), making sure it's well-drained, aerated, and has good water- and nutrient-holding capacity. Specialty mixes for particular plants are unnecessary. Note that the soil tends to "shrink" over time. If the plant doesn't need a new home, add more soil and lift the plant higher in the pot.

Fertilizer: Indoor plants don't require a great deal of fertilizer due to their relatively low-light environment. I prefer liquid fertilizers and apply them only when the plant is actively growing.

Container: Most any kind of container will do, but be sure the pot has drainage holes. If it doesn't, fill the bottom with broken clay pot pieces and rocks. This will create a space where excess water can go without soaking the soil and causing root rot. The clay pieces also serve to retain some moisture, a nice safeguard when watering is temporarily forgotten. Glazed pots retain moisture in the soil longer than raw terra-cotta pots, which allow rapid evaporation through the porous material.

Cleaning and Grooming: To remove dust and grease, allowing for better transpiration and breathing, periodically clean the leaves of your plants with a very, very mild solution of water and detergent. Or place your plant in the shower or outside under the hose. Be sure the outside temperature does not vary much from that indoors, and do not let the water pelt the plant.

If your plant seems to be hugging the sides of the pot, growing too big for it, lightly tamp it out of the pot if possible. If the roots are large and curling tightly around the sides of the root-ball, it's probably time to give the plant a larger home. Break up the root tangles with your fingers and put the plant in a larger pot with more soil, being sure to keep the top of its root-ball at the top of, and not below, the soil line.

Remove dead leaves, stems, and spent flowers as you see them and trim scraggly growth.

Water: This is without a doubt the most confounding cultural requirement for most plant stewards, but the principle is simple for most plants: water when there is very little or no moisture in the soil. Check by sticking your finger down an inch or more into the soil; do not water just because the soil surface is dry. After time, you can gauge water needs by the weight of the pot. If your plant is wilted, do not assume it needs water since it may be wilting because it has too much. Fluoride-treated tap water is fine for most indoor plants; rainwater from your roof is better. You should leach (wash) the salts from the plant soil periodically by watering thoroughly in the sink or outdoors (if the temperatures are not too different than those inside). Also, get rid of excess water sitting in the pot saucers after each watering.

Trial and error will likely dictate your watering success, as will an understanding of the factors contributing to your plant's needs: plant size, container size, soil type, temperature, and humidity. Note that you will probably have to water more often in the winter since heating systems draw lots of moisture out of plant soils. Also, indoor plants love to be misted. Tropical in nature, they are used to 40–60 percent humidity, so use a spray bottle and spray away.

One final note on water: Have you ever wondered what the water droplets you sometimes see on some of your plants' leaf tips or edges in the mornings are? The oozing, or guttation, is actually xylem sap that cannot transpire through the leaves because the stomata are closed or narrowed (common at night when photosynthesis is not taking place) or because of environmental conditions such as soils highly saturated with water or high humidity, when water won't evaporate. So, when water is drawn into the roots by the ever-present osmotic equalization process, is pushed by root pressure up into the plant, yet does not have its normal vaporous escape through the stomata of the leaves, special leaf pores called hydathodes allow it to exude in liquid form, along with sugars and minerals and other organic solutes. The pores were developed in certain species to allow a plant to get rid of excessive salts. Salt on the leaf edges after the droplets evaporate may be an indication of excessive salt in the soil, probably from fertilizer. (See Lesson 1 for more details on root pressure, transpiration, and osmosis.)

Propagation: Without making a fuss, you can add to your plant party. Use the clippings from grooming, or take cuttings (stems with one or two leaves). Place them in a glass of water in a window and see if they will root. You'll be amazed at how many will. After the roots have grown thick and substantial, plant the babies in a very small pot of soil until fully established. Then pot them up into a larger container.

Problems: I highly recommend you purchase a comprehensive book about indoor plants and their care. Read only about the particular cultural requirements of the indoor plants you select for your home. Then, if a problem arises, consult the book and try to diagnose and remedy the ailment. You may find, for example, that the wilting you see is due to overwatering, the gradual defoliation is a result of inadequate light, the rapid defoliation is because of shock from moving a plant to a different environment, the strange foliage color is because of insufficient fertilization, the scorched leaf tips are from overfertilization or salt buildup, or the stickiness on the leaves is due to insect infestation. Or you may find that some other situation is responsible for these conditions. Look it up or consult your local Cooperative Extension Service for help. They are impressive at diagnosing problems, especially if you take the plant (or plant part) to them—being careful, of course, of drastic outdoor temperatures during transport!

LESSON 11 ✿ November 26–December 2
The Essence of Things

If facts are the seeds that later produce knowledge and wisdom, then the emotions and the impressions of the senses are the fertile soil in which the seeds must grow. The years of early childhood are the time to prepare the soil. Once the emotions have been aroused—a sense of the beautiful, the excitement of the new and the unknown, a feeling of sympathy, pity, admiration or love—then we wish for knowledge about the object of our emotional response. Once found, it has lasting meaning. It is more important to pave the way for the child to want to know than to put him on a diet of facts he is not ready to assimilate.

—Rachel Carson
The Sense of Wonder

The Amazing Grace of the Changing Seasons

MY CHILDREN ALWAYS USED TO ASK me what my favorite holiday is. I think they wanted me to say Christmas, but I couldn't. It's Thanksgiving—without a doubt, hands down. The string of days beginning on Wednesday has always held special sway with me for reasons sensuous, sentimental, and sublime.

For me, fall is intense. It's all new beginnings, new challenges. Once, it was school for me, then it was school for my children. New sports, new patterns at work, new goals, the renewal of meetings and friendships faded during the summer months, and renewed spirit. That intensity drives the days, working toward the climax of the holiday season, beginning with Thanksgiving. It's the first breath, the first reprieve from the fervor, and it used to be the first chance I had in months to go to Social Circle, Georgia, to visit my father's parents, Granny and Grandpa.

That trip, that day of Thanksgiving, was the most wonderful day of the year. I saw cousins, uncles, and aunts whom I hadn't seen since our first-Sunday-in-August reunion. I gorged on plate-fuls of the best Southern cooking imaginable. And I reveled in the warm sunshine out in the yard under the pecan trees, inhaling the syrupy sweet aroma of the elaeagnus bushes that bordered the back line near the barbeque pit that became filled with Grandpa's shucked oyster shells over the years. Oh, there was nothing like it.

If I was lucky, we stayed late in the day, or on occasion spent the night. Either way, I was afforded the grandest pleasure watch-ing the sun set. Bright reds and oranges, with the slightest hint of green just above, emblazoned the country sky across the flat fields. It was a sunset I could not see through the tall oaks at home in Atlanta. It was the kind of sunset my father first pointed out to me as he stood in awe and commented on its magnificence and the incredible, simple complexity of nature. It was a sunset of winter waiting.

At Thanksgiving I realized the seasons had changed while I had been busy hurrying helter-skelter toward . . . well, I'm not really sure toward what. But I embraced the change. I loved it, and I was thankful—for Granny and Grandpa and the home they opened up

At age 88, Granny (Georgia Ann Adams Godwin) prepares for Thanksgiving dinner, 1985.

to us, the food they prepared and shared with us, and the family that gathered together. I was thankful for Social Circle and for the changing seasons.

Yes, the seasons change—all of them. Our family tradition continued throughout the first forty-plus years of my life. My grandfather passed away in 1978, two months after I married. But Granny lived on, and on. She entered a long-term care facility in the 1990s but left her house just as if she would return, and she did return for Thanksgivings and family reunions. But the number of family members joining our festivities dwindled over time. By 1998, there was no Thanksgiving dinner at her house. And in 1999, Granny passed on at the age of 102.

I was left with some of Granny's household items, knick-knacks, and personal effects. These things remind me of her and of certain events, people, holidays, celebrations, and gatherings. But they are more like botanical books that list, define, and describe plants—conjuring up images and smells, but failing to describe the true sensory impact, the essence, or the spirit of the plant; failing to describe the indescribable impact of the plant on the observer, the participant in its life; failing to describe the world in which the plant grows. So too, Granny's things fail to describe, to emit her essence, her spirit, and the stage on which her life and mine merged. The seasons, sunsets, traditions, cycles, love—none of these things can be described. They must be observed, they must be lived, they must be held in awe, for they fulfill you. They are part of your substance and your spirit. If you could describe them, in your very breath of utterance you would lose their essence, and a part of yourself, to the ether.

So I don't attempt to describe. I just mourn. I mourn a season's change. I weep. I ache and I am sometimes lost. It's been hard accepting a new season, a new landscape. It's been hard departing the pecan trees dropping the most delicious, plump, moist nuts on the leaf-strewn grass and letting the warm November sun shine through the breeze-tossed remnants of lonely leaves dotting their branches. It's been hard departing the aromas, the tastes, the familiar voices and stories, the walks down the main street—to the store, cemetery, to friends' and families' houses. It's been hard departing the placid escape from the hectic pace we set for ourselves, the love and amazing grace given in peculiar ways. It's been hard departing the sunsets.

Six and a half years after Granny's passing, just as I was resurrecting my writing of this book, my father passed. While arranging his memorial service, I described to the minister a man who had opened my eyes to the awesome beauty of nature by revering the Social Circle sunset. It was my father's gift to me, one that has given me constant beauty by validating the mere act of observation; one that has given me anchorage in the knowledge of the constancy of nature when all of my moorings seem to be cut loose; one that has defined my very existence, having woven a steadfast thread through the patterns of my past, binding it to my present, securing its integrity for my future. With this gift, I can continue, part and parcel of what has come before. If I'm lucky, I'll remember always. And if I'm smart, I'll continue to live each moment observing, embracing, loving, and learning. My past and my present will become my future as my seasons change.

Thanks be for the seasons, for my family, for amazing grace. Thanks be for the Social Circle sunsets.

LATIN NAMES ARE UNIVERSAL

JUST AS IT'S NOT POSSIBLE to adequately describe the grace of my Thanksgivings because of a transcendence that's indescribable, it's not possible to convey the essence of a plant through use of its name. But language is our means of labelling and communicating so that we have some connection in thought. Plants, therefore, have names—several of them.

It's the Latin names that amaze me. Actually, it's the plantspeople, including my husband, who use them that amaze me. They rattle off the botanical name of a given plant like a well-known jingle—they speak Latin, regularly, fluidly, and easily. I just can't do that.

While lots of folks think the ability a showy, useless thing, most people don't realize that the common names they use when referring to plants often apply to three or four very different plants, depending upon their region, or that one plant may be known by three or four different common names. It gets confusing! The botanical name clarifies the situation, in most instances, although plants are often recategorized and renamed, leading to a confusion of proper plant taxonomy and nomenclature for many years, until eventually the dust settles. Nevertheless, the common name of many plants is its botanical genus or species name—not so difficult, except when writing about them and deciding the proper form (capitalized or italicized or not).

IT'S A MATTER OF FACT

Squirrels love pecans, eating an estimated ten million pounds each year. Did you ever see that commercial with the industrious squirrel skittering in and out of someone's office, grabbing Post-it Notes, and sticking them to the walls of his hollow home with reminders of where he has hidden his nuts? I love it! Must be the middle-age thing about not being able to remember stuff unless I make a note. Anyway, squirrels do gather nuts for winter food. And they do hide them, just as a dog buries his bones, waiting for just the right time to eat them. Nuts are a one-celled fruit wrapped with a dry shell. When squirrels forget where they have placed them (as those who do not use notes often do), the nuts germinate into seedling trees. Some trees, like oaks, have developed a mechanism (made possible by its mast, or nut production) to prevent the population growth of healthy predators, whose numbers can become great enough that they eat all of a tree's nuts, leaving none for reproduction. The tree will cease to produce nuts for a few years, starving predators, or at least discouraging their continued presence. Then the tree will produce a large crop of nuts, more than the reduced population of predators can possibly eat; some nuts then will be left for rooting and reproduction.

A botanical name starts with the genus, the group of plants to which it belongs and with which it shares many characteristics; when written, the genus is capitalized and italicized. The second word in the name delineates the species and is descriptive of essential identification characteristics common to the subgroup; the species epithet is lower cased and italicized. Varieties or subspecies, individual plants that have a marked difference in nature to the rest of the species, are denoted by the inclusion of "var." or "subsp." or "ssp."

Cultivars (*cultivated varieties*) are those cultivated plants that are clearly distinguished from the rest of the species by characteristics that are physiological, chemical, etc., and that retain those characteristics when reproduced (see Lesson 52). Most are notated by capitalization and single quotes. Thus, *Vitex agnus-castus* 'Shoal Creek' is the cultivar Shoal Creek of the species *agnus-castus* of the genus *Vitex*, otherwise known commonly as chastetree or bee tree. Because cultivar names cannot be trademarked, some cultivars are further identified using a trademarked name that is user-friendly and descriptive but of no taxonomic validity. The cultivar name stands and the additional name bears the ™ symbol or, if registered with the U.S. Office of Trademarks and Patents, uses the mark ®, giving a nursery or plantsperson the exclusive right to use that name. For instance, *Hydrangea macrophylla* Endless Summer® The Original ('Bailmer') carries a trademarked and cultivar name. When referring to the plant, taxonomists use the cultivar name 'Bailmer', whereas the nursery that introduced the plant uses the legally protected name Endless Summer® for marketing purposes. (You may see ™ attached to a plant name, and later ®, as has been the case with Endless Summer, which bore a trademark [™] when I first wrote this section, but now bears a registered trademark [®] for the collection name. Actually, because there is now more than one Endless Summer hydrangea, the first introduction, 'Bailmer', has been given the name The Original, to distinquish it from the others.)

This branding sometimes leads to multiple trademarked names for the same plant; they're produced by different nurseries but are the same botanically. The loropetalum Plum Delight® is the same as Pizzazz™, and both are the cultivar 'Hines Purpleleaf', for instance. And some cultivars commonly known by one name are now being marketed under trademarked names, but they are the same plant. For example, *Ilex vomitoria* 'Shadow's Female' is now sold also as Hoskin Shadow™.

Another relatively new marketing strategy is grouping plants into "collections" and "series." The collection or series name is usually trademarked as in, for example, The Knock Out® Family of Roses, Encore Azalea® Collection, The Razzle Dazzle® Crapemyrtle Series, and The Glowing Horizons Loropetalum® Series. Some nurseries and innovators in managing the patenting, branding, and licensing of new introductions create collections of plants, which may include several entirely different types of plants that are common only in their proven reliability and appeal. The Gardener's Confidence® Collection (by McCorkle Nurseries) and the Southern Living® Plant Collection (by PDSI® [Plant Development Services, Inc.] and Southern Living®) are but two examples.

Not only do plantspeople have a way to protect the name of a plant, they have a way to protect the plant itself, preventing anyone from legally reproducing it through propagation or otherwise without their "permission"—a plant patent. Anyone reproducing a patented plant must pay the patent holder (usually the breeder or introducer) a fee for each occurrence. If a patent is pending, the plant name may include the acronym PPAF, "plant patent applied for," as in *Lantana camara* 'Chapel Hill Gold' PPAF. If the patent has been awarded, the name includes the acronym PP, meaning "plant patent." *Abelia* × *grandiflora* 'Kaleidoscope' PP#16,988 is an example.

According to the U.S. patent office, plants can be patented only if they are "invented or discovered and, if discovered, that the discovery was made in a cultivated area." In other words, they must be "new" plants. So, for instance, Bloom 'N Again® azaleas cannot be patented because they are simply old azaleas that have been selected by a nursery, grouped because of similar characteristics as a brand, and marketed under the trademarked collection name. In contrast, Encore® azaleas, which are cultivars newly developed through breeding, are patented.

Because of these complicated monikers and their tendency to change over time, there is a great deal of inconsistency and incorrectness in the green industry when citing various plants. When researching one rose collection for this book, I was greatly confused by the official collection Web site listings. Upon contacting the company to inquire about the correct reference for their roses, I was told that their Web site was incorrect, and I was given the proper names by e-mail. I have found other errors on the Web sites of some plant developers themselves, as well as in their catalogs. So just know that this matter of plant names is confusing, not only because of the marketing ploys, but also because of the failure of some members of the green industry to be correct all of the time in usage. Also know that I have attempted in this book to denote plants as accurately as possible, but some appellations will have changed by the time you read the book, and some may not be quite right, at my hand, because of the noise of it all—forgive me.

So let's get back to some basics. Cultivar names are usually descriptive of some outstanding characteristic of the plant, but some are the name of public figures or fictional characters as well as foreign expressions, and almost anything else. Often, however, the cultivar name is the name of someone or place having some connection or significance to a plant's breeders, introducers, or the plant itself. *Legends in the Garden: Who in the World Is Nellie Stevens?* by Linda L. Copeland and Allan M. Armitage is an engaging book that tells the stories behind the naming of many such cultivars.

Most of the descriptive species names are easy to learn or decipher and give clues about the appearance, origin, or habitat of a plant. As a sampling:

- azurea   sky blue
- citrina   yellow
- purpurea   purple
- rubra   red
- buxifolia   boxwoodlike
- parvifolia   small
- alta   tall
- capitata   headlike
- compacta   compact
- contorta   twisted
- elegans   slender
- nana   dwarf
- reptans   creeping
- australis   southern
- chinensis   of China

- Canadensis   of Canada
- phyllus   leaf
- cornuta   horned
- densi   dense
- florida   free flowering
- fulgens   shiny
- lobata   lobed
- macro   large
- radicans   rooting
- rugosa   wrinkled
- scabra   rough feeling
- longifolius   long leaved
- punctatus   spotted
- virens   verdant green
- rigens   stiff
- serotinus   late
- flora   flowers
- armata   armed
- riparia   of riverbanks
- perennis   perennial
- reflexus   bent back
- odoratus   fragrant
- multifidus   with many divisions
- latifolius   broad leaved
- planus   flat
- cordatus   heart shaped
- humilis   low growing
- frigidis   growing in cold places
- calidus   warm, hot
- tardiflorus   late flowering
- longissimus   very long

The list of descriptive terms is extensive.

LESSON 12 ⌁ December 3–9
Holiday Hollies and Poinsettias

I prefer the winter and fall, when you feel the bone structure in the landscape—the loneliness in it—the dead feeling of winter. Something waits beneath it—the whole story doesn't show.
—Andrew Wyeth (b. 1917)

Hollies Highlight the Holiday Season

IT'S HOLIDAY TIME, with expectations of presents and decorations, which often include sprigs of holly—as in "deck the halls with bows of holly, fa-la-la-la-la, la-la-la-la." The holly tradition derives from the days when ghosts and demons were said to howl in the winter winds, and, because hollies are evergreen, it was believed they were magical and could chase evil away if placed over the home door. Sadly, the holiday hollies most often seen today in homes are artificial. More disheartening, the plastic imitates holly leaves with prickles, reinforcing the common misconception that all hollies have sharp spines and are, in many instances, undesirable in the landscape. After all, who wants to be pricked?

As a genus, hollies (*Ilex*) are, in fact, some of the most misunderstood landscape species. Contrary to popular belief, they don't all have prickles, and they come in all sizes, shapes, and habits. You should select them based upon your intended use, the planting site, and their compatibility with other landscape plants.

For year-round color, there are hundreds of varieties of evergreen hollies. And the increasingly popular deciduous hollies, while not green during the winter, provide contrasting texture and lively berry color in the season.

Dwarf hollies are marvelous additions to rock gardens or landscaped areas with taller shrubs. Medium-height hollies are good choices for foundation plantings, and taller hollies (sometimes referred to as trees) make excellent screens, windbreaks, hedges, specimens (singular planting), standards (limbed up with single trunk showing), or tree-formed (limbed up with multiple trunks exposed) highlights.

Berry color may be a consideration when choosing a holly. Japanese and inkberry hollies bear black berries; most others have red berries, but some have yellow or orange ones. The red berries make some hollies look like natural Christmas trees in the yard. The birds adore the red treats and will grace the winter landscape because of them. Although not as delectable to our feathered friends, the yellow and orange berries are showier and more visible on gray winter days and in shadowy areas.

The list of hollies hardy to our area is extensive, and several are basic additions to the Southern landscape. Here's a sampling:

- **Japanese Hollies** (*Ilex crenata*): People are most confused about these hollies because of their small, oval-shaped, non-spiny leaves that are similar in appearance to boxwood. In fact, a common name for Japanese holly is box-leaved holly. It's not unusual at the nursery for folks to come in with a leaf sample of a Japanese holly growing in their yard, thinking it is boxwood, and wanting more of the same. But it's easy to determine whether you have boxwood or Japanese holly: the leaves of boxwood are opposite one another on the stem whereas the leaves of Japanese holly are alternate. The most popular Japanese holly varieties are 'Compacta' and 'Helleri.' 'Green Luster' and 'Soft Touch', with their prettier, darker, shinier leaves, are excellent substitutes for the commonly used 'Compacta.' These relatively small, shade tolerant varieties are used extensively in foundation plantings since they can be easily shaped and maintained. Some upright Japanese holly varieties, like 'Chesapeake', can be used as substitutes for *Ilex × attenuata* 'Fosteri' (Foster holly) or other pyramidal forms in shaded areas. Different cultivars can be planted together to form screens from 2- to 12-feet tall.

- **Chinese Holly** (*Ilex cornuta*): These hollies are larger leafed than Japanese hollies and generally will not tolerate much shade. The species is sometimes seen in older landscapes, but newer cultivars are very popular. 'Burford' and 'Dwarf Burford' are probably the most popular, growing 8–25 feet tall. 'Needlepoint' is similar to 'Dwarf Burford', but it has a slightly longer leaf and heavier fruiting habit. 'Rotunda' and 'Carissa' are smaller forms (3–4 feet high and slightly wider) of the Chinese holly. 'Rotunda' reminds people of the Christmas holly with its spiny leaf shape and red berries. The 'Carissa' leaf shape is similar to 'Needlepoint' but longer. It does not fruit, but is a good, small holly. 'Dazzler' is a mid-sized upright (to 10 feet) that is very heavily berried with fruits larger than 'Burford'.

- **Yaupon Holly** (*Ilex vomitoria*): A small-leafed (1/2-inch wide by 1-inch long), no prickles holly with shiny red berries and many uses, yaupon grows 15–25 feet tall and will tolerate very wet soils and shade or full sun. Good for screening, it's easily sheared but looks nice in a loose, natural form. When tree-formed, the convoluted, sprawling branches create a jigsaw puzzle–like design beneath the leafed canopy. My favorite upright yaupon is 'Shadow's Female,' which has a slightly larger and rounder leaf and produces berries abundantly at an early age. Weeping yaupon varieties make unusual specimens, while dwarf varieties are similar in shape to 'Helleri.' Yaupons are good to use as foundation plantings around houses with no gutters or under downspouts, especially where there's heavy clay soil (i.e., where there's lots of water).

- **American Holly** (*Ilex opaca*): This is the native holly you see growing in the woods, the result of seed dispersal by birds, most likely. It is loose like many understory trees in that shady habitat, but when grown in full sun, it is large (up to 50 feet), pyramidal, and dense, with red (sometimes yellow) berries. Although there are over

1,000 cultivars, 'Greenleaf', with its glossy, medium green, spiny foliage and bright red fruit (born at an early age), is one of the most popular ones. American hollies make nice, single-trunk trees and work well as singular specimens or in groups as screens. But many other sun-preferring hollies that have a similar upright pyramidal shape are available, making them suitable replacements. For instance:

- Savannah (Ilex × attenuata 'Savannah'): Very similar in appearance to American holly, 'Savannah' has lighter leaves (especially in winter and early spring), faster growth, and more berries.
- Nellie R. Stevens (Ilex × 'Nellie R. Stevens'): Very dark green lustrous leaves dress this holly, which is wider at the base than many other upright hollies. Nellies are the most popular screening holly.
- Emily Bruner (Ilex × 'Emily Bruner'): Similar in growth habit to 'Nellie R. Stevens', 'Emily Bruner' has larger, spiny leaves and is slightly lighter in color.
- Foster (Ilex × attenuata 'Fosteri'): Slower growing than many uprights, this holly has slender, dark green leaves and outstanding berry production. Fosters prune nicely into single-trunk trees.
- Lydia Morris (Ilex × 'Lydia Morris'): This holly is a good choice for a smaller area since it grows to only about 12 feet high and wide. It has cardinal red berries and small leaves that are extremely spiny.
- Lusterleaf (Ilex latifolia): I love this one! The large leaves are up to 8 inches long. This holly looks somewhat similar to a magnolia from a distance, but it has berries and less leaf drop. It's very substantial, full, and regal looking.

- **Inkberry Holly** (*Ilex glabra*): This plant is a native, small-leafed holly that is rapidly gaining in popularity as new cultivars are introduced. It tolerates shade and wet, even swamp-like, conditions and is cold hardier than Japanese or Chinese hollies. Compact forms stay as low as 3 feet, while others grow to 10 feet. The bushes sometimes tend to lose their lower leaves and have a loose habit, but they can be pruned to promote fullness. The black fruits are not very showy. 'Shamrock' and 'Nigra' are dwarf varieties that hold their lower foliage well. I'm partial to this dark green shrub that has a lustrous sheen as it waves when the wind blows.

- **Winterberry Holly** (*Ilex verticillata*): This is another native, which loses its leaves in winter (deciduous). The females set a display of bright red fruits. It tolerates wet soils and some shade or full sun. Winterberry can be used as a small tree and makes a good substitute for a dogwood in wet areas. There's good fall color on some hybrids like 'Autumn Glow' and 'Harvest Red' that are crosses with finetooth hollies (*Ilex serrata*).

- **Possumhaw Holly** (*Ilex decidua*): This is another native deciduous holly that grows larger than winterberry (up to 30 feet in the wild, but usually only about 15 feet or so in cultivation) and bears fruits that persist into spring. 'Warren's Red' is the most popular cultivar.

Hollies are the most durable, hardy, easy to maintain, bread-and-butter shrub/tree for your landscape, with many choices for a variety of sites. They highlight your winter landscape with their leaves and berries and will dress your house if you pick the sprigs of the spiny crew for that traditional holiday look.

I have made hollies the subject of one question on the employment test for our nursery: "How many prickles does a holly have?" The responses of the vast majority of applicants demonstrate that they think all holly leaves have spines and that the number of spines is the same for all varieties. But the correct answer that I look for is: "It depends upon the variety, and not all hollies have prickles." Remember that, when someone suggests hollies for use in your landscape, or you apply for a job at our nursery.

Have a happy hollyday.

Postscript on hollies: We learned during our exceptionally wet, heavy, 7- to 8-inch snowstorm on March 1, 2009, that some hollies just can't take the weight and break dramatically under such stress. In our fields, yaupons of all sizes and tall Savannahs sustained the worst injuries.

IT'S A MATTER OF FACT

Holly was an important emblem for Native Americans, so much so that various groups traded the berries with tribes located where holly did not grow naturally. Because of its evergreen character, it symbolized courage and everlasting life and was painted, embroidered, or pinned on the clothes of warriors going to battle.

POINSETTIAS ARE PICKY ABOUT LIGHT

HOLLIES MAY HIGHLIGHT the holiday season, but poinsettias brighten it. They are pink, rose, white, and red hot—the biggest single holiday flowering crop. Breeders keep developing new varieties of them to meet the demand and to add some glitter to the traditional red offerings, which still manage to hog the market share of sales.

The newest cultivars come in multiple colors as well as some less traditional hues such as a purple introduction from the Paul Ecke Ranch in California, a leader in the poinsettia industry. Leaf colors may also vary from the usual green, as do the flowering times (from early to late season).

White poinsettias aren't yet true white, but the breeders are working on it. In the meantime, they've managed to develop some interesting colorations in the 'Jingle Bells' releases, which have red bracts speckled with pink, and the marbled varieties with variegated appearances. If you're confused by bracts, flowers, and leaves: The colorful "flower" of the poinsettia is not a flower at all, but bracts (modified leaves) that have changed color and surround the small yellow true flowers. The green leaves below the bracts are just that: simply leaves.

It's usually not worth the effort to keep a poinsettia for subsequent holiday season color. But if you want to try, here's what you'll have to do:

- After the bracts have faded, grow your poinsettia like any houseplant, under high light.
- When the weather permits, move the plant outdoors, and fertilize and water regularly throughout the summer.
- Prune and shape the plant throughout the summer, but do not prune after the first of September.
- Take your poinsettia back indoors when night temperatures drop below 55°F.
- To produce the colored bracts again, put the plant in complete darkness for 14 continuous hours every day starting October 1 until about Thanksgiving when the bracts are fully colored.
- Do not cheat and peek at your veiled poinsettia. Just a bit of light can throw off the photoperiod that's required to make the bracts color. Cover it with a box, put it in a locked dark room, or whatever. But don't peek for 14 straight hours.
- During the other 10 hours of the day, put the plant in bright, high light daylight.
- Do not let the temperature where you keep the plant fall below 60°F.
- Continue to water and fertilize your renewing poinsettia.

I've carried a poinsettia from Christmas until the following frost and enjoyed it as both an indoor and patio plant. But I have yet to make the effort to force "reblooming." It's another one of those time, patience, and inclination things. Better sometimes to bite the bullet and buy another one next year. Go ahead, support those nursery folks and make their holidays just a little bit brighter!

LESSON 13 ❧ December 10–16
Evergreens

Any landscape is a condition of the spirit.

—Henri Frederic Amiel (1821–1881)
Journal, October 31, 1852

Live Christmas Trees Provide Lasting Benefits

Did you know that the Christmas tree tradition has roots from as far back as 2000 B.C. and stems from the celebration of the winter solstice? Did you know that for many today this centerpiece of holiday decor and activity stands as a symbol of eternal life? What better way to celebrate eternal life than with a *live* Christmas tree, placed indoors or out. What better time to place a live tree indoors than during the week just prior to Christmas day.

Before selecting a live tree, be sure it will survive your climate after planting. For instance, we can't count on a blue spruce or Fraser fir to survive in our Piedmont area. Although I've seen one or two small ones spotted around our vicinity, they are aberrant and not likely to grow to maturity since they need the cooler temperatures of the North Georgia Mountains and beyond.

Norway spruce is only marginally hardy here and requires care in the picking. Purchase one that is balled and burlapped, but be sure the ball is large enough to support the tree. A 5-foot tree with a basketball-size root-ball is not going to survive.

White pine is another marginal possibility. These trees are great for decorating since they have wide spaces between the tiers of branches, and in maturity they are challenging climbing trees. But they just don't seem to reach those golden years in this area. Again, they need slightly cooler temperatures. Ditto: noble fir.

If you're starting to think that this discussion is purely academic, rest assured that it's not; there are several great choices for live Christmas trees that will survive in our region. Try an Arizona cypress, for instance. The cultivar 'Carolina Sapphire' has the same blue tinge of blue spruce, will grow 30–40 feet with a width of 15–20 feet, and prefers hot, dry conditions with well-drained soil.

Another great choice and dominant feature in our landscape in the past 10–20 years is Leyland cypress. It enjoys full sun and will grow 60–70 or more feet. Buy your Leyland cypress in a container since it does not transplant well as a balled-and-burlapped tree.

A sure bet for survivability is native Eastern red cedar. My grandmother always had one (cut, not alive) in her living room for Christmas. In fact, a great Southern Christmas tradition included a trek along the edge of the woods or fence lines to select and cut a red cedar. Needless to say, the larger ones are now hard to come by due to the demand. I've even found a few missing from my land throughout the years. But there's no need to trespass and steal since you can find these natives live at your local nurseries—and besides, it's just plain wrong. Plant them in full sun for the fullest growth, and expect good longevity in clay or sandy, low or high pH soil.

If you prefer or need a smaller, very slow-growing Christmas tree, try a dwarf Alberta spruce. The 12- to 24-inch containerized sizes make excellent tabletop decorations. Larger sizes are also available but are somewhat costly.

One final possibility I'd like to mention is the fantastic landscape specimen deodar (meaning timber of the gods) cedar. In 1920, Altadena, California, started its mile-long "Christmas Tree Lane" by decorating 200 flanking deodars with 10,000 multicolored lights. I suppose that's nothing compared to today's Christmas light spectaculars, but what a spectacle that must have been back then. The deodar grows slowly and has a graceful habit. Horticulturist Michael Dirr suggests that its useful garden life in our area is 10–20 years with a maximum height of about 40 feet. (They grow much taller in other areas.)

If you choose to set your live tree indoors, first put it in an unheated, sheltered area but do not expose it to freezing temperatures. After a few days of transition, move it indoors and make its stay as short as possible. You do not want it to break its dormancy, making it prone to cold damage when placed back outside. Because our houses are so dreadfully dry in the winter and furnaces suck moisture out of everything, be sure to keep your tree adequately watered. Check the soil 2–3 inches down for dryness, water thoroughly, and use a spray bottle to mist the foliage periodically—a good measure not only for the health of the tree but also for fire prevention. Unplug any ornamenting lights and be sure not to dowse them with the spray, and allow a drying period before reconnecting them.

When you're ready to move your tree back outside, again give it a few days in an unheated, covered area, protecting it from sun, wind, and extreme winter cold. After the transition period, plant the tree and water it. If we get our normal winter rains, you shouldn't

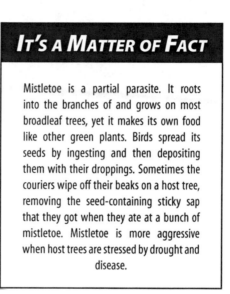

IT'S A MATTER OF FACT

Mistletoe is a partial parasite. It roots into the branches of and grows on most broadleaf trees, yet it makes its own food like other green plants. Birds spread its seeds by ingesting and then depositing them with their droppings. Sometimes the couriers wipe off their beaks on a host tree, removing the seed-containing sticky sap that they got when they ate at a bunch of mistletoe. Mistletoe is more aggressive when host trees are stressed by drought and disease.

have to worry with watering much, but check for dryness every 4–5 days. Be sure to mulch around the base of the tree to protect it from severe cold and to retain moisture.

The most gratifying way to enjoy a live Christmas tree is to buy one to plant immediately in your yard while using a cut tree inside the house. Decorate the outdoor tree with or without lights and other colorful additions. Or decorate it for the birds, which will love feasting on strings of red cranberries and popcorn, suet balls, peanut butter and birdseed balls, and oatmeal raisin cookies.

Start a new tradition by planting a tree each year in honor of a loved one. Consider it your Christmas gift to Mother Earth for all the bounty and beauty she bestows on us throughout the year. Or simply enjoy it as a perennial reminder of the gifts of love and eternal life.

In the tradition of my grandparents and those before them, we went out and found and chopped down a tree to serve as our Christmas tree in 1959. This pine came from our young tree farm in Loganville. As was most often the case on Christmas morning, we (left to right: me, my sister, Elizabeth, and brother, Thomas) were tired from little sleep and an early morning look under the tree for Santa's gifts.

EVERGREENS FOREVERMORE

WE'VE JUST EXPERIENCED the decay of the annuals, the decline of the herbaceous non-evergreen perennials, and the ultimate dance to dormancy of the deciduous trees and shrubs. We see death. We feel cold. But we have been given the evergreens, which keep our landscape from becoming totally barren in the winter—another sign of amazing grace.

Evergreens are plants that maintain green leaves year-round. Osmanthus, loropetalum, Indian hawthorn, gardenia, camellia, leucothoe, waxmyrtle, anise, nandina, juniper, some azaleas, some magnolias, some hollies, abelia sometimes, and many conifers help us get through the dormancy and mysterious renewal of wintertime with their color.

Evergreens shed and replace their leaves continuously, rather than all at once like the deciduous plants that lose their leaves in fall and remain bare for part of the year. On most evergreens, one leaf stays three to four years. But there is great variation among the plants. For example, rhododendron leaves fall after as little as six months while pine needles (leaves) may fall after as much as nine years. You'll often see lots of yellowing leaves during the "spring flush" of evergreens because, while the new spring growth is demanding more nourishment, many older leaves turn yellow and are pushed off. Magnolias and Savannah hollies are notorious for causing concern about their health during this flushing time.

As if they want to be evergreen, some trees keep holding their brown, dead leaves throughout the winter. They are deciduous, but their mechanism for dropping leaves is not fully developed, so they hang onto them until new spring growth pushes them off. Again, we are blessed with the beauty of their crinkled, dry foliage as it catches the light during the winter. The sight of glistening, bouncing beech leaves on an immature, smooth-barked tree in the understory of a winter forest is akin to the vision of a young, naked model posed for portrait, adorned only with jewels. And the sound of those leaves is the sound of spirit, ever present in the decaying woods.

As we approach the calendar mark of the commencement of winter, evergreens remind us that the landscape is fully alive and never really dead—the perpetual course of nature remains apparent. It's an incredible thing we have to enjoy; there's never a dull moment.

WINTER

As THE SUN LIES LOW in the sky and the light is least, I think of the ancients who feared the dormancy of winter and questioned whether the life-giving source of light would disappear altogether—whether a future would be. But as I am captivated with the beauty of the winter landscape, any fears of fate I may have inherited are silenced.

I know the Earth is simply resting, fitfully preparing for the spring fling. I feel the cold, wet winter wind saturate my bones, yet I witness the warming, nurturing beams of the midday sun. I feel the rawness of the barren trees and frozen waters, yet I witness the fresh buds and running brooks. I feel the veil cast by the dreary, thin, gray clouds, yet I witness a glow periodically breaking through—creating an aura of anticipation.

As the drama of winter unfolds and progresses toward the next act, the characters assume their roles and don their costumes on the earthly stage. The slanting rays of sun pierce the dusty air, bounce off luminous leaves of evergreens, and illuminate grassy plumage. The bright berries of bountiful bushes reflect the light and demand the attention of hungry birds. The forests—stripped of their tent of leaves, snaky vines, and underskirts—stand naked in the light, revealing their alluring curves and contours.

I wrap myself in the comfort of the cocoon of winter, secure in the knowledge that there is light after darkness, life after death—eternity in the endless cycle.

LESSON 14 ∽ December 17–23
Holiday Toys and Tools

*The thumb is our chief tool in the garden, and if we wield it
particularly well, such that nature's ways and our desires are made to
rhyme, it may be said to be green.*

—Michael Pollan (b. 1955)
Second Nature: A Gardener's Education

Gardeners Like Holiday Gifts Too

IT'S ALMOST CHRISTMAS DAY. Your loved ones have expressed how distressed and dumbfounded they are because they have no gifts for you. But you're a gardener, and gardeners have lots of wishes. Perhaps the following list, which you can pass along, will give those benefactors some ideas, and perhaps they'll give you what you want. With the possibilities for giving to a garden lover endless, my suggestions are just a start:

- Gardening journal: to keep tally year to year of weather, growth punctuations, and natural happenings.
- Gardening jewelry: to demurely advertise ones passion.
- Gardening T-shirt: to loudly proclaim one's passion.
- Starter pots: for indoor windowsills, particularly above the kitchen sink.
- Decorative pots: for indoor or outdoor plants. Be sure of weatherability.
- Tools: those with a lifetime guaranty, and worth the additional dollars.
- Hooks: for hanging indoor or outdoor plants. See decorative pots above.
- Bird feeders and houses: to invite life into the landscape during the frigid winter, as well as the rest of the year.

- Hose guards, soap sheds, and other gardening helpers: to make life in the garden easier.
- Figurines, sculpture, and other weatherproof objects: to enhance the landscape artistry.
- Benches: for the weary gardener and the meditative soul.
- Water garden additions: statuaries, sculpture, fountains, and decorative rocks.
- Decorative canning labels: for the vegetable garden enthusiast. You can probably count on some yummies coming your way next summer.
- Botanical stationery: to thank folks for gifts and good times.
- Gardening attire: botanical T-shirts (not to be confused with gardening T-shirts mentioned above), gloves, hats.
- Labor-soothing devices: knee pads, stool with tool compartment, and koozie for cold drink.
- Gardening books: practical, inspirational, idea-generating, or just plain pretty.
- Potted indoor plant: to bring the outdoors in.
- Membership in a botanical garden: usually includes admission, educational programs, publications, discounts in the gift shop (hmm . . . next year's gift-giving season is closer than you think).
- Botanical pictures: too late to frame now, and color selections may not suit anyway, so just give the picture.
- Stepping-stones: inscribed or plain, inspirational or not, to help one down the garden path.
- Plants: Gee, what a novel idea! Has your garden lover always wanted a foxglove or Japanese maple? The cool season remains a suitable, if not perfect time to plant trees, shrubs, and perennials, at least in this area. But some plants don't look so hot in the winter, like the dead-to-the-ground perennials. A gift certificate (see below) might be better if your recipient likes a particular plant that won't look good until spring. (Be careful about bringing landscape plants into the heated house.

Save that for the last minute or leave them in the garage or other protected, but unheated area.)

- Gift certificates at garden centers or nurseries: This gift may be a last resort, or perhaps the best idea—a matter of philosophy, perspective, personality, and practicality. Gift certificates are a great way to deal with plants like perennials that now appear lifeless but are waiting for rejuvenation in the spring, when the gift certificate can be used to pick out that perfect specimen. As for all of the other gifts mentioned above, your loved one might just as soon pick out her gloves or gardening book. And it might be more feasible to send a gift certificate than a bulky present to your far-away recipient, allowing him to purchase the perfect gardening present close to home. It's easy to purchase them with a phone call or on the Internet.

So there you have it: a rough and ready list to share with others to make their shopping for you easier. Tell them that most of these items can be found at garden centers and many of the nurseries that sell to the public and are so much fun to visit—away from the hustle and bustle of the commercial centers during the busiest shopping season. They'll thank you for the reprieve.

Now that you've taken care of *their* shopping, what about yours? Here's an idea: While you are shopping for others, think of ways to share the joy of nature with them. And if it's your passion, give yourself a holiday treat by shopping plants and shopping gardening. Remember that the love and joy you put into your giving, and the holiday spirit you maintain, will come back to you many times over. So be good to yourself; the joy will spread.

IT'S A MATTER OF FACT

Watering cans are tools, and like other tools, they come in all sizes, shapes, and materials. Because of its durability and feel, galvanized steel used to be the material of choice. Traditionally, folks had two cans— one was covered with red enamel and was designated for soluble fertilizers, the other was green and held pure water.

Use Tools, Not Toys, to Tend Your Yard

Having the right tool for the right job—that's the mark of a professional, and the smart amateur alike. There are all kinds of gardening tools, from shovels to pruners to hoses and wheelbarrows. The quality varies immensely and is virtually always reflected in the price. But, like most everything, if you pay for and get good quality the first time, you won't be replacing tools and ultimately spending more money in the long run. In fact, most high-end tools have 5- to 10-year or lifetime warranties with full replacement at no cost. Now you do the math.

What tools does a gardener need? That's an easy question with a not-so-easy answer. The gardener will figure out what's needed as his work progresses; the kind of work determines the kind of tool. For instance, digging may require a shovel (rounded, squared, scooping, or trenching). Or it may necessitate a spade (long-handled, draining, root-ball, or serrated). But maybe the digging actually

We maintained a gift shop we called The Garden Hearth at the nursery for many years. In addition to gardening items, we carried works by local artists and artisans. John and I also had fun during the holidays selling poinsettias and providing materials and greens from our field stock for customers to make wreaths on site. This 1996 photo was used for advertising.

calls for forks (spading, composting, scooping, or bedding). Or for those really hard digs, picks and mattocks might be in order.

That's just the digging. What about cultivating (hoes, weeders, etc.) or planting (dibbles, trowels, bulb planters, and containers)? Pruners, shears, and saws are needed for cutting; hoses, sprinklers, and cans for watering; and buckets, baskets, and wheelbarrows for help in hauling and holding. Rakes and brooms are used in cleanup just as lawn mowers, edgers, rollers, and aerators are needed for lawn maintenance. Composters use special riddles and bins. And propagators use knives, potting benches, and coldframes.

The tools need tools for sharpening, oiling, and other routine maintenance. The gardener needs tools on the body—boots or shoes, gloves, hats, and pocketed clothes and jackets. And all the tools need storage— shelter, hooks, bins, etc.

Exhausted yet? Feeling broke? Overwhelmed? Don't be. Let's simplify. Start with the most essential and basic tool of all—you. Now let's add tool number two, a pair of gloves. Put some on your hands, go out into your yard, and the rest will take care of itself. If you're so inclined, you will stoop over and pick just that one weed, protecting your hands and making the job easier. And if you are even more inclined, you will then bend over and pick, oh, just one more weed. But, oh, don't you need to trim that dead stem from that shrub? It's been bothering you for so long. Don't you remember having some pruners somewhere? Weren't they conveniently stored in a bucket in the garage? Or will the search go on until dinner? Just how important to you is removing that twig anyway? And so it goes—or doesn't. Regardless, start with the gloves, always. If you and the gloves aren't going to work, nothing else will either.

You might be able to measure a gardener's degree of zeal and understanding of the vocation of gardening by his tools, but the tools do not a gardener make. And the lack of tools does not diminish the degree of love and devotion the gardener has for the art, or her skill, determination, and patience in practicing it.

LESSON 15 ❧ December 24–31
The Winter Solstice

The sun illuminates only the eye of the man, but shines into the eye and the heart of the child. The lover of nature is he whose inward and outward senses are still truly adjusted to each other; who has retained the spirit of infancy even into the era of manhood.

—Ralph Waldo Emerson (1803–1882)
Nature

The Winter Solstice Brings Light to Our Landscape

IT'S THE TIME OF THE WINTER SOLSTICE—when the sun passes low in the southern sky, making its briefest visit of the year in the Northern Hemisphere. By meaning, it's when the "sun stands still" and is actually an exact moment in time—when the sun reaches its greatest angular distance on the other side of the equator from us. According to today's Gregorian calendar decreed by Pope Gregory XIII in 1582, that moment occurs sometime between December 20 and December 23. But December 25 was established in the Julian calendar in 45 B.C. as the winter solstice and, by decree of Pope Julius I in the fourth century A.D., remains the date of one of the most significant winter celebrations in our Southern culture, Christmas.

By all rights, now should be a time of mourning, recognition of the darkness and death all around. But this late-December, midwinter period is a festive time in most cultures—a time of holidays, celebrations, and gatherings, most in recognition of the power of the sun, the return of light, and rebirth. Worshipping sun gods and goddesses, as well as gods of wine and merriment, were common themes in many societies. For example, Mithra, the Persian god of light, was honored when the sun lay reposed far from those lands. It was said that he rose from the dead on the winter solstice, symbolizing the promise of new life to all who followed him. The Mithraic feast, Brumalia, honored the invisible sun and was incorporated into Saturnalia, the wintertime festival of Roman tradition that started on December 17 and ended with a celebration of the birth of the sun on December 25.

But the Christian church attempted to squash such paganistic practices by invoking its celebration of the birth of Jesus Christ, establishing December 25 as the day of observance even though many believed that the actual birth date was some other time of the year. Despite the eventual shadowing of the solstice observations, the Christmas tradition incorporates many of the symbols and rituals of its predecessors, with plants, particularly mistletoe, holly, and ivy, maintaining a considerable role in the celebrations.

Mistletoe, commonly used in Christian homes today for one to stand under and receive a kiss, has a rich tradition in other cultures, ancient and modern. It was sacred to the Druids, along with oak, the tree they most connected with the partial-parasite. Meaning "all-healing" by their naming, they believed mistletoe had medicinal powers, despite its poisonous properties, and considered it a symbol of fertility. To this day, Aboriginal people in Australia believe spirit children live in the plant, and Swedes hang sprigs of "thunder-broom" over their doorways or on their walls to protect them from storms.

Holly, an evergreen representing immortality, has deep roots in mythology. Gifts of the plant were given during the Roman Saturnalia, which ended on the winter solstice. And the Holly King, who vied with the Oak King for the fair maiden's hand, would win at midsummer, while the Oak King would win at midwinter, assuring the smooth flowing of the seasons. Holly has been used in homes to ward off elves and fairies during winter and in stables on Christmas Eve to bring luck to the animals.

Ivy, whose leaves formed the poet's crown in ancient times, is associated with the Egyptian sun god Osiris, as well as Bacchus, the Roman god of wine and intoxication, who wore a wreath of ivy and grapevines and whose wand was encircled with both. It has a mythic past that intertwines with that of holly. Considered a male plant because of its prickly leaves and bright red berries (see Lesson 12 to correct that catchall description), holly complemented the female-characterized ivy. In Greek mythology, the god Dionysus (the Roman Bacchus) watched a girl dance passionately to her death at his feet, and, being moved, put her spirit into the plant, which has since borne her name and has clung to and embraced all that comes close.

Later drama portrayed holly as "king" and ivy as "queen," and Christian tradition speaks of ivy representing the pale innocence of the Virgin and holly representing the spiked crown of the Crucifixion. Being evergreen and not dying or withering in the winter, both plants, along with other evergreens, were used in winter festivals because they symbolized the undying gods of the natural world, the hope of continuation, and the rebirth assuredly to come in spring. They both grace Christian homes and churches today during the holiday season, but it is believed by many that such greenery should not be taken into the house until Christmas Eve; otherwise, bad luck will ensue.

> ## IT'S A MATTER OF FACT
>
> The winter solstice marks the first day of winter on our calendars. But our coldest times will come in January and February, after the summer and autumn heat absorbed and retained by the Earth and its oceans is finally dissipated. Cultures vary on when they consider winter to begin. New Englanders, for example, think it starts on the first full moon after the middle of November. Meteorologists say winter starts on December 1 (with March 1, June 1, and September 1 being the start of spring, summer, and fall respectively). Botanists say the season begins when the average daily temperature falls below 43°F, which is approximately when sap stops flowing and plant growth ceases, and leaves, stems, and flowers wither and die. Obviously this occurs at different times in different locations, but there is some certainty: On average, the seasons progress up and down the globe at about one hundred miles per week.

Although not specifically tied to the winter solstice, the Green Man is perhaps the most interesting source of confluence between mythology and the Christian church and is primarily a symbol of rebirth, which starts at the winter solstice when the sun begins its return from darkness. The Green Man has parallels with many dieties such as the Greek Pan and other characters of lore like Robin Hood and Peter Pan. And his likeness has been carved in wood and stone in churches, cathedrals, and other Christian establishments since the eleventh century. Today this embodiment of the life force, of all things green, is considered by some to be the patron of the environmental movement.

There's a reason why the myths and traditions surrounding the celebration of the winter solstice and considered pagan were often incorporated into the Christian traditions, as well as many other cultural practices around the world. They, like Christianity, address the darkness, death, anxiety, and fright associated with the lack of sunlight, and they speak to the anticipation, hope, and faith of rebirth—that the light will return, bringing life, growth, and creativity in its path.

Religion and cultural practices take many forms, but they all seem to attempt to institutionalize a spirituality that can only arise from one's relationship with the physical universe. My spirituality derives from, is nurtured by, and depends upon my awareness of and participation with my natural surroundings. It is impossible for me look at, smell, feel, and otherwise take in the majesty of the outdoors without believing in something greater than myself. And for me, as for the ancients perhaps, the message I receive is most powerful now, when we lie farthest from the sun, the light is least, and the Earth seems to pause and question continuation. For me, as for the ancients and Christians alike, I seek comfort where fear resides.

At this time surrounding the winter solstice, I see the landscape best. I see beyond the manipulation by humankind, beyond the décor and ornament, beyond the wishes and desires. I see the inconsequence of man in the raw supremacy of nature. I see a mighty drama orchestrated by a universal power binding all into one—a ceaseless energy. I see simply what is—dressed nakedness and lively death.

I hope you enjoy this time of the year as much as I do. Regardless of your beliefs, despite your celebrations, and in spite of (or to spite) your stress, give yourself a gift no other can. Go outside. Spend *at least* a minute or two, particularly as the sun rises or as the sun sets. Look, listen, and feel. Close your eyes and breath. Experience a moment in silence. And thank your God for the winter solstice and a clearer vision of the landscape.

Maple trees late in the afternoon in the nursery during the March 1, 2009, snowstorm. The flakes were as large as or larger than golf balls. We tend to take lots of pictures of snow events since they are special in our neck of the woods.

THE TREE IN WINTER

IF YOU HAVE BROADLEAF TREES in your landscape, you are blessed. If those trees are mature, with height and fullness, you are doubly blessed. If you take time in the winter to take stock of the grace of those trees, you are truly blessed. And if you can view your trees against a winter sunset, you are surely in heaven.

We all know that our broadleaf trees provide us shade in the summer, creating a cozy canopy from the sun and a cooler to combat its heat. They turn a sweet, light green in the spring as new leaves emerge, filling the air with anticipation. And they turn again into warmer hues during the fall, readying us for the onset of winter.

But it's the winter tree that most enlivens my soul—the trunk, rising and radiating into naked branches that stretch skyward with ever-diminishing size until their tips pierce the air. Black against the sky, the creature's silhouette begs my attention, claiming its place in the landscape. It leaves no doubt that it is alive, a formidable presence—a spirit requiring my respect.

I am exceptionally fortunate to be able to watch the brilliant winter sunsets behind a distant rise stretching across the western horizon at our farm. Perched on that rise is a forest of oak and hickory trees; spotted some distance in the forefront along a fence line are a few smaller persimmons and wild cherry. As the sun slips to the point where the air cools quickly and the shadows stretch so they all but disappear, those trees darken in stark contrast to the ever-enlivening sky. They appear as angels, standing guard at the gates of heaven, giving me pause to think, to contemplate my worthiness in their sight.

And as the sunset subsides and the gloaming casts its veil, the sky turns gray like ash from the inferno. And those trees—those trees remain stationed and black, sentinels slowly eclipsed as the darkness of night obscures their outline.

Oak and pecan trees in our backyard in December, 1997, following a dusting of snow. Fog settles in just before sunset.

LESSON 16 ᔐ January 1–7
New Year's Time

Given time—time not in years but in millennia—life adjusts, and a balance has been reached. For time is the essential ingredient; but in the modern world there is no time.

—Rachel Carson
Silent Spring

New Year's Resolutions to Grow On

IT'S A NEW YEAR—a mark on the calendar telling us it's time to begin again. We'll demand ourselves into action by resolving to make *it* happen. We'll reignite projects lost long ago to procrastination. We'll stop whatever pains us or start whatever pleases us. And usually, we'll set ourselves up for failure, disappointment, and shame as the days tick by and the habits of old surface once again.

So let's forget about resolutions—the word itself suggests failure. Think instead about growth, about developing yourself in a more healthful, fulfilling way. If your idea of a better life includes being a better, more knowledgeable gardener, having a prettier yard and healthier plants, or sharing a harmonious, peaceful relationship with your landscape, there are many activities you can do in working toward that goal. I have several suggestions, with a warning attached. If you become stressed by any of the activities and they become a chore, don't do them! Keep the journey enjoyable and realize your goal in the journey itself. If you don't like the journey, in all likelihood you don't really desire the destination.

- Start a gardening calendar. What's the weather like? What changes did you notice in your yard today? What are the animals doing? This is an excellent way to get to know your landscape, year after year, and to learn what to expect so you can plan your gardening activities accordingly.

- Start a gardening journal. See above and expand upon it. How did all of these happenings make you feel? Take pleasure in reviewing your entries periodically. Are your plants growing healthily? Are you?

- Add your name to gardening mailing lists. You'll receive lots of free information and perhaps discounts on gardening supplies and plants.

- Subscribe to gardening magazines, newsletters, e-newsletters, and other publications (only if you will take the time to read them). Again, they are terrific sources of information and inspiration.

- Create a file or notebook for garden-related articles, book titles, and other interesting things you come across. Start an index by subject matter so you can find information when you're ready to use it.

- Read that gardening book you coveted in the library, store, or catalog. Still no time? Then put the name, author, and source in the notebook mentioned above for later reference.

- Watch the newspapers and other sources for gardening shows and note them on your calendar. They are pleasurable respites during the cold months while waiting patiently for spring to come.

- Can't be patient? Are those reminders of spring-to-come too enticing? Then get outdoors and garden. If the ground isn't frozen, plant that live Christmas tree you bought, after giving it a transition period of a few days in your garage or other mild location. Decorate it with popcorn, cranberries, peanut butter, suet, and birdseed for our feathered friends.

- Invite more birds into your yard by filling your long-empty bird feeder with seed. Buy a bag or bucket. Open. Pour. Nothing to it. The pleasures far, far outweigh the simple task.

- Use the inevitable, unseasonably warm, January thaw days to start working your beds for spring planting. Churn the soil, mix in compost, and let it all start working. Smell the moist, earthy richness.

- Use the same thaw days to plant trees and shrubs. The plants will become better established than your later spring plantings, and they'll withstand the rigors of their first Southern summer more easily. Warning: Don't buy the plants, succumb to laziness, and leave them exposed to the cold nights as the roots may be damaged. Plant them when you buy them.
- Start a compost pile with the remains of autumn that you haven't yet cleaned up. Satisfaction guaranteed.

Note that there are no *shoulds* in this list, just suggestions. Don't tell yourself that you *have* to do any of these activities. Just consider whether an activity will help you improve as a caretaker of the landscape, given your time and resources.

Whatever you choose to do or not do, please strive for a stress-free, peaceful, and happy new year. Start by playing in your yard.

IT'S A MATTER OF FACT

A calendar day has not always started at midnight. Although the Chinese and Romans used that moment to commence their reckoning of the Earth's rotation, the Egyptians used dawn and the Babylonians used dusk. The division of the day has had a varied history, including the Christian monastic canonical hours that divided the day into eight three-hour intervals based upon devotion times. Early divisions of the day for the period from dawn to dusk resulted in hours that were longer in summer than in winter. Although these temporal hours were replaced with twenty-four equinoctial hours of equal length in the second century B.C. for astronomical purposes, it was another 1,000 years before the common folk adopted such a measurement.

Do You Have the Time?

ALTHOUGH THE NUMBERING of the years may be arbitrary to some people, divine to others, the calendaring system is, for the most part, based upon the predictable cycles of nature. Since time

immemorial, man has ordered time, starting with the measurement of the flow of natural phenomena—the sun, moon, Earth,
and stars—to help plan for seasonal changes. Days are based upon
the Earth's revolutions. Seven-day weeks approximate the length of
one phase of the moon. Months (moonths) approximate the lunar
cycles during a year, the number of days in each month having
been manipulated over the years to fit the fancy of some politi-
cians. And the years are based upon the orbit of the Earth around
the sun.

It's the seconds, minutes, and hours that are most arbitrary.
Timekeepers, clocks, and watches have ticked away, chasing each
moment to the next. Most recently, the master clock of the world,
the atomic clock, marks the *official* world time. It measures time
based upon the oscillation rate of metal cesium: 9,192,631,770 oscillations per second, or more important, 290,091,200,500,000,000
oscillations per year. But like all of the calendars and timekeepers
used through the centuries, it too is inaccurate because the Earth
itself is not entirely perfect. The clock has to be recalibrated periodically to account for the wobbles and wiggles that cause fluctua-
tions in the Earth's rotation and length of a day.

Man now uses those natural and something-less-than-natural
measurements to regulate business, commerce, politics, religion,
and other social conventions. He uses them to assert power over
others with appointments, to dictate behavior with deadlines, and
to alter the natural flow with schedules. Nevertheless, this ordering
of time is apparently alluring; most humans (at least in the developed world) live by the clock and calendar. We allow the conventions of society to dictate the movement of our days, the timing
of our thoughts and activities. We fill each moment with activity,
with something to be done, some place to be, someone to meet.
We fit our lives into the pages of our Day Runners, checking off
each event, racing against the tick of tardiness, collapsing in relief
at the end of the day. We have an allotted amount of time, and we'd
better fill it.

But what time is it that we are allotted? Is it not just each
moment, one at a time? The present is all there is; it digests our
past and fertilizes our future. The past cannot be changed nor the

future determined. The two flow together, uninterrupted—except by us and our clocks, watches, timepieces, and alarms. Rather than rowing our boats gently down the stream (so that life is but a dream), we're like boulders in a gently moving stream, disrupting its peaceful journey.

In the midst of our modern conventions and constraints we have to reclaim our own time. We have to listen to our hearts and bodies, align ourselves with the universal mechanisms, and heed natural time. When the sun is rising, it's time to listen to the multitude of birds singing their joyous tunes. When the sun bears down in the middle of the afternoon, our food is digesting, and mind and body are tired, it's time for a siesta. When the sun is setting, it's time to breathe, take a moment to reflect, give thanks for the sustenance given that day, and watch our awesome source of energy drop below the horizon.

To the ancient Greeks time had a dual nature. *Chronos* was the time of clocks, calendars, and schedules. *Kairos* was the time of infinity, transcendence, and the sacred. In chronos time we make resolutions and attempt to beat the clock to fulfill them so we don't waste time. In kairos time we escape ourselves and allow the breath of God in; we give ourselves time and make dreams into desires and desires into reality.

LESSON 17 ⤳ January 8–14
Camellias

To the attentive eye, each moment of the year has its own beauty, and in the same field, it beholds, every hour, a picture which was never seen before, and which shall never be seen again.

—Ralph Waldo Emerson (1803–1882)
Nature

Camellias Thrust Their Color into the Winter Landscape

YOU WOULD THINK IT SPRING, looking out our window. The barren landscape is brightened and cheered by the camellias, neatly tucked on the western side of a large oak tree, protected from the morning sun.

How lucky we are in the South to have flowers in winter. Pansies, hugging the ground, shrivel and expand as the temperatures fluctuate, and ornamental cabbages and kale dot beds with rigid openness and warm colors. But camellias thrust their color into our landscape, like rouge on Nature's winter complexion.

From early November (although mid-October is apparently becoming the new norm) until April I enjoy my evergreen, flowering members of the tea family, Theaceae. My *Camellia sasanqua* blooms first, displaying a mass of dark pink flowers. Primarily fall bloomers, sasanqua varieties grow from 6–10 feet and have white-to rose-colored flowers that are 2–3 inches wide.

A Japanese camellia (*Camellia japonica*) outside my kitchen window, with buds that swell as the year winds down, starts blooming mid- to late January (again, however, an earlier bloom time is becoming the norm). Mine is a dark red, some are white, and some range in-between with a multitude of variations on color striations. Japanese camellias (common camellias) grow larger than sasanquas, reaching a height of 20–25 feet. The 3- to 5-inch-wide flowers of *C. japonicas* are larger and fuller than those of *C. sasanquas*; the wax-like leaves are larger as well.

In addition to the Japanese and sasanqua camellias there are numerous other species, including *Camellia sinensis*. These are smaller shrubs with smaller flowers that bloom earlier than the two above-mentioned varieties. But they are hard to find in nurseries and rarely seen in the Southern landscape.

You can select any number of appropriate sites for camellias. Place them in a line at the rear of shorter, bordering shrubs; spot them under shade trees or in woodland areas; or tuck them in the corner of a courtyard garden. They will flower best if planted in partial to full shade. The larger leafed varieties prefer more shade than the smaller leafed ones.

To prevent camellia flowers from browning, plant the bushes in a spot where the morning sun will not touch them until after the frost has dried. To protect the flowers, buds, and leaves from freeze damage caused by temperatures below 15–20°F or so, throw a sheet over the bushes, but be sure to remove the covering during the day if it's sunny. Planting semi-double flowering varieties rather than big doubles will yield more flowers with less freeze damage since the semi-doubles tend to open more quickly, giving them less time to catch the damaging cold halfway during development.

> ## IT'S A MATTER OF FACT
>
> You can induce earlier and larger flowering on your camellias by gibbing. Twist out the vegetative (leaf) bud that is next to the flower bud. Put a drop of gibberellic acid solution in the old bud cup. The flower bud will swell in as little as two weeks. If you do this in September, your early-flowering camellias will bloom in approximately 30 days. Later varieties will bloom within 60–90 days.

Camellias need moist, very well-drained, acid soil that's rich in organic matter. Their roots are particularly shallow so they shouldn't be planted too deep and should be mulched liberally. Prune camellias soon after the flowers have dropped, being sure not to wait very long since, if you do, you might cut off buds forming for next year. Also, don't prune too much or you'll probably destroy the beauty of the natural shape. Tame some scraggly branches, cut out dead wood, and slightly shape if necessary, but don't prune your camellia into a ball like a lollipop.

Even before spring arrives, bees appear on camellia blossoms on warm days. *Camellia sasanqua* 'Kanjiro'.

There are literally thousands of camellia hybrids and cultivars among the *sinensis*, *sasanqua*, and *japonica* groups. For the most prolonged winter delight, starting as early as September and ending as late as April, plant at least one variety from each group. Your *sinensis* will bloom first, followed by the *sasanqua*. Then the Japanese camellia will bloom and warm your heart during the most numbing days of winter and into the spring-flowering months.

As you stare out your window at your spring-in-winter, think about this: Nature is the ultimate cinema, constantly entertaining us with movement and color. Even in the depths of winter, the frames keep rolling, providing viewers with the best and cheapest of pleasures. But you cannot rewind the film and see the same again, since each moment is unique and cannot be reproduced.

So savor each moment. Ingest each moment. Become one with each moment Nature provides.

COLD-TOLERANT CAMELLIA CULTIVARS

SOME OF THE COLD-HARDIEST camellias are tea-oil varieties (*Camellia oleifera*). Although they are rarely found in cultivation, some have been hybridized with *C. sasanqua*, *C. hiemalis,* and *C. japonica* varieties, resulting in extremely tolerant, fall-blooming specimens. 'Winter's Star' and 'Pink Icicle' are two examples. The Ackerman hybrids are not quite as nice as *C. japonicas* and *C. sasanquas*; but I'm glad for their flowering at our mountain cabin, where the standards would not otherwise tolerate the cold.

Many *C. japonicas* and *C. sasanquas* also tolerate some of the coldest weather found in the mid-South (-10°F to 0°F). However, their chances of surviving a winterkill are diminished if you apply excessive fertilization and irrigation after spring growth and if you prune them late (September-November). A few of the most popular hardy varieties are as follows:

Camellia japonicas:

 'Governor Mouton': red and white variegated, semi-double to peony-form flowers.

 'Kramer's Supreme': fragrant, deep red, large, peony-form flowers.

 'White Empress': early white, semi-double flowers.

 'Bernice Boddy': early, semi-double, shaded light pinkflowers.

 'Pink Perfection': perfectly pink double flower.

 'Mathotiana': red, rose form, double flower.

Camellia sasanquas:

 'Daydream': single, large, white-edged deep rose flowers.

 'Jean May': semi-double to double, large, shell pink flowers.

 'Yuletide': single, red flowers with yellow stamens.

If your camellia flower is browned on the outer edge of the blooms, it has probably been damaged by cold or wind. But if the petals have brown patches near the center of the bloom, moving outward, it probably has flower blight, a fungus. In that case, remove the diseased blooms from the bush and the ground underneath and burn or deeply bury them.

LESSON 18 ⮎ January 15–21
Birds

I once had a sparrow alight upon my shoulder for a moment while I was
hoeing in a village garden, and I felt that I was more distinguished by that
circumstance than I should have been by any epaulet I could have worn.

—Henry David Thoreau (1817–1862)
Walden

Birds Love Your Trees and Shrubs

I ALWAYS VIEW THE BIRDS in my yard with a sense of good fortune. Never knowing what I might see in any given day, I'm always
grateful for each surprise.

Many days it's blue jays, which assert their claim—with
cacophonous clamor—to rule our landscape. But other species
have proven tenacious in maintaining their territorial privilege. In
fact, we have some visitors whose presence always evokes a "call-
to-view" from me to the rest of the family. "Look out the window!
Hurry! Look—on the side of the pecan tree," I yell. With absolute
delight, I point to the large pileated woodpecker, with its bright
red head the shape of a bike racer's helmet, rapping the trunk in
search of food. Then I quickly direct attention to the birdfeeder
for a look at a yellow-shafted flicker, (another woodpecker with
red on the nape of the neck), tail wrapped under the feeder edge,
flicking seeds to the ground below, where a mourning dove awaits
his share. Perched on a bush nearby, a northern cardinal and cedar
waxwing bide their time until the flicker leaves the feeder, while a
nuthatch, head down, repeatedly pokes its beak beneath the bark
of a neighboring oak tree. The excitement remains, for me at least,
until our guests disappear, taking temporary leave until it's feeding
time again.

We've always had tons of birds in our yard, which lies adjacent to fields of nursery stock. The trees and shrubs attract the large and diverse population that nests in the foliage and branches and feasts on the delicacies of various plants.

Birds are drawn to the brightly colored fruits of plants, especially those with agreeably pulpy, nutritious flesh. If the pits are hard, birds will frequently discard them, sometimes after flying to a new perch. Smaller seeds often withstand a bird's digestion; they are transported until expelled, becoming candidates for germination in the new location. Plants have evolved many other strategies for seed dispersal by birds. For instance, mistletoe seed is disagreeably sticky. After getting his full, a winged snacker rubs the seed off his bill onto tree bark, the very place where this partially parasitic plant prefers to grow.

There are many trees and shrubs you can grow to provide inviting seed and shelter for the birds, while assisting the spread of their plant seeds for regeneration. Following are some examples:

Chionanthus virginicus (Fringetree or Grancy Gray-beard): This is an old-fashioned favorite with white whiskery flowers that sweeten the air in spring and dark green leathery leaves that turn a clear yellow in fall. A graceful shrub or small tree, it can be planted as a small specimen or as part of a shrub border along a woodland edge or stream. Many birds favor the dark blue, egg-shaped fruits that appear in late summer. Bobwhites, mockingbirds, gray catbirds, robins, and starlings feed on and nest in this deciduous plant.

Cornus florida (Flowering Dogwood): A Southern favorite, this spring-flowering delight is also a choice of many bird varieties, which use the tree for cover, nesting, and a source of food. Bobwhites, bluebirds, gray catbirds, mockingbirds, robins, sapsuckers, starlings, red-bellied woodpeckers, quail, and many others visit this native that is best loved for its spring display of white flowers. The dark green summer leaves turn red and purplish-red in fall, and the glossy, red fruits ripen September to October. Dogwoods prefer acid, moist, and well-drained soil and do best in partial shade.

Ilex glabra (Inkberry Holly): Bluebirds, bobwhites, northern cardinals, cedar waxwings, towhees, robins, yellow-shafted flickers, and several others flit furiously for food around this spineless evergreen. Mockingbirds and robins also use this shrub for cover and nesting. Inkberry makes a good hedge or screen and combines well with deciduous trees and shrubs. The berries are ink colored and last from September through May, and the leaves are lustrous dark green, small, and wide, providing shelter for birds. Reaching about 8 feet in height, this shrub is easy to grow, tolerates shade or sun, and wet or dry soil.

Ilex verticillata (Winterberry Holly): This relatively small, deciduous holly grows 6- to 10-feet high and 8- to 12-feet wide. It has red fruit and orange, yellow, or red color in the fall. There are many cultivars with varying characteristics. Some cultivars of the hybrid combination of *I. verticillata* and *I. serrata* that I find particularly pleasing are 'Autumn Glow' and 'Harvest Red'. Compared with *I. verticillata* varieties, these hybrid varieties are faster growing, heavier and earlier fruiting, and have a reddish tint to their new growth; their red berries bleach out in the winter to a yellow-white on the sun-facing side of the plant, adding an interesting dimension to the landscape. These hollies enjoy visits from bobwhites, flickers, mockingbirds, brown thrashers, robins, cedar waxwings, and gray catbirds.

IT'S A MATTER OF FACT

Always provide water for our feathered friends. During drought, they will flock to water sources—lakes, ponds, streams, and birdbaths. If you've got the best or the only one around, they'll visit, and eat your insects in thanks.

Ilex opaca (American Holly): If you are starting to see a trend here, it's because hollies are some of the best bird attractors as well as some of the easiest, most hardy plants to grow for a variety of purposes around your yard. (See Lesson 12 for a more comprehensive discussion of hollies.) American holly is a time-honored plant found wild in the woods and known for its holiday greenery and berries. Growing at a medium rate, it's a broadleaf evergreen that is dense and pyramidal when young, becoming more open with age. Its fruits mature in October and persist well into winter, inviting the presence of bluebirds, bobwhites, northern cardinals, gray catbirds, cedar waxwings, yellow-shafted flickers, robins, woodpeckers, brown thrashers, towhees, purple finches, cardinals, and many other birds. Several birds, such as mockingbirds, gray catbirds, brown thrashers, robins, and cardinals, use this plant for cover or nesting.

Liriodendron tulipifera (Tulip Poplar): This member of the Magnolia family is the tallest deciduous hardwood in North America, making it a good choice as a stand-alone tree or on an expansive property. The tree was named for its greenish-yellow and orange, tulip-shaped spring flowers. Northern cardinals and purple finches use the loftly tree for nesting. Many birds eat the tree's seeds; among them are bobwhites, Carolina chickadees, cardinals, grosbeaks, purple finches, and ruby-throated hummingbirds.

Nyssa sylvatica (Sour Gum or Black Gum): Bobwhites, woodpeckers, crows, purple finches, yellow-shafted flickers, blue grosbeaks, tufted titmice, brown thrashers, bluebirds, robins, and many other birds enjoy the dark blue, fall fruits of this native tree. It makes a great specimen planting or addition to a woodland setting. Its thick, shiny green leaves are often the first to turn color in fall, exhibiting shades of brilliant red, orange, and gold. The scaly bark and horizontal branching is picturesque in winter and is adorned with bright red buds in early spring.

There are numerous other plants that coax birds toward their food and shelter. Beech, red maple, white pine, hemlock, flowering crabapple, spruce, mulberry, box elder, wild cherry, hawthorn, hemlock, and red and white oak are just a few. Fruit-bearing shrubs and vines adored by birds include pyracantha, honeysuckle, blueberry, blackberry, raspberry, and viburnum. And many annual and perennial flowers such as sunflower, aster, daisy, verbena, poppy, and cosmos attract visitors.

While writing this lesson, and many others in this book, I've been blessed each day with a visit by a female cardinal. Her staccato "wheet-wheet-wheet-wheet" grabs my attention from the books and keyboard. Without fail, I rise to view the feeder just below my office window, and there she is, poking and picking at the seed I keep there to insure such pleasures. I gaze across the room and through another window to see several other cardinals, male and female, perched in a Japanese maple. They're always there too, encouraging a break and a smile. It only takes a moment like this to clear my cobwebs, to find my spirit, to regroup. What great rewards for such little effort!

"Once birds sang and flirted among the leaves while men, more helpless and less accomplished, skulked between the trunks below them. Now they linger in the few trees that men have left standing, or fit themselves into the chinks of the human world, into its church towers, lamp-posts, and gutters." Consider these words of Jacquetta Hawkes, an English archaeologist and writer. And remember that birds are as much a part of the landscape as plants—the two are inseparable. So entice them and allure them. Plant plants they need and love. Add feeders to enhance your landscape and the food supply year-round. Place birdbaths and water containers in your yard, particularly in the summer. Then sit back and enjoy the sights and sounds.

How Hummingbirds Hover

ALTHOUGH WE WON'T BE SEEING these jewels until spring when they are first spotted migrating through our area (about mid- to late March), I want to talk about them while we're on the subject of birds because, unlike many other birds, hummingbirds fascinate people who don't otherwise pay much attention to our winged companions. I remember the first time I saw one up close. In fact, I saw several of these tiny, too-fast-to-really-see-them-clearly birds feeding on hanging fuchsia in a patio area of an inn in the Berkshire Mountains of Massachusetts. I was mesmerized and awe-struck by their incredible speed and agility.

I now see hummingbirds quite regularly in the North Carolina Mountains, where they whiz by my head, buzzing like a huge bug and chirping in soprano voice. And each occasion is special, drawing my attention like the sighting of a porpoise that's rising and dipping through the ocean. I have to keep my eyes peeled or I will lose my glimpse of a wondrous event.

Hummingbirds are intriguing birds, the only ones that truly hover in still air for any length of time, which they must do in order to insert their slim bills into the depths of nectar-producing flowers. Their agility depends upon their unique flying technique.

When they beat their paddle-shaped wings that act like hands that swivel at the shoulder, the tips draw a figure-of-eight in the air. The lift produced on each loop is of equal strength, providing stationary flight. A slight change in the angle propels the bird forward—or backward.

At 25–200 beats per second, hummingbird flight requires a tremendous amount of energy, fueled by nectar that may be gathered as much as 2,000 times each day. When the day is over and the hummingbird cannot see to fly, it allows its muscles to cool. Its heart slows from the daytime 500–1,200 beats per minute to an almost undetectable throb, and its breathing slows dramatically. It, in essence, hibernates.

The hummingbird's iridescence is another captivating feature. The feathers are flattened and twisted with their broad sides facing outwards. The filaments have to be detached from one another in order to develop this way; consequently, they lack tiny hooks that would otherwise link them to adjacent feathers. Within the filaments are microscopic layers of melanin particles that split the light, creating colors that vary depending upon the angle from which you see the bird.

In Georgia, we have the ruby-throated hummingbird, which is attracted to bright red flowers that are long, tubular, and preferably drooping. Spring-flowering azalea and columbine; summer-flowering bee balm, cardinal flower, and scarlet sage (salvia); and fall-flowering trumpet vine are good attractors. Other nectar producing flowers for hummingbirds are nasturtium, honeysuckle, petunia, impatiens, and the horse chestnut tree.

LESSON 19 ✒ January 22–28
January's Flowers

A child's world is fresh and new and beautiful, full of wonder and excitement. It is our misfortune that for most of us that clear-eyed vision, that true instinct for what is beautiful and awe-inspiring, is dimmed and even lost before we reach adulthood. If I had influence with the good fairy who is supposed to preside over the christening of all children I should ask that her gift to each child in the world be a sense of wonder so indestructible that it would last throughout life, as an unfailing antidote against the boredom and disenchantments of later years, the sterile preoccupation with things that are artificial, the alienation from the sources of our strength.

—Rachel Carson (1907–1964)
The Sense of Wonder

Winter's Yellow Is Fool's Gold

Each year, late in January, I'm fooled by the imprinted childhood thought that spring is right around the corner. The fallacy emerges when I spot an arching mound or cascade of yellow flowers. At first glimpse, I always mistakenly think the yellow congregation is forsythia, since as a child that's what I always thought it was. As an adult, that's what I'd like it to be because, in these parts, forsythia is *the* harbinger of spring.

But my January sightings are not of forsythia at all, but of winter jasmine. Both members of the Oleaceae family, these shrubs make equally generous additions to the Southern landscape and add varying dynamics year-round. Both don bright yellow flowers, providing a lengthy, late winter/early spring show, with jasmine blooming first, followed by forsythia. But the two shrubs are quite different in their habit.

Winter jasmine, or January jasmine (*Jasminum nudiflorum*), is a deciduous, mounding shrub that grows rapidly to reach 3–4 feet in height and 4–7 feet in width. It can be trained to grow on walls or trellises with 12- to 15-foot extensions. Its trailing branches will root when they come in contact with the soil and will form new plants.

Winter jasmine starts blooming in January and continues into March. Its display is not as full or brilliant as that of forsythia, which blooms profusely in a short period. It's a great plant for banks or other areas where erosion is a problem and is showiest if planted in masses. Cascading over walls, it exhibits its blooms and four-angled branches.

IT'S A MATTER OF FACT

In his book, *The Future of Life*, Edward O. Wilson defines biophilia as "the innate tendency to focus upon life and lifelike forms, and in some instances to affiliate with them emotionally." He says that the acquisition of biophilia comes in stages and states that studies of childhood mental development indicate that knowledge of and interest in the natural world rises sharply in children aged 9 to 12, and a "moral feeling toward animal welfare and species conservation" develops between the ages of 13 and 17.

Forsythia (*Forsythia × intermedia*) (called Yellow Bells by some, in deference to the appearance of its flowers) starts blooming later than winter jasmine—usually in February with peak bloom in mid-March. Encouraged by the warmer spring air, the fresh green leaves of this deciduous shrub quickly displace the colorful blooms. True to its reputation, forsythia bridges winter to spring, from bloom to leaf.

Forsythia is most effective when planted on banks, for borders, and in groups. It also serves as an exceptional accent plant with its wispy, graceful branches. A young shrub will look spiky as the branches grow upward, but the aging bush will present winsome, drooping whips, flowing up and then falling like water from a round fountain.

Forsythia does have a tendency to dominate an area and needs some pruning simply to keep it from taking over. After its spring bloom, you can master its growth by selectively cutting interior canes. However, do not severely prune or shape the younger bush since its arching, tentacle-like branches make a dynamic statement when left alone. The loose yet full natural form of the older bush is also best when pruning is conservative.

Forsythia is a low-maintenance, easy-to-grow shrub that requires full sun for the best bloom. Give it plenty of room to grow since it will rapidly reach heights of 8–10 feet and widths of 10–12 feet. It looks great against a backdrop of evergreens and will relax the most formal landscape, like loosely falling, long blonde hair on a black-suited lady lawyer. When picking a site for your plant, bear in mind that it often displays a pleasant, maroon-like color in fall.

Perhaps the best forsythia for our area is 'Lynwood Gold' (more properly called 'Lynwood'). Its flowers are more open and have better distribution along the stems than those of 'Spectabilis', the standard forsythia by which others are judged.

If the proximate blooming of winter jasmine and forsythia is not enough to confuse, the latter's blooming is followed by the yellow flowering of *Gelsemium sempervirens*, or Carolina yellow jessamine (often incorrectly called jasmine). This fast-growing evergreen vine forms mounds or climbs whatever it can cling to, reaching 10–20 feet. Its funnel-form flowers are fragrant, blooming from February into April. I planted one of these natives near my back door among other shrubs and had to be vigilant about its wiry stems that seemed to encircle neighboring branches overnight. Furthermore, it didn't flower a great deal because of the crowding and relatively shady spot. It was in the wrong spot—so I moved it after many years.

I see more and more winter jasmine each year. At first sight, the nudge of childhood misconceptions creeps across my mind— it's forsythia and spring is near. But alas, now I pretend adulthood, know slightly more, and quell my spring-is-coming excitement by reminding myself that my January sightings are of jasmine, not forsythia. And, just like an adult, I also temper the temporary thrill with the nasty knowledge that if it is forsythia blooming in January, we will surely have a disastrously flowerless spring—a fate I dread each year as our winters become warmer while early spring cold blasts continue to threaten.

The unrestrained, misconceived thoughts of childhood were exciting, sometimes daunting, and ofttimes the progenitor of imaginative illusion—or destructive delusion. Hope prevailed, however, and carried me through time, however prolonged or distorted. Spring always came. Ah, to keep that youthful faith in the midst of adult sabotage.

BUT IT'S NOT A ROSE

THE FIRST TIME I SAW a flowering Lenten rose while on a walk in the shade garden at the State Botanical Garden of Georgia, or at least the first time I noticed it and became aware of it, my life was changed. Never before had I appreciated the demure statement of such an elegance. Never before had I understood that the beauty of blossoms persists through the coldest months in Georgia. Never before had I been captivated by a plant—one whose name suggests a holiness in its blooming.

Lenten rose (*Helleborus orientalis*) is a 6- to 8-inch-high evergreen perennial that reaches 10–14 inches when flowering. It blooms with nodding blossoms that range in color from white to light purple, to deep pink/rose or light green. Bend down, rotate the stems upward, and peek at the inside of the five-petal cup; you'll find an enchanting, animated life smiling at you. As the flowers age, they effuse new life with spring-green snow pea–like pods shooting from the center of their faces.

H. × hybridus is the species name for some of the vegetatively-propogated cultivars being bred that augment or change certain characteristics of *H. orientalis* and some of the other *Helleborus* species. More colors, more spotting and doubling, and blooms that smile upward are just some of the "improvements." (Watch for names like 'Pink Lady' and 'Ivory Prince'.) Despite the breeding efforts, most hellebores found on the market are seedlings. It's difficult to assure consistency of their flower color, but the randomness of colors in a bed of seedlings is enjoyable.

I've witnessed Lenten roses blooming as early as December—during some of our milder winters. Generally, however, they start blooming in our region around the end of January and continue for months, usually into April, although I've also seen blooms in May. Each bloom persists for 6–8 weeks. If planted in the soil they prefer—moist, fertile, well-drained, and neutral—they will flourish with flowers.

I took a picture of this Lenten rose in my backyard while lying on my stomach looking up into the flower faces, wondering about their secrets.

Lenten roses are replete with the plant qualities most gardeners seek. They are low-maintenance, relatively free of diseases and pests, and deer don't like them. Requiring shade, especially in the late afternoon, they're a wonderful complement to other shade-loving plants like hostas and ferns. Furthermore, they will easily and inexpensively fill a bed if you divide them during the cooler months. I have lots of volunteers coming up in my yard; birds or the wind apparently spread the seed.

While the rose of Valentine lore may be the most revered flower since antiquity, the Lenten rose is mine. It sneaks its beauty into the winter landscape, and I grin as I imagine the secrets we share of the hidden wonders constantly surrounding us.

LESSON 20 ∽ January 29–February 4
Landscape Planning

The frog does not drink up the pond in which it lives.
—Indian proverb

Planning for Spring Planting Is Practical

IT'S THAT TIME OF YEAR when I find myself happy for cloudy, gloomy days—days that tell me it's okay to stay inside, okay to escape the endless motion of the outdoors, to block out the ceaseless sounds and noise, to pause from the intensity of Nature. "Thank heavens, the sun has gone in, and I don't have to go out and enjoy it," as Logan Pearsall Smith said.

But as the minutes march on and become hours, sometimes turning into days, in those precious moments I find myself looking out the window, wondering about things to come. I begin to plan for the inevitable spring planting, even though most planting would have been best done over the past few months.

For some, spring planting is simply a matter of replacing a dead shrub. For others, it's a whole lot more—a partial or entirely new planting or design for the yard, whether for emotional, physical, or financial reasons.

If you are of the latter group, you'll find that there are many factors to consider when planning a new landscape: use of space, materials (plants, hardscaping, sculpture, and so forth), location, size and shape, function, style of composition, and your likes and dislikes. And before you begin, be sure to understand what you have to start with as well as where you want to go. Save yourself lots of money and disappointment by assessing your assets first, before jumping into a full-scale project.

First and foremost, the lay of the land, how it handles water, whether it is shaded or sunny, and whether it's protected from extreme weather conditions, are all factors to consider. Whether you are starting from scratch or completely redesigning, these elemental features may require some substantial grading, soil addition, and general restructuring of your yard. You will most likely want to use someone with expertise and appropriate equipment to help you with this phase of the landscaping. (See Lesson 27.)

Similarly, take note of all existing hardscape features such as walkways, fences, and retaining walls. Do you really want to move them, or can you work them into your plan? What about the natural features of your yard? Do you like the existing contours, for instance? Are the boulders or rock outcroppings something you can maintain and work into a design that's pleasing to you? Is there an irrigation system to contend with? And what about practicalities? Do you have an access point into your yard for heavy-duty tools and equipment when there's work to be done? Can a truck full of mulch get into the backyard?

In conjunction with the general lay of the land, take special note of your views from all angles. Are they open or confined, sweeping or fragmented? Do you want to screen an obtrusive or disconcerting object from sight, or do you want to open up a vista, carrying you to the far away? Does noise need to be dampened, or do you want to embellish the echo from a valley below?

Finally, when assessing the existing situation, look at the flora already present. Do you have mature, healthy trees that should, by all rights, be left standing? What about other mature or well-established trees and shrubs? Can you keep them and work them into your new design? Are there some that have been in the ground for less than three years and are still relatively easy to move and relocate if necessary? What about your neighbor's flora? Do their trees shade your yard? If so, count that as a given you cannot control.

Having assessed your situation, start to get more specific about the plants you want. If you don't have a professionally drawn plan or want to insert your own ideas, you need first to understand that one of the most important aspects of plant selection, other than survivability in a particular climate, is mature size, allowing for at least 10 years of growth. Shrubs, for instance, shouldn't be too close to the house foundation when they are full-grown. Shrubs used for hedges should be planted close enough to touch within several years without crowding each other out after ten years.

Plant selection also depends upon sun and shade requirements as well as proper moisture and drainage. For particularly sensitive plants, protection from frost pockets, which are usually at the bottoms of hills, and winter winds or frequent, strong winds that will burn their leaves or misshape them is a consideration. Intensely bright, reflective spots near white walls or fences must be noted as should dark walls and structures that heat up and create a torrid environment.

If you have a plan for your yard drawn by a landscape architect or designer, I heartily suggest that you first take that plan to a nursery, inspect the plants called for in the design, and be sure you like them. You may find, as do so many of our customers at the nursery, that you don't like the plants specified. Or you may find that some of the plants are not available from any growers, and you will be forced to select substitutes. (Note that if a particular plant is not grown by any of several local nurseries, there's probably a good reason; often it's not culturally suited to the area.)

Having said all of this, I'm exhausted. There's too much to think about, too much to know. How can you ever have the yard you want? It's simple, really. Just use some observation, a touch of common sense, a bit of sweat-breaking work, and your imagination and desires. Maybe start backwards like I do. First, decide upon the plants you want and the aspects of your natural yard that you like. Then work your design to make your choices happen, giving credence to the laws of water flow, the existence of sun and shade through the seasons, and the natural and man-made barriers or protections you already have or can create.

Above all, remember that your yard is not static; it will change over time. Trees and shrubs will grow, shading spots that once were sunny. Plants will die, leaving spots to be filled. Trees may fall from storms or disease, baring once shaded plants to the sun. And how wonderful it is—all the new opportunities created so you can play with the ongoing development in your garden. So don't get hung up on perfection now or expectations for the future. They don't exist.

Whatever you do, when planning your landscape, make it *your* landscape, *your* garden, *your* yard. *Your* image, *your* dream, *your* desire, *your* taste.

Although fall and winter are the best time to plant in this area, most folks tend to wait until spring. In the nursery, we plant during the winter months, and in early spring if we are behind schedule. Here, the field rows have been thoroughly subplowed and are ready to receive bare-root liner plants. An implement called a transplanter is pulled behind a tractor while one or more people stand inside the cage-like tool. A shoe at the front end of the transplanter makes a trench in which someone (here: Jon Hobus) inserts the plants as the tractor moves down the rows. Then two coulter disks at the rear push the soil back together, and two tires pack it down. This run was our second-year planting at our Madison County nursery in 1990.

XERISCAPING IS WATER-WISE LANDSCAPING

As I WRITE THIS WINTER lesson in early May, we are in the midst of a terrible drought. I anticipate the upcoming summer and am forced to guess how the weather will be. I hope we will have plenty of rain, but the lessons of experience fight with my faith. Whether it rains or not, we'll undoubtedly continue to have water woes. In fact, I imagine we'll have watering concerns from here on out since increasing demands are surpassing supplies (or at least those made available). So regardless of our rainfall, I urge you to pay heed.

By altering the design of your landscape, you can reduce its demands for water while eliminating some of your workload. Water-wise landscaping was devised in response to a prolonged drought in Colorado in 1981, and the term xeriscape was born. There's nothing particularly ingenious or unusual about xeriscaping; it's simply

IT'S A MATTER OF FACT

Petrichor ("stone-essence") is the name given to the scent of rain on dry earth. The pleasant smell comes from volatile oils that are released by plants and collect on clay-based soils and rocks. Rain reacts with the oils, which combine with the organic compound geosmin ("earth-smell"), and creates an aerosol. The resulting aroma is strongest after a dry spell.

the application of sound horticultural practices to produce and maintain a quality landscape while minimizing water use and protecting the environment. The seven principles of xeriscaping should be practiced at all times, and you will have the natural results of less water consumption and lush, low-maintenance landscapes.

Group plants by water needs (determined after the first 6–8 weeks of planting), creating zones. Locate medium water use (occasional) zones next to the high water use (often) zones. Place low-use (natural rainfall) zones on the peripheries of your landscape. High-use zones require watering on a regular basis, unless it rains, and perhaps even if it rains. Medium-use zones require supplemental watering during hot, dry spells. Low-use zones need little or no supplemental water. Incorporate plants that will shade any hot hardscaping, like brick walls and gravel walks.

Optimize soil conditions to use surface water more efficiently and promote better root growth and plant health. Be sure the structure of the soil provides good drainage while allowing for water penetration and moisture retention. For a small fee, the Cooperative Extension Service will provide a soil analysis, so take several samples from different areas of your yard to your local office.

Choose plants that thrive naturally in your climate and that suit your landscape needs and desires. Look for adaptability to the area, effect, color, texture, and mature plant size. While arranging the plants to fulfill your needs and aesthetic tastes, as I've mentioned, group them according to their water-use requirements. So, for example, put low-water crapemyrtles in the same watering zone as drought-tolerant verbena. But concentrate high-water-use flowering annuals in the high visibility, segregated beds next to your walkway. Don't let your plant selection be limited by the water-zone concept; just be more conscious about placement, using the water-zone technique as one additional criterion for your placement choice.

Limit your use of lawns and grassed areas. They are high-water-use areas. Make them just another element in your landscape, not the main thrust around which everything revolves. Use turf areas with function in mind and limit their size. Separate turf areas from ornamental plant beds to accommodate the differing watering requirements.

Water only when needed, deeply. Do not water frequently lightly. Rather, use prolonged, as-needed watering to promote deep root growth, which will encourage healthy development and more drought tolerance. If possible, use a drip irrigation system, soaker hose, or micro-sprinklers on ornamental plants.

Place mulch 2–4 inches deep around plantings and in beds. Organic, fine-textured, no-matting mulches are preferred. Pine bark, shredded or in mini-nuggets, is the best mulch. Pine straw works well too but does not last as long, look as good, or provide the soil-building benefits that pine bark does. Do not use mulch composed of chopped wood like pallets or discarded building material since, when it breaks down, wood ties up the nitrogen in the soil and also attracts termites.

Practice appropriate maintenance. If you follow the first six principles, this maintenance principle is easier and cheaper! You'll need less fertilizer, pesticides, and other chemicals. Specifically: Don't give plants high-nitrogen fertilizer during dry periods, or you'll encourage water-hungry new growth. Selectively prune, don't shear, plants for the same reason. Watch for pests regularly so you can destroy them before they weaken a plant, which will then want more water. Finally, don't mow your grass more than one-third its height, and, during drought, raise your mower blades higher than usual.

Note: I originally wrote this Lesson in 2000. The drought that I mentioned above that we were experiencing then lasted from 1998–2002. Now, in late 2008, we are in another long-term drought, which started in 2006 and is more severe in impact than previous ones because there are even greater demands on our water supplies due to increased population and development.

LESSON 21 ∿ February 5–11
Grasses

When, as a very small child, I was playing with a horsetail that had been growing as a weed in one of our flower-beds, dismantling it section by section like a constructional toy, I remember how my father told me it was one of the oldest plants on earth, and I experienced a curious confusion of time. I was holding the oldest plant in my hand, and so I, too, was old.

—Jacquetta Hawkes (1910–1996)
A Land

Ornamental Grasses Animate Your Yard

I'M STARTING TO SEE the blocks of blades, sheared sharply, like bristled crew cuts squared on top. But I'm also seeing silvery plumes left standing, dancing in the wind and glistening with the illumination of the low-lying winter sun. It's hard to let go of the plumage, but it's time for the once-a-year maintenance check on some of the grasses—preparation for new spring growth.

I'm speaking of the ornamental grasses that are increasingly adorning our landscapes and providing perhaps the greatest design versatility of any plant. They are at the end, and beginning, of another cycle. Now, and until late March, is the time to start hacking back the stems and bleached flowers and await the emergence of new spring shoots. But beware: the blades are sharp-edged and can snake up a pant leg with cruel intentions, so wear gloves and be careful. If you wait until late March, you can avoid the cutting chore all together by burning the plants, which promotes faster spring growth and kills nesting insects and their eggs. By waiting and burning, you'll also get more mileage out of the unique winter drama the lingering flowers provide, but do be sure that burning is allowed in your area before planning this approach.

Because ornamental grasses come in a multitude of sizes, shapes, textures, and colors, by using each feature to advantage, you can place these perennials strategically in your landscape. By selecting the proper variety, you can brighten a dark corner; add movement to a stiff, formal scene; lend flowing texture where coarse evergreens prevail; create height to bridge two areas of the landscape; create a double-row hedge or screen; or simply highlight the incredible beauty of a single grass plant by prominent placement.

Although there are hundreds of varieties of ornamental grasses, some have gained particular popularity because of their pest-damage resistance and low-maintenance requirements. These sun lovers are also easy to grow.

Maiden grass (*Miscanthus sinensis*) has clumps of narrow foliage that grow 1–8 feet in height. Its panicles (floral clusters or plumed flowers) bloom in early to late autumn and remain throughout the winter. The cultivar 'Gracillimus' has green foliage.

Variegated silver grass (*Miscanthus sinensis* 'Variegatus') has an arching habit of green foliage with creamy-white stripes running along its ½-inch-wide, vertical blades. Its cousin, **zebra grass** (*Miscanthus sinensis* 'Zebrinus'), has yellow or white horizontal bands across the green leaves. Hint-of-pink flowers grace 'Variegatus' in late summer while 'Zebrinus' has yellow flowers in early autumn. Both cultivars grow 4–6 feet in height with a 3- to 4-foot spread. 'Variegatus' tolerates partial shade.

Probably the most visible grass in contemporary landscapes is **pampas grass** (*Cortaderia selloana*). Its 1-inch-wide leaves rise up 8–10 feet in clumps, eventually spreading as wide. It flowers in late summer, shooting large plume heads several feet above the foliage. The feathery floral clusters remain well into winter, although rains that are cold and heavy often erode their beauty.

A good alternative to the massive pampas grass is its dwarf cultivar, 'Pumila'. The gray-green leaves are smaller, only ½-inch wide, and the creamy ivory flower plumes of the female are very showy and prolific. The dwarf stands at a relatively diminutive 5–8 feet and spreads to equal width.

A much more delicate grass than maiden or pampas grasses is **fountain grass** (*Pennisetum alopecuroides*) with arching stems and bottlebrush clusters of fuzzy flowers that are showy, soft, and cylindrical. The 4- to 5-inch flower plumes are tan or buff to a creamy white in midsummer/early fall and turn to reddish, copper-purple in fall, lasting into winter. The leaves become streaked with yellow-gold in fall and reach heights of 1–3 feet with a 2- to 3-foot spread. Fountain grass tolerates drought and light shade and is slow growing.

One of my favorites, **purple fountain grass** (*Pennisetum setaceum* 'Rubrum'), has soft, purplish red flowers on shoots that arch over its narrow purple leaves. The flower clusters are 9- to 12-inches long, bloom in late spring to late summer, turn pleasingly brown in fall, and last into winter. A terrific motion and accent plant, it should, however, be treated as an annual in the Southern climate due to unreliable hardiness.

> ## IT'S A MATTER OF FACT
>
> Despite its enormous size, bamboo is a grass. It grows extremely fast because it grows at more than one point. While other plants grow at the tips of their stems only where meristem is present, bamboo has meristem at each node and grows at each of these points. The distance between each node increases with the growth, creating space between nodes—the hollow tube. Bamboo dies after it blooms, but blooming may not occur for 10 to 120 years. Clumping varieties are best for cultivated landscapes since they spread more slowly than the running varieties.

Another personal favorite is **pink muhly grass** (*Muhlenbergia capillaris*). This finely textured grass with needle-like foliage is stunning in the fall when its pinkish purple flowers create an airy aura. When planted en masse, the floral display looks as though tightly grouped, wispy clouds have settled just above the ground. Although it is sun loving, pink muhly tolerates partial shade and will grow in harsh conditions. It is tolerant of deer and drought as well as poorly drained soils.

Extremely interesting as it changes colors through the seasons, **Japanese blood grass** (*Imperata cylindrica* var. *rubra*) is slender and upright. Its 1-foot-long green leaves emerge in the spring with red tips that turn bright blood-red. The intensity increases throughout the summer into fall and fades to a coppery tan in winter. Please be warned: you need to be careful of this grass's invasive tendency.

Choose a variety of ornamental grass based upon your needs and its characteristics and growth requirements, but don't hesitate to be bold and experiment. Because they are easy to grow and require little maintenance—and should you change your mind—you can afford to move or replace the clumps without much setback.

Ornamental grasses have a way of adding unanticipated dynamics and effervescence to an otherwise humdrum scene, and they particularly enliven the winter landscape. So keep those plumes through the winter, and watch the grasses blow in the wind, swaying to and fro. Watch the grasses glisten in the sun, illuminating shafts of light. Hear the grasses rustle with the winter winds, whispering Nature's incantations.

THE PARADOXICAL GRASS

GRASSES ARE PERHAPS THE most paradoxical plant used by man. They have been part of the landscape forever, from the grasslands of our ancestral Africa to the tallgrass prairies of the North American continent. Grasses have provided food and forage for roaming animals like elk and buffalo. They have provided food for human beings— barley, corn, oats, rice, rye, sorghum, sugarcane, and wheat—and thatch and sod for roofs and homes; reeds for musical instruments; and blades for hats, baskets, and other utilitarian items. They have filtered and held wetland waters. And—now here's the paradox—they have carpeted the soil of most typical American homes and businesses.

The benefit of the native tallgrasses to our ecological health is convincing. The detriment of the manicured turfgrasses to our environment is frightening. If we use the beauty of the taller, ornamental, non-turf grasses for dramatically embellishing the landscape while eliminating some of the lawn grasses, we'll have less chemically-dependent, water-wasting yards that are far more appealing and self-sufficient. And we'll move toward greater harmony with nature.

LESSON 22 ⟡ February 12–18
Roses

These roses under my window make no reference to former roses or to better ones; they are for what they are; they exist with God to-day [sic]. There is no time to them. There is simply the rose; it is perfect in every moment of its existence.

—Ralph Waldo Emerson (1803–1882)
Essays: First Series, Self-Reliance

Roses Are Scent from Heaven

IT'S VALENTINE'S DAY TIME. For many a lucky lady that means long-stemmed, red roses from a sweetheart. For me it means it's time, once again, to decide whether I want to take a stab at growing those royal reflections of beauty and love. You see, I've been raised to believe, and my husband continues to tell me, that roses are a pain in the backside to grow and maintain. Let's examine that assumption.

My study starts in memory. When I was growing up, Louise Orahood, my then best friend of grade school, Girl Scouts, and summer camp, invited me each year in April to her birthday party. To this day, I can't tell you a thing about the cake, games, or presents. But I can tell you about the massive display of Lady Banks' rose growing up the side and across the top edge of her carport. The tiny yellow flowers lay abundantly within the willow-like green leaves and daintily brightened the air with their spring beauty. I loved them.

Then, when I returned to Georgia in 1981, following a nine-year sojourn in New England and marriage to one of them damn Yankees, my husband and I built a house, and planted. He got his lilac bush (*Syringa patula* 'Miss Kim', a heat tolerant variety rather than the common lilac, *Syringa vulgaris*, which is not prosperous in Zone 7), and I got my Lady Banks' rose. That rose overtook an entire chain-link fence and arched dramatically to either side, creating a shaded area, perfect for a bench. From my breakfast room window above, I could watch the birds coming and going to their nests carefully built in the protective vines.

I did nothing but plant the Lady Banks', watch it grow, and, on occasion, prune back some stems that had simply grown too much. Not much effort there. So what's fact or fiction about rose cultivation? The *fiction*, I have learned, is that *all* roses are *difficult* to cultivate; the *fact* is that *many* roses are relatively *easy* to grow.

First, it's important to understand that, absent an official scheme for the thousands of rose varieties, they are classified in a number of ways. The American Rose Society uses three main categories: species, old garden, and modern. Lady Banks' and Cherokee rose (the Georgia state flower) are examples of species, or wild, roses. The oldest of the genus *Rosa*, species roses are native or naturalized varieties that have been propagated and sold commercially. Generally—classification opinions vary here also, resulting in less than accurate summations—they have five petals, are usually thorny, have self-pollinating hips (the red "berries"), and will breed true from seed.

By most standards, roses that predate the introduction of hybrid teas in 1867 and that have maintained their genetic purity are referred to as antique, old, or old garden roses. They are usually white or pastel in color and fragrant. Their successors are the modern roses, which developed as a cross between tea roses and hybrid perpetuals and include hybrid teas, floribundas, and grandifloras. Rich colors and multiple bloomings make these roses more appealing to some than the paler, once-a-year-flowering antiques.

The roses of Valentine's Day are modern roses, generally of the hybrid tea type. Over the years, crossbreeding has produced flowers in a multitude of colors, shapes, sizes, and textures, but fragrance, a recessive trait, was all but lost among the modern roses until greater attention was given by breeders to that intoxicating, seductive characteristic. Similarly, many of the roses' natural resistances were lost in modernization resulting in roses that are more prone to disease and insect infestation—a fact that puts me back to my original query, with an answer of sorts.

Generally, antique and species roses are the easiest to grow and maintain, while hybridized, modern roses are more troublesome. With that in mind, let's ramble through some particulars of cultivation.

In our climate, you should plant bare-root roses between November and March. Containerized roses can be planted November through May. Choose a location with at least six hours of sun each day, opting for morning sun that will dry the dew, helping with disease resistance, and avoiding the late afternoon sun that may scorch the plant. Be sure the rose bed is well-drained, well-aerated, and moderately fertile with neutral to slightly acidic soil.

Prepare a rose bed as you would any other planting area, being sure to dig deeply and mix in organic compost. Then, for bare-root stock, dig a hole 12- to 14-inches deep and wide, making sure that the roots will not be crowded. With soil, build a cone-shaped mound in the hole and spread the roots over the mound, setting the swollen part of the main stem of grafted varieties about one inch above ground level. Add soil to the hole until it is about two-thirds full, eliminating any open spaces. Water thoroughly. Fill the remainder of the hole with soil and water again.

Plant containerized roses in similarly large holes but without the mounding. Loosen the root system of any root-bound plant before placing it in the hole. Be sure to plant the rose no deeper than it was in the container—the surface of the root-ball should be at the same level as the surface of the ground, or even slightly higher.

Mulch newly planted roses with 2–3 inches of pine bark, cypress chips, pine straw, or fall leaves. Water deeply (about one inch) once or twice a week, keeping the water off of the leaves to prevent fungus diseases. Fertilize at least three times each year—in early spring, when buds appear, and in midseason—using a blend that has 12–16 percent nitrogen.

Most roses should be pruned in late winter or early spring, before new growth emerges. The more hybridized the rose, the more finicky it is about pruning. For the modern aristocratic roses, use a sharp, clean, rounded shear and cut at a 45-degree angle, one-quarter inch above, and slanted parallel with, an outward-facing bud. Bushy and climbing species and antique roses can withstand a whacking with hedge clippers. All roses will benefit in health and appearance from grooming throughout the growing season to remove dead wood and unruly branches.

For successful floral production, the aristocrats also require frequent dusting and spraying. Weekly applications of fungicides and insecticides are needed for disease, insect, and mite control, especially in our humid climate. Always be sure to read the chemical labels before applying. The preventive approach is best since, once infected or infested, rose ailments are hard to control.

To encourage modern roses to set more flowers, remove the spent blooms, preventing the formation of hips. Although you can simply pinch off a bloom, deadheading roses is best accomplished by cutting below the spent blossom where the stem is at least pencil thick, above an outward-facing bud, and above a five-leaflet group.

Roses grown for other than perfect Valentine's Day flowers are far easier to maintain than

It's a Matter of Fact

Because of its beauty, durability, and fragrance, the rose has symbolized love for ages. Cleopatra used rose petals in her love nest pillows, and Nero showered them upon his guests. The Persian word for rose, *gul*, was close to the word *ghul*, meaning spirit. Love is the fulfillment of spirit, the essence of life.

the modern hybrids. You prune them less often, and some even thrive better without pruning. You use less or no fungicides and pesticides, and you still get abundant flowering, even without the tedious removal of spent blooms. In fact, with no deadheading, the hips produced add their own special effect to the rose plant and some will self-pollinate. Also, some birds are attracted to the bright fruit.

Now, with a partiality to antique roses, I'd like to mention some incredible new rose introductions that, although cultivated by the hands of man, are akin to the antiques in their appearance, growth habits, and ease of care. Perhaps the best to reach the market is the Knock Out® family of patented shrub roses. (See Lesson 11 regarding patents.) These continuous bloomers bear flowers throughout the growing season and into late fall without the need to deadhead.

They have glossy, dark green leaves and medium-sized clusters of flowers. The earliest members of the family are pink to cherry-red, depending upon the variety. The newest addition, The Sunny Knock Out® Rose ('Radsunny'), is my favorite rose color—yellow. Unlike the others, it's fragrant. There's also the 2007 All-America Rose Selections (AARS) winner, The Rainbow Knock Out® Rose ('Radcor'), which is coral pink with yellow centers. Virtually maintenance free and resistant to black spot, powdery mildew, and aphids, these roses quickly grow to about 4 feet by 4 feet. They tolerate our Southern humidity and will grow with as little as four hours of sun.

So, my generalized conclusion about roses is: If you want to produce picture-perfect roses on long stems, be prepared for lots of maintenance. But if you are happy with a more naturalized look, a beauty that speaks of love and the spirit, consider the antique roses.

A final word about roses: The care of many roses is so particular that you should read one of the many, many books that discuss their cultivation. Furthermore, you should decide how much work you are willing to perform, what kind of flower you are after, and how much fragrance you desire. Again, the hybridized modern roses have many positive characteristics, like repeat blooming, large flowers, and almost shocking colors. But the old roses are more natural looking, require little care, have exceptional fragrance, and, for me, are the ones most scent from heaven. I will forever love my Lady Banks' rose.

Postcript: As I was working through yet another edit of this book in December 2008, I attended a memorial service for Louise (Orahood Ray), whose passing was untimely. I was reminded by another friend in attendance of the treasure hunts we had at those birthday parties mentioned, and Louise's mother confirmed my memory of the Lady Banks' rose. For Louise and her kind friendship, I dedicate this Lesson in her memory.

The Goods on Grafting

MOST ROSES BOUGHT TODAY are grafted. Although it is becoming easier, once again, to find and buy "own-root" roses, they are not always the varieties sought and found in the grafted hybrids. Roses grown on their own roots maintain their own heritage,

Louise (left) and I goofing off, circa 1967. We had different talents, yet shared similar joys. I loved waking up in her room that was decorated in pinks and greens, always feeling like spring was in the air.

genetic disposition, and character, and they tend to be more disease resistant, easier to grow, easier to maintain, and more fragrant than their hybrid counterparts.

Hybrid or grafted roses are those that have been vegetatively propagated by uniting the parts of two separate plants, combining some of the benefits of each parent. Sometimes the rootstock has a valuable quality, which, when combined with equally good qualities in its partner, makes for an exceptional plant. Both parents are often of the same species, but must be at least of the same genus.

Plant breeders have used grafting as an asexual propagation method for over 2,000 years. One of several techniques, notch grafting involves the breeder taking a rooted plant, called the rootstock or stock plant, and cutting it off square first, then cutting it with a downward V-groove. The second plant, which is to be reproduced and must have at least three buds, is known as the scion. It is cut in a wedge shape and inserted into the notch of the rooted stock. The cambium (growing tissue) of each plant is aligned—the surfaces are cut clean and put in close contact. The union is wrapped with a special tape that has a biodegradable cloth backing, and all cut surfaces are covered with grafting wax or mounded soil. By the time a bud sprouts, the tape has disintegrated. And a new rose grows to maturity.

LESSON 23 ∽ February 19–25
Pruning

> *Trees are poems that the earth writes upon the sky. We fell them down and turn them into paper that we may record our emptiness.*
> —Kahlil Gibran (1883–1931)
> *Sand and Foam*

Proper Pruning Is Based upon Plant Physiology

PRACTICALLY EVERY PERSON is perplexed, particularly about principles pertaining to pruning. Say that three times . . . real fast. Now see . . . that wasn't so bad. And neither is pruning. You just have to know *what* to prune *when*, *why*, and *how*. Okay, not so easy. Perhaps the following discussion of the basics will help you.

We prune to help plants. Beneficial pruning means removing plant parts to get rid of dead and dying material; to strengthen the plant and encourage fuller, healthier growth; to rejuvenate old plants; to stabilize weak or damaged plants; to encourage fruit and flower production; and to create special effect.

There are four basic kinds of pruning: pinching, cutting back, thinning, and shearing. Pinching back stem tips of new growth helps promote branch development, ultimately resulting in a compact, bushy plant. Cutting back, or heading back, shortens branches and is used to remove branches damaged by cold or storm, to limit plant size, or to produce more and better flowers or fruits.

Thinning involves removing whole stems at their point of origin, reducing the bulk of the plant while maintaining its size and shape. Thinning allows light and air into the interior of the plant, eliminates competing branches, and removes unproductive stems. Generally, plants should be cut back at the same time they are thinned, to prevent long, floppy, weighty branches that will break when stressed.

The fourth method of pruning is shearing. Traditional hedges are sheared. Topiaries are sheared. Any bushes you want to look rigid, starched, and unnatural are sheared. It's the easiest, low-maintenance pruning technique for bushes, but not always the prettiest since it restricts the natural, flowing form of a plant.

IT'S A MATTER OF FACT

Cutting tools have evolved since the first pruning with a falx (sickle) of the grapevine in Armenia around 6000 B.C., roughly the beginning of the modern era. The Romans also used the falx with its recurved blade. Although wheat was originally harvested by pulling the plants out of the ground, Middle Eastern farmers began harvesting with a scythe, which evolved from the falx and was refined through the years, becoming a prized possession of medieval farmers, costing them as much as one-quarter of their annual income. The advent of the fifteenth- and sixteenth-century demand for well-trimmed hedges required smooth and efficient cutting tools, leading to the invention of hedge shears, the first scissor principle tools. As gardening developed, so did the variety of cutting tools, which, by the nineteenth century, included shears, saws, axes, bark scalers, chisels, scythes, moss scrapers, and pruners. All have changed in form over the years, and many new additions and numerous specialty tools have been added to the list.

The most common question about pruning is *when*? The answer is, it depends. Although you can prune almost any time of the year, plants are best pruned at particular times, determined by their flowering or their sap flow (as is the case of many trees).

Generally, you should prune spring-flowering shrubs and vines immediately after their blossoms have fallen. This group includes azalea, beautybush, bigleaf hydrangea, spring-flowering spirea (like bridalwreath), camellia, some clematis, climbing roses, deutzia, doublefile viburnum, flowering quince, forsythia, Japanese kerria, Japanese pieris, lilac, mock orange, pearlbush, pyracantha, rhododendron, shrub honeysuckle, sweetshrub, weigela, winter (fragrant) daphne, and wisteria. Do *not* prune these now; wait until after they have finished blooming, but don't wait too long. If you prune spring-flowering shrubs after their new woody growth has started, you diminish or eliminate flower growth the following year.

The kind of pruning required differs for various spring-flowering shrubs. Bushes like forsythia and Thunberg spirea should be cut back and thinned to remove long, wispy branches. Do not shear them; rather, cut extra-long branches halfway or so down. On the other hand, bushes like azaleas and camellias may require a little shaping, but again, not shearing. Using hand pruners, cut stems to approximately equal heights/widths but do not create a ball of a bush.

Summer-flowering and autumn-flowering shrubs and vines should be pruned in late winter or early spring, before spring growth begins. Some of the most common of these are beautyberry, chastetree (vitex), cranberrybush viburnum, crapemyrtle, floribunda roses, grandiflora roses, glossy abelia, Japanese barberry, summer-flowering spirea (like 'Anthony Waterer'), nandina, Rose-of-Sharon (althea), oakleaf hydrangea, and witchhazel. We're nearing the end of the pruning season for these plants and need to be wary about pruning too late, especially if it's been another unusually warm winter.

Trees are best pruned when they are dormant, but they are not all ready for pruning at the same time. Prune deciduous trees during the cold months, but not after the buds are swelled. Usually you can safely continue pruning them through mid- to late February. However, spring-flowering trees, such as flowering pear, dogwood, crabapple, flowering almond, redbud, saucer magnolia, star magnolia, flowering cherry, and flowering peach, should be handled selectively and sparingly since you do not want to remove too many of the spring blossoms that are already present and ready to burst forth. These are best pruned November through January. Summer-flowering and autumn-flowering trees, like goldenraintree, mimosa, and sourwood, can be pruned into late February, before spring growth begins.

Plants have individual pruning needs. Some require heavy pruning each year; others need light pruning every few years.

And some demand remedial pruning due to accidental damage. Reading about pruning and observing the growth of your plants and their response to pruning are the best ways to determine their pruning needs. In addition, here are some common pruning matters that may provide some guidance for you:

- Prune hollies, osmanthus, and most broadleaf evergreens almost any time of the year. They put out a flush of growth 2–3 times per season and after pruning or injury. Pruning after the first flush of growth helps keep these plants at a lower height. Pruning them in midsummer helps keep the overall growth of the plant in check. Severe late-winter to early spring pruning can be harmful to the plants because the new growth that is promoted will likely be harmed by a frost, causing tissue damage. Pruning young plants often promotes faster, fuller growth. Do note that if you want an abundance of berries on your hollies, do not prune them after they flower in spring, so the berries will set.

- Never prune junipers, pines, cedars, spruces, Leyland cypress, arborvitae, cryptomeria, and other evergreen conifers any further back than the previous season's growth. Unlike broadleaf evergreens, these plants cannot send out new growth from just any place on the stem. Prune creeping junipers by lifting the top branches and cutting the larger branches underneath; the younger growth on top will then hide the cuts. Prune pines in the spring by cutting part or most of the new "candle" growth.

- Do not prune shade trees in early spring since they are putting all of their resources into new growth. Removing this growth before the leaves have had an opportunity to gather and send nourishment back to the roots will stress the trees. Prune *large* shade trees in late June after the leaves have come out and hardened off. This early-summer pruning is often preferred since all of the dead and unhealthy branches can be identified by lack of leaves.

- Do not prune large limbs at their base. Rather, leave a ¼- to 1-inch stub to promote faster healing.
- Do not use wound paints and sealers to protect trees after pruning. They have been proven ineffective.
- Prune bigleaf and oakleaf hydrangeas (*Hydrangea macrophylla* and *H. quercifolia*, respectively) shortly after bloom but not in late winter or any time before bloom because these hydrangeas bloom on the previous season's growth. Note, however, that the new repeat-blooming *H. macrophylla* cultivars such as those in the Endless Summer® Collection bloom on old and new wood, so you can prune them almost any time. And you can encourage more flowers on them by pruning back flowering stems to a pair of healthy buds, as well as by deadheading. When cutting hydrangeas, on each stalk leave 2–4 new stems or leaf buds, which will form new stems. If you're not sure how to do it and can't find detailed instructions, remember that no pruning is better than improper pruning of a hydrangea.
- Do not prune forsythia or other early spring–flowering shrubs in the winter. They bloom on the previous year's growth; so pruning any time other than just after bloom reduces the amount and intensity of bloom the next year. Any pruning should be very reserved since forsythia and many other spring-flowering shrubs are loose growing and not meant to be shaped into round balls or boxes.
- Prune clethra, butterfly bush, and chastetree almost anytime before or during the growing season, despite their flowering.
- Avoid "crape murder" of your crapemyrtles. (See Lesson 46.)
- Be aware that there are three types of buds. Cutting the terminal buds at the ends of stems makes a plant become bushier since its energy is directed to growth along the stems. Cutting lateral buds on the sides of plant stems encourages taller, skinnier shapes. If a plant has any

latent buds that look like nubbins on the stem, removing growth higher up the stem causes them to sprout.

- Don't try to keep a plant "tame" in its location by frequently pruning (most likely shearing) it. If that's necessary, the plant is probably in the wrong location for its naturally mature size, and it will ultimately fail in health and aesthetics.

- Use the proper pruning tool, sharpened, for the job at hand. Don't, for instance, try to use hand pruners to cut a 2-inch branch from a tree. Loppers and saws were invented for that purpose.

- Prune to expose the greatest beauty in plants by enhancing their natural character and habit, not to bend them to your will.

There are numerous illustrated books and pamphlets available in libraries, bookstores, and local Cooperative Extension Service offices that describe pruning techniques and times for individual types of plants. Use them. Then, by carefully experimenting with pruning and watching the results, determine your plants' particular requirements. If you prune a plant incorrectly or at the wrong time of the year, you may severely alter its temporary growth and ultimate shape. But it's unlikely you will kill it.

Proper pruning is based upon plant physiology. Understanding the basics will help you in the art of nurturing the healthy growth of your plants and awakening their intrinsic, natural beauty. It may sound too scientific, but it's not. Just take the time to educate yourself a little. And be bold. Or, hire a professional, but be sure she *is* a professional, since "mow, blow, and go" lawn maintenance folks often do not know about proper pruning.

Just as we have to weed out, redefine, and refine our undesirable traits to more fully develop our growth as human beings and reach our fullest potential, we have to cut out undesirable and unhealthy plant parts to encourage hearty development, renew vigor, and enhance beauty. It often smarts when we make the cut, and the latent artistry does not always present itself immediately; but in time, the benefits of our work are revealed and we are greatly rewarded.

PLANT A TREE ON ARBOR DAY

IN GEORGIA, THE THIRD FRIDAY in February is celebrated as Arbor Day. Most states observe the national homage to trees and tree planting on the last Friday in April; but Georgia, like several other states, chooses to coincide its celebration with tree-planting weather.

J. Sterling Morton, a journalist, moved to the Nebraska Territory from Michigan in 1854. To his surprise, there were few trees. Morton used his position as editor of the first Nebraska newspaper to spread the word about the importance of trees: they act as windbreaks to keep the soil from blowing away, provide shade from the hot sun, and serve as fuel and building materials. He used his potent power-of-the-journalist's-pen to urge individuals and civic organizations to plant them.

At Morton's suggestion, the Nebraska State Board of Agriculture had a contest, offering prizes for those planting the largest number of trees on April 10, 1872. One million trees were planted in Nebraska that first Arbor Day. In 1885, Arbor Day became a legal holiday in Nebraska with Morton's birthday—April 22—becoming the date for its permanent observance, until 1989 when it was changed to the last Friday in April. Other countries around the World have adopted similar days or periods of action and observation. (April 22, 1970, was observed as the first annual Earth Day and marked the beginning of the modern environmental movement.)

A single person can make a difference to the life of this planet, using the gifts given him. Morton used his love of plants and his talent with the pen to enhance the quality of life and landscape in Nebraska. His legacy lives on, as each year we are reminded of the importance of trees. Plant a tree each Arbor Day. Encourage a neighbor to plant one too. Just think of the possibilities.

LESSON 24 ✍ February 26–March 4
Conifers

We don't mind growing trees in the South; it's a good place for silviculture,
sunny and watery, with a growing season to make a Yankee gardener weep.
What we mind is that all of our trees are being taken. We want
more than 1 percent natural stand of longleaf. We know a pine plantation is
not a forest, and the wholesale conversion to monocultures is unacceptable
to us. . . . When we say the South will rise again we can mean that we
will allow the cutover forests to return to their former grandeur and pine
plantations to grow wild.

—Janisse Ray
Ecology of a Cracker Childhood

Conifer Collections Are Cool

MY CHILDHOOD NEIGHBORHOOD was filled with broadleaf trees—
mostly tall, stately oaks, with a mix of hickory, sweetgum, dogwood, and, I'm sure, many others that I did not identify at the time.
But there were patches of pines in the vicinity too. On the Emory
University campus, we sledded on cardboard down a hill covered
with pine needles slickened by snow—yes, it did snow in Atlanta
back then—and the playground behind our church had towering
loblolly pines shading the picnic tables and seesaws.

Despite these neighborhood enclaves, my relationship with
pine trees was fashioned in the country at a farm we visited sporadically on weekends. Virtually the entire acreage was covered
with loblolly pines that had been planted on terraces remaining
from abandoned cotton fields. On sunny, not-too-hot days, my
father and I walked through those pine trees until we found the
perfect spot to lie down on the pine needle bed. With no effort

at all, we napped—lulled to sleep by the dampened whistle and whoosh of the breeze through the needles above.

My husband and I moved to that pine tree farm and, before starting our nursery, planted Virginia pines in one field to sell as Christmas trees. Upon arrival, we gave the farm its name in deference to a name my sister had once pegged on the place—Pinebush. She thought the reforesting 4- to 5-foot seedlings sprouted all about looked more like bushes than trees, and she called them pinebushes.

Those pines, and cut Christmas trees enjoyed throughout my childhood, were about the extent of my knowledge of, involvement with, or appreciation for conifers. If I were to ask any Southerner to name some conifers, I bet *his* first thoughts would be of the tall pine trees and any number of cut Christmas trees too. After all, the long-needled pines *Pinus taeda* (loblolly), *Pinus elliottii* (slash pine), and *Pinus palustris* (longleaf pine) are mainstays of our Southern landscape, filling abandoned cotton fields, dotting forests, and creating stands for turpentine, pulp, and timber harvest. And the Christmas trees—well, many are cut, imported from foreign climates, and always a welcome addition to our homes during the sun-depressed holiday season.

But there are so many more conifers that make fantastic additions to the landscape, either as specimens (stand-alones) or in groups, including cedar, cypress, redwood, cryptomeria, false cypress, fir, hemlock, juniper, larch, spruce, pine, arborvitae, and yew. With the abundance of broadleaf, deciduous plants in our landscapes, conifers add interest and beauty in the winter. Various shades of green, brownish purples, silvers, grays, yellows, and blues accent the dull gray scene. And the various shapes, textures, sizes, and silhouettes provide form in the seemingly lifeless picture.

Conifers are gymnosperms, meaning *naked seed*, and are part of the non-flowering portion of the plant world. Most conifers are evergreen and have cones (their flowers), although some have more fruit-like seed carriers, and most have leaves that are needle-like. All carry their male and female sex organs in separate "flowers," some on the same tree and some on separate trees. All have two-layered bark. And all provide texture and contrast to the broadleaf ornamentals.

Conifers enjoy moist, well-drained, richly organic soil, and most (especially non-green varieties) like sunny spots. Some, though, prefer partial shade and show burn from direct sun, and many do quite well in heavy shade. Although they tolerate drought and hot weather, conifers (other than junipers) do not like sites where the summer heat is intensified by southern exposure, stone walls, or the like.

Many quick-growing conifers make good windbreaks and hedges and are easily maintained at low heights by frequent trimming. On the other hand, many conifers are slow growing and virtually maintenance free, requiring only slight pruning for shaping. Prune conifers on new wood during the growing season before bud set (midspring to late summer), but do not prune them in August or September.

IT'S A MATTER OF FACT

One of the most devastating stories of environmental destruction in our nation's history is that of the 300-year exploitation of white pine in the eastern United States, resulting in the complete loss of those virgin forests. The noble tree, whose wood was used for boats, bridges, millwork, houses, shingles, cabinets, etc., was coveted by the British and colonists alike and became a chief economic factor contributing to the rising storm toward revolution. In 1761, the Crown ordered the New Hampshire royal governor to include a clause in all land grants "to reserve all white or other Sort of Pine Trees fit for Masts, of the growth of 24 Inches Diameter and upwards at 12 inches from the Earth, to Us our Heirs & Successors, for the Masting our Royal Navy, and that no such Trees shall be cut—without our Licence—on Penalty of the Forfeiture of such Grant, & of the Land so granted reverting to the Crown...."

I've grown fond of many conifers over the years and have selected a handful to give you some flavor of my favorites and possibilities for your landscape:

Chamaecyparis pisifera (Sawara or Japanese Falsecypress): The wild species are tall, pyramidal trees with loose, open habits.

But the numerous cultivars tend to be substantially smaller, with narrower or columnar shapes. They are called "false" because the leaves have a flattened profile, different from the true cypress's more three-dimensional sprays. 'Gold Mop' is a low-growing cultivar with thread-like leaves that combine to look like a golden mop of hair. The plant flops over the ground, making it a great rock garden addition. It does not burn in bright sun and will remain golden if kept out of the shade.

Chamaecyparis obtusa (Hinoki Falsecypress): These plants have spreading branches and drooping, frond-like branchlets. The ever-popular dwarf cultivar 'Nana Gracilis' has dark green foliage and grows slowly to about 6 feet with a 3- to 4-foot spread, making a pyramidal bush. The cultivar 'Nana Lutea' has foliage formed in wavy fans arranged in tiers, giving a sense of movement on the most windless of days. Its golden yellow becomes greenish yellow on the underside and in the shade. 'Nana Lutea' is another good rock garden plant that is very slow growing.

Tsuga canadensis (Canadian [Eastern] Hemlock): When crushed, their leaves smell like the herb hemlock. The foliage is flat and needle-like, joined to the shoot by a short projection. Some varieties grow 40–70 feet or more while some cultivars remain quite low. This tree is marginal in Zone 7 because of the heat and requires partial shade. I am heartbroken that we are losing our hemlocks—*Tsuga canadensis* and *Tsuga caroliniana*—to the hemlock woolly adelgid, an aphid-like insect introduced from Asia that infests the trees from southeastern Maine to Northeast Georgia and kills them in as little as four years. The loss of these majestic giants in our Appalachian Mountains and forests will devastate those ecosystems as we now know them. Hemlocks grown in nurseries can be protected from the invasion, but once they are put in the landscape they will require continuous protection by observation, good cultural practices, and spraying or injection. Nevertheless, we are being encouraged to keep planting them so that some of the species will survive extinction—perhaps.

In addition to the conifers that add visual delight to the landscape, there are many that serve important, practical functions as well—screening and ground cover quickly come to mind. Junipers are the leaders in the field and have two important traits to remember: they require very well drained soil since they don't like wet feet, and they will look horrendous if you don't prune them properly.

Leyland cypress (*Cupressocyparis leylandii*) has become the conifer of choice for screening purposes, but in my humble opinion, it's overused, as is often the case with a popular plant like the red tip photinia and Bradford pear of years past. Furthermore, the recent drought years have encouraged the growth of the deadly bot canker and other fungul diseases on Leylands, which can wipe out an entire screening because of the monocultural planting. Watch for a welcome movement toward the use of 'Yoshino' Japanese cedar (*Cryptomeria japonica*) and Atlantic whitecedar (*Chamaecyparis thyoides*) to hide or separate you from the rest of the world.

Another Leyland alternative, 'Green Giant' arborvitae (*Thuja plicata*), has extremely vigorous growth, a dense habit, and bronze coloration in the winter. 'Carolina Sapphire' Arizona cypress (*Cupressus arizonica*) is another very fast growing Leyland substitute that has a superior silvery blue color and a much softer, relaxed habit. While extremely drought tolerant, this conifer will not tolerate too much water; consequently, many are seen dying in urban landscapes due to too much irrigation. (See Lesson 20 regarding xeriscaping and the use of zones for different watering needs.)

There are many, many low-maintenance conifers that will add an incredible mix of interest to your landscape. It's worth your time to look through some books, stop at some nurseries, and discover the possibilities. You may even want to consider creating a cool conifer collection in a small part of your yard. I have seen one that was fashioned as a rock garden on a sloping bank that extended into a shaded area, which sported all types of conifers, each with an individual personality to entertain the senses.

Cultural Diversity and Pine Plantations

Georgia takes pride in its forestry industry and particularly in its coniferous pines. The numbers are impressive: As of 2006, there was approximately $22.7 billion worth of direct and indirect economic impact and 145,000 jobs supported by the industry in

Georgia, which compensates employees and business owners more than $3.3 billion, making it the second highest paying industry in the state. Georgia is in its fourth generation of commercial forests that were begun in 1926 when James Fowler, a farmer/business-man from Soperton planted 10 acres of pine seedlings. Ultimately, he planted 7,000,000 of them on 10,000 acres in his lifetime. Of the 37 million–acre total land area of the state, there are now about 22.5 million acres of forestland available for commercial use.

Tree plantations proliferated during the twentieth century. A direct response to the devastatingly barren landscape left from eighteenth- and nineteenth-century clearing for pastures, farming, and development; a need for jobs in the depressed South; and newly discovered uses for pines led to the development of an industry that grows trees as a consumable crop. In 1932, Charles Holmes Herty discovered a way to make paper from pine trees. The ensu-ing industry still maintains a large presence in the state. Numerous other uses for wood and its by-products have been developed over the years, including cellulose gum used in syrup to make it flow consistently; tree fibers made into viscose pulp that is made into rayon for clothing; cellulose acetate that becomes photographic film; cellulose derivatives made into hard plastic items like combs, toys, and screwdriver handles; microcrystalline cellulose that gives antacid its creamy texture; cellulose that coats easy-swallowing caplets; specialty grade cellulose that becomes artificial leathers used in wallets, belts, and shoes; pulp process by-products made into paints, polishes, perfumes, and soaps; nitrocellulose used to add the gloss to nail polish; and wood residues and pulping liquors burned and used to fuel the pulp mills. Most recently, in response to the need for alternative fuels, Georgia has been selected as the location of the nation's first plant to process pine trees and pine scraps into ethanol.

This is all wonderful and good, but it is important to note that reforestation in the form of tree plantations is not the same as natural reforestation or virgin forests. Tree plantations do not have, create, or maintain a true ecosystem. They are a monocul-ture and do not encourage natural selection of the species or the introduction of other species. The biodiversity of flora and fauna that naturally occurs in a true forest does not exist, and the need to keep the monocultural agricultural crop pure and healthy requires management that includes herbicides and pesticides. The natural interdependence found in an ecosystem is lost.

Reforestation in the form of tree plantations is good for the economy, good for consumerism, and better for the environment than wasteland. In fact, in a salute to the environmental importance of tree plantations, during the 2008 election, Georgia voters approved a constitutional amendment giving preferential tax treatment to owners of large tracts of forestland, the espoused purpose being to preserve Georgia's forests and save them from the ravages of development, which is more likely to occur as property taxes rise. But despite these admirable goals, one has to ask: Are monocultural plantings good for the perpetuation of biodiversity? Are they good for life on Earth? Are they good for your soul? Like so many other issues confronting us as we grapple with our wants and needs and our over-consumption and destruction of the environment to meet those wants and needs, we should consider this issue also.

Pines are a staple in Georgia, even on Stone Mountain. In 1990, during one of our many climbs to the top, James found haven under one.

LESSON 25 ⤳ March 5–11
Azaleas

> [T]he fiery Azalea, flaming on the ascending hills or wavy surface of the
> gliding brooks . . . that suddenly opening to view from dark shades, we are
> alarmed with the apprehension of the hills being set on fire. This is certainly
> the most gay and brilliant flowering shrub yet known.
>
> —William Bartram (1739–1823)
> *Travels through North & South Carolina, Georgia,
> East & West Florida*

Azalea Picks Are Boundless

Evergreen Azaleas

BLOOMING EVERGREEN AZALEAS are some of the most spectacular and common sights in our Southern landscape—they have
become synonymous with our spring fling. However, they offer far
more than a colorful spring. Properly selected and placed, they can
be a vital component of your garden year-round. But you should
familiarize yourself with the plant characteristics and plan your
landscape for the best results.

To take advantage of their perennial appeal, consider several
elements when selecting your azaleas: size, shape, flower color,
winter foliage color, texture, bloom time, compatibility with other
plants in your landscape, and cultural requirements.

Size and Shape: When referring to an azalea's size, Fred C. Galle,
former Director of Horticulture at Callaway Gardens, cited its
mature height at 10 years of age. Thus, an azalea that is up to 3-feet
tall is called *low* (Satsuki varieties); *medium* azaleas grow 3- to 6-feet
tall (Kurume varieties); and *large* ones reach over 6 feet (Southern
Indian, Kaempferi, and Glenn Dale varieties). The ultimate size

of your azalea, however, will depend not only upon its natural habit and age but also upon the care you give it and its location.

Azaleas may be upright (erect and taller than broad), spreading (erect and broader than tall), or compact (small, dense, and twiggy). Their shape may change as they mature, and location influences their growth. Furthermore, the blooms themselves vary in size and shape. There are singles, doubles, semi-doubles, and hose-in-hose blooms in all sizes.

Blooming Period: In our area, the bloom time for most evergreen azalea varieties spreads from March through June. But some are repeat bloomers. For example, varieties from the Bloom 'N Again® and Encore® collections put forth a second time during the fall months. Most azalea blooms last one to two weeks, but by selecting several varieties, you can have uninterrupted color for months.

Colors: Because there are so many azalea colors, there is a standardized color classification scheme used to describe each tone. Whenever possible, Galle used the National Bureau of Standards (NBS) Special Publication 440, Color Universal Language and Dictionary. He also referred to the Royal Horticultural Society Colour Chart (RHS) when available.

Flower color is affected by altitude, temperature, light, soil chemistry, and abnormal growing conditions such as drought. Color intensity in any one azalea may vary from year to year depending upon climatic and environmental factors.

Site Selection: Be sure your azalea will grow in the location you have selected. Generally, is it suitable to your hardiness zone? And, more specifically, does the selected site have proper sun/shade and soil requirements? Furthermore, will the mature size and growth habit of your selection fit the area and design you have in mind? Will your selection outgrow its site?

Azaleas are shade tolerant. But constant, heavy shade or a north side location may be too extreme. More than four hours of sun each day is probably too much, and direct midday or late afternoon sun should be avoided. Tender varieties require some protection and should not be placed on windy corners or in frost pockets. Good air circulation and drainage is necessary for good health.

Cultural Requirements: Evergreen azaleas like acidic soil with a pH of 4.5 to 6.0. The best soil for these plants has sufficient amounts of organic matter and is loose and crumbly, a rarity around houses or in developed areas. So you will probably have to improve your soil. Add organic matter such as leaf mold, pine bark, compost, or well-rotted leaves. However, do not use peat moss since, in our clay soil, it retains water and causes clumping, the very problems you are trying to cure. Mix the amendment with the loosened and chopped clay six inches or more deep and let the mixture settle for a week or more before planting. If you have very little or no topsoil, you will need quite a bit of organic matter. Similarly, you will need to improve the soil if trash, mortar, or free lime was left around your house when it was built.

> ## IT'S A MATTER OF FACT
>
> William Bartram marveled at the flowering rhododendrons (sisters to azaleas in the same genus *Rhododendron*) of the Blue Ridge and Great Smoky Mountains as he traveled through western North Carolina in early summer. A pantheist, he believed each plant embodied the essence of divinity and had a soul. He wrote, "Perhaps there is not any part of creation, within reach of our observations, which exhibits a more glorious display of the Almighty hand than the vegetable world."

The factors to consider when selecting your azaleas are no different than those for other plants you plan to add to your landscape. It's just important that you remember that the decision is not simply whether you want an azalea, but which azalea. To answer this question, you will have to look at the special characteristics of each variety you are considering, looking for compatibility with the rest of your landscape and surrounding architectural features, as well as compatibility with your needs and tastes.

Consulting a book that lists varieties and their characteristics may be helpful when selecting your azaleas. An excellent source is *Azaleas* by Fred C. Galle, but it is dated and does not include the newer varieties, many of which deserve attention. Plant tags at the nursery are also helpful. Try not to get stuck with the comfort of the azaleas whose names you know. Rather, stretch out and try something new.

The Japanese believe that when Ninigi descended from heaven and created their empire, the Kurume azalea sprang from the soil of their Mount Kirishina—a mystical plant that became a mainstay of the Japanese landscape. Azaleas were a part of my childhood landscape also. I recall my mother's obsession with her bed of 'Coral Bells' Kurume azaleas with their tiny pink flowers. She gave them more loving attention than any other plants in the yard, ritualistically watering them many afternoons, or having me do the same. But I also recall the azaleas fronting our next-door neighbors' house. They were quite different in their height, looseness, and flower size;

Mom's favorite Coral Bells azaleas had their own bed next to the driveway. She, and I, watered them quite frequently the first several years they were in the ground becoming established. My brother, Thomas, seen next to me, didn't help with that routine, but he had plenty of time connecting with Nature while earning his Eagle Scout status. I too was a scout and to this day relish the experience and lessons learned, particularly the camping, trail blazing, hiking, and making S'mores. 1965.

they were Formosa azaleas. I liked them both. It doesn't matter which type *you* like since, by carefully selecting, placing, and caring for your azaleas, you too can create an enchanting landscape that will create lasting memories.

Deciduous (Native) Azaleas

The evergreen azaleas are typically native to Japan, but all azaleas that are native to North America are deciduous—they lose their leaves in the winter. Native azaleas have many attributes that distinguish them from their evergreen counterparts. In addition to the obvious difference in appearance in the winter when their bare branches grace the landscape, the natives' summer leaves are larger than those of the evergreens. The flower colors of the native azaleas do not cover quite as large a spectrum as those of the evergreens, but the palette does include yellow, a color not seen in the evergreen clan.

Although they like the shade, deciduous azaleas will tolerate full sun, but their blooms won't last as long as those grown in shade. Most pleasingly, native azalea flowers are more fragrant than those of the evergreen varieties.

There are sixteen azalea species that are native to the United States, with fourteen in the Southeast. Based upon their flower color, the three general groups of these azaleas are white, pink, and orange. Bloom time and other characteristics distinguish the various plants within these basic groups. For a listing of the native azaleas with bloom times and colors, visit the Azalea Society of America's Web site.

There are two series of native azalea cultivars being produced that I find exciting. The first is the Maid in the Shade® series, native azalea cultivars that represent several different species, cultivated by the Beasleys of Transplant Nursery in Lavonia, Georgia. Some of the varieties are as follows:

- 'Camilla's Blush'—Ball-shaped trusses. Soft pink blossoms. Fragrant. Early bloomer.
- 'Lisa's Gold'—Bright gold flowers. Early bloomer. Fragrant. 10–12 feet.
- 'My Mary'—Large, pure yellow flowers. Thick, dark green foliage. Early bloomer. A hybrid.

- 'Nacoochee Princess'—Large, slender white flowers with slight tinge of pink with blue undertones. Very fragrant. A hybrid.

The second is the Confederate Series, hybrid native azalea cultivars developed by Tom Dodd III, an Alabama plantsman. Heat and cold tolerant, the plants are pleasantly fragrant. Some of the varieties are as follows:

- 'Admiral Semmes'—Large inflorescences (flower groupings) with big, yellow flowers.
- 'Col. Mosby'—Large, fragrant flowers in big inflorescences. Start deep pink and fade to lighter pink with yellow blotch.
- 'Robert E. Lee'—Red flowers in spring. Fragrant.
- 'Stonewall Jackson'—Orange flowers in spring. Fragrant.

Native azaleas are a must for woodland settings and yards with lots of trees and good shade. Their color pokes fun with the dappled light and invites you closer, into the woods. And that's a good place to go for a change.

THE BARTRAM TRAIL COMES MY WAY

WILLIAM BARTRAM TRAVELED through my area, and according to one map I have seen, he traveled right by our nursery spot, going up what is now Georgia Highway. 106, after passing close to the present site of the State Botanical Garden of Georgia in Athens. I feel a particular kinship to him, a knowing that comes from our common ground—as close as that can be, with 200 years separating our lives.

Bartram was one of the first spiritual naturalists, using the word *sublime*—meaning noble, exalted, or majestic—to describe the nature he saw and traveled through in the Southeast colonies from 1773 to 1776. His descriptions of the flora and fauna, the wilderness, and the native peoples were considered overly romantic by many in his day, but writers and poets Thoreau, Emerson, Wordsworth, Southey, Coleridge, and Carlyle were impressed, as were many landscape artists.

William Bartram was the son of John Bartram, the "King's Botanist" (George III) in the colonies and a naturalist, paleontologist, scientist, and herbalist. John introduced over 500 new species of plants to the Old World, took an expedition through South Carolina, Georgia, and Florida with William (1765–1766), discovered the rare *Franklinia altamaha* tree (now *Gordonia franklinia*), and supplied British gardeners with New World plants during the eighteenth-century time of gentleman gardening and horticultural experimentation.

Inheriting his father's passion for plants, William ultimately illustrated them, as well as birds; started the nation's first nursery; and published the first plant catalog in the United States. In 1773, he started a four-year journey through portions of the lower South, including Florida, Georgia, South Carolina, and North Carolina, during which he wrote his *Travels*.

'Admiral Semmes' azalea (a Rhododendron Exbury hybrid cross with *R. austrinum*, for cold *and* heat tolerance) is a fabulous deciduous azalea from the Confederate Series with orangish yellow flowers that are very fragrant. It earned a spot on the 2007 Georgia Gold Medal list, and its namesake was "Commander of CSS Alabama during 'the recent unpleasantness,'" according to Dodd & Dodd Native Nurseries, the breeders. The long stamens and pistol of the native azaleas give them a wispy, loose feel, different from that of many of the evergreen azaleas. Specimens found in the woods are superb surprises to happen upon during a walk.

LESSON 26 ∽ March 12–18
Hedges and Screens

The old Lakota was wise. He knew that man's heart, away from nature,
becomes hard; he knew that the lack of respect for growing,
living things soon led to lack of respect for humans too. So he kept his youth
close to its softening influence.

—Luther Standing Bear (1868–1939)
Oglala Lakota Sioux Wise Man

Hedges Hide Your Neighbors

WHEN I WAS A CHILD, I darted across the neighbors' backyards, following the well-worn paths that tunneled through the hedges dividing the territories. During the earlier years, most of the bushes were privet, elaeagnus, and abelia, sometimes choked with strands of honeysuckle. But stiffer, more regal hollies of the prickly kind began to appear as fortunes were made, decorum became important, and privacy was of greater concern. It was hard to squeeze between those stately shrubs, and some were placed along newly constructed wooden fences meant to ensure protection to the fortresses. Visits down the street took longer—took a degree of planning, in fact. So they waned along with the spontaneity. Friendships followed suit.

I loved those loose, living fences. They were just enough to make a statement of domain, but lively enough to meld into the landscape and give a sense of continuation to the next yard, a sense of neighborliness. If unpruned and left to grow tall, broad, and virtually weeping, they harbored scores of birds and small wildlife and made terrific play areas for kids. My children and I temporarily lost that sort of living fence in our backyard at the nursery—John insisted that the 15-foot-high, broad, scraggly privet hedge be removed for a layered buffer of hollies and other evergreen shrubs. It's now an impenetrable barrier—with the invasive privet gradually growing to former proportions in any area it can. So, once again, privacy prevails and the birds feed and nest.

Hedges, usually considered dense, single rows of one type of plant, serve many purposes. They define spaces; integrate man-made structures with the remaining landscape; connect points in the landscape; and provide intimate, framed spaces. They are formal or informal, evergreen or deciduous, short or tall, mono-tone or colorful. Most folks think about hedges when they want to hide something. But what they really need is a *screen*—a multiple-rowed, possibly multiple-species planting. Perhaps a matter of semantics to some, there is, nevertheless, a difference between a hedge and a screen when viewed from the utilitarian desire of blocking an unwanted view of the neighbor's shed, backyard, pool, road, parking lot, factory, you name it. For the sake of simplicity, I use the words interchangeably here.

As with all landscape situations, to decide which plants make the best screen for your situation, you first have to determine the cultural requirements of the site: Will the screen be in sun or shade? Will it be at the bottom or top of a hill, subject to frost pockets or not? Does it need to grow fast?—basically a useless question since everyone seems to want tomorrow today. Does the site require a formal or informal look? Is the area particularly wet? How much room is there; how big can the screen get?

After figuring out the culture, select plants based upon your needs. To screen something year-round, opt for evergreens that grow vigorously and densely and reach medium to tall heights. Some deciduous shrubs work for screening, but they should be extremely twiggy and preferably bear leaves early and hold them late. In all cases, choose plants based upon their mature size. Plants do best if allowed to grow to their mature heights, with occasional pruning as necessary. It's okay to keep a formal hedge sheared, but be sure your plant choice will tolerate the frequent pruning.

To keep people and some animals out of an area (or in an area), select wide, medium-height, thorny or prickly plants with dense branching to the base. There are evergreen and deciduous varieties that suit the bill. To create a wall effect, use evergreens that are densely twiggy, slow-growing, small-leafed, with little or no fruiting or flowering. You can also create a wall with some deciduous shrubs that are dense and stiff.

To make a formal living fence use shrubs that are slow-growing, tolerant to frequent shearing, and finely textured with leaves and twigs all the way to the base; those with a rigid branch structure are best. To muffle noise, pick an evergreen that is wide and dense, thickly branched to the base, and pollution tolerant (and note that some experts now say that plants do not buffer noise). A windbreak hedge should be drought-tolerant, evergreen, tall, wide, and dense with branches to the base; the wider, the better.

It's a Matter of Fact

The word garden derives from the word for enclosure in Old German, and the word yard comes from the old English word for enclosure. Most gardens throughout history have been fenced or walled. But the American concept of gardens—exclusive areas cultivated with flowers and other ornamental plants—has become confused with the concept of a yard, generally meaning a lawn, with some ornamentation spotted around. Most Americans today have yards, but many aspire to have gardens, of the ornamental type. Nevertheless, most gardens in America today are vegetable gardens.

It's important to be flexible in your thinking about your hedge. If it's going to cover a good distance, it's likely to pass through differing cultural climates. For instance, it may encounter full sun all day on one side of your yard but lie in shade cast by your neighbors' trees on the other side of the yard. So you may need different plants along the course of the hedge. Transitioning from one species to another and using multiple rows is an effective and pleasing design.

There are advantages to using a variety of plant species to create your screen. For instance, lower growing bushes used in front of taller ones will hide bare lower branches while adding another dimension to the screen and providing additional buffering. However, if you don't want to add the lower row, you can usually prevent bare lower branches by keeping the top of the hedge narrower than the bottom, thus allowing sunlight to reach down and promote growth. Also, periodic renewal pruning (severe pruning, but not below the point where leaves still grow) can rejuvenate lower portions of many plants.

Multiple-species screens may also help prevent the spread of diseases and harmful insects. Monocultures, like a single-species hedge, are at high risk of disease and insect destruction since infestations easily hop from one plant to the next. Mixing species provides breaks that act as barriers to any spreading.

Because of their size, hedges are usually major investments in the landscape. Unfortunately, if they are single-rowed, a loss of one plant can mean a loss of purpose or aesthetic value. But planting a hedge in multiple layers, particularly one that is used for screening, can help with any unsightliness resulting from the loss of a single plant. It also provides coverage more quickly since the spaces between plants are masked by the growth of plants staggered on another row. And multiple-row planting is healthier for the plants since you're less likely to plant them too close together; in the competition for nutrients, overcrowding slows growth.

If you have problems with a hedge, ask yourself several questions: Is this the proper climate for this plant? Was the planting done in properly prepared soil? Has the planting been watered enough or too much? Are my neighbors' habits affecting my hedge—do they use herbicides, have excessive water run-off, etc.? Is my hedge that's close to the road pollution tolerant? Are the plants getting enough sun or shade? Is the soil around the plants too compact due to foot traffic or past activities? Is the soil pH proper for the plants—has it changed over time and is now in need of amendment? Is my hedge subject to too much wind? Is it properly pruned, allowing sunlight to the lower branches?

You can be neighborly when hiding your neighbors. The very act of establishing a living fence rather than a structural one is, in itself, a friendly gesture—and respectful.

ON SPACING AND PLANTING HEDGE PLANTS

MOST *SINGLE-ROW, FORMAL HEDGE* plants should be spaced apart about one-half to three-quarters the normal mature width of the plants (more or less, depending upon how fast you want them to fill in). For example, if a plant will grow to be 6 feet wide, plant it 3 feet from its neighbor; the two will meet and grow into one another, creating a dense marriage. Deciduous plants are best planted closer together than evergreens, but planting too close together will result in a short-lived hedge. Suckering plants, like privet, nandina, and mahonia, can be planted as close as one foot apart.

If you want a *screening hedge* to appear to grow together faster, to be more informal looking, and to appear shorter and wider than a single-row planting, do a double row, zigzag planting. For instance, a double row of Green Giant arborvitae (with an approximate mature width of 20 feet) will consist of two rows that are 10 feet apart, with plants in each row that are each 20 feet apart. (Distance is measured from the center of the plant.)

To create an impenetrable hedge, plant two rows in zigzag formation, using one-half to three-quarters the mature width between plants in each row and between rows. So, for instance, a double-row screen of hollies, with an approximate mature width of 12 feet, will consist of two rows that are 6–9 feet apart, with plants in each row that are each 6–9 feet apart.

The list of possible plants to use for hedges and screens is virtually endless. Table 1 includes some commonly used varieties, their sun/shade tolerances, and water tolerances. In selecting plants, know their mature size, being sure you have the proper information for the particular cultivar or variety you select. Follow the spacing guidelines mentioned above.

To plant a hedge, prepare a trench twice the width and depth of the root-balls, the entire length of the hedge. Till the soil until it is pulverized, then till in organic matter until it is mixed thoroughly with the soil. Use a shovel to dig a hole for each plant, placing the surface of the root-ball at the surface of the ground or higher. Lightly tamp the ground around each plant to slightly compact the soil. Water thoroughly and deeply. If the plants seem to sink, dig

Table 1: Screening Plants

Plant	Sun/Shade	Tolerates Wet Area?
Evergreen		
Boxwood	sun/part shade	no
Japanese hollies (ex: compacta)	sun/shade	no
Chinese hollies (ex: burford)	sun/part shade	no
Hybrid hollies (ex: Nellie R. Stevens)	sun/part shade	no
Inkberry hollies	sun/part shade	yes
American hollies	sun/part shade	no
Yaupon hollies	sun/shade	yes
Pfitzer juniper	sun	no
Anise tree	sun/shade	yes
Carolina cherrylaurel	sun/part shade-shade	no
Ligustrum	sun/shade	no
Elaeagnus	sun/shade	no
Southern waxmyrtle	sun/part shade	yes
Azalea	sun/part shade	no
Agarista (Leucothoe)	shade	yes
Loropetalum	sun/part shade	no
Arborvitae	sun	no
Leyland cypress	sun	no
Cryptomeria	sun/part shade	no
Virginia pine	sun	no
Eastern red cedar	sun/part shade	no
Atlantic whitecedar	sun	yes
Arizona cypress	sun	no
Deciduous and Semievergreen		
Pyracantha	sun/part shade	no
Forsythia	sun/part shade	no
Barberry	sun	no
Privet	sun/part shade	no
Abelia	sun/part shade	no
Burning bush	sun/shade	no
Viburnum	sun/shade	no

John stands next to a nursery row of Nellie R. Stevens hollies, which are the most popular holly used for screening today. We always use John in our plant pictures in the field so folks can judge the size of the trees and shrubs. Of course, we also use a measuring stick to gauge the exact height and then say what it is in trade terms. In this case, the Nellies are 14-16 feet. They will be dug with a 48-inch root-ball and will weigh about 3,000 pounds.

again and pull them carefully to the surface, then push more soil underneath. Cover the entire bed with mulch, 2–3 inches deep. Do not let the mulch hug the trunks of the plants. Note that it is absolutely 100 percent worth the investment to rent a tiller for the day, or if you are planting large stock, you may want to hire someone with a tractor and plow.

SPRING

As the peepers fill the spring evenings with their din—gleefully announcing the warmth of waters in their soggy habitats—I can't help but feel the tug to tour the woodlands. There are few greater gifts than the early spring sight of fern fiddleheads unfurling and soon-to-be-flowering perennials poking their nascent stems of fine freshness through the rich moistness of decayed leaves and humus, anxious to reach the renewed warmth offered by the sun, as the days grow longer.

So I go and I smell the richness, the odor of decay reformed. I feel the urge—that primitive call of Nature—to view new birth, to participate in the rites of celebration for new life bestowed, rising into existence. My nostrils flare and I breathe slowly, deeply, grabbing every morsel of aroma that floats midair. I taste it, I feel it in my gut, I absorb it.

Life—wrought by spirit. Life—born to live in dying. Life—springs eternal.

LESSON 27 ⤳ March 19–25
Landscaping

[Be] willing to cultivate [your] connection to place, little by little, season by season, before making any changes. Sit and watch, listen and learn, in the place you envision as your Sanctuary Garden. Whenever you feel ready to dive in, do so humbly, with a beginner's mind, open heart, and an empty bowl of gratitude.

—Christopher Forrest McDowell and Tricia Clark-McDowell
*The Sanctuary Garden: Creating a Place of Refuge in
Your Yard or Garden*

The Vernal Equinox Springs Life

IT'S THE WEEK OF THE VERNAL EQUINOX—when the sun crosses the equator on its return voyage from the lands down under to the lands up top. Days and nights are equal in length; the weather is moderate. Soothing greens and warmth encourage naps in the sun; bright, invigorating colors and growth incite renewed spirit, racing hormones, and spring fever.

There's a lot of movement this time of year. Birds migrate; plants are transplanted. And many people buy or build new homes, moving to new locations. But while they might put tons of time, money, and effort into finding or building the perfect house, they don't always think about the yard, the landscape.

If you are moving but don't have the time, inclination, or resources to seriously consider your landscape, don't despair. You can create your paradise, and take the time to enjoy the process! Consider these pointers:

If you purchase an old house:
- Be patient. Wait a full year before making any drastic changes to the landscape, and go through the seasons

with your yard to see what surprises may await you in the beds. Before pulling out and digging up for the trash heap, give yourself time to discover the well-established, spring-flowering bulbs buried next to your stoop, the clematis that climbs the fence, and the spider lilies that suddenly sprout their flowers, without the normal warning of leafy stems that draw attention.

- In similar fashion, watch for plants that you can't identify, and don't be hasty to pull them up. You may be lucky enough to harbor an endangered native plant or a plant that has yet to be officially identified and named. Over 1,000 species of plants have been newly identified in the United States in the past 25 years. One, a clematis named Morefield's leather flower, was found in a vacant lot in the middle of Huntsville, Alabama, and is now on the endangered species list.

- Don't hesitate to do remedial pruning to tame and shape overgrown or unsightly trees and shrubs. Just be sure to prune at the appropriate time for the particular plant. (See Lesson 23.) Then observe the plant for a year to see what it offers your landscape.

- If the lawn is in decent shape, start and continue a maintenance program. Lawns won't wait. You have to keep up with their fertilization, liming, mowing, aeration, and reseeding requirements. Otherwise, they will deteriorate and you will be faced with much greater cost to revitalize them.

If you purchase or build a new house:

- If you're building and hire a landscape architect, involve that person from day one to assure proper grading and hardscape and house placement.

- If the building site is already set, don't feel compelled to complete your landscape immediately (except, of course, the minimum required by your lender, neighborhood covenants, homeowners' association, or governmental authority for closing). Wait to see where your water runs, the kids walk, and the dog trots. These paths-of-least-resistance probably won't change, so you should design with them in mind.

- Don't feel compelled to stick with the minimal plantings the builder completes to close the deal. Use them as a starting point, or move them to other, more suitable locations in the yard.
- Go ahead and design your yard as completely as possible. Then muster up all the patience you can and break the installation into stages of development, growing your landscape as your time and money allow.

Some general suggestions:

- Bed preparation is the most critical aspect of landscape gardening. If you don't spend the time and money to properly prepare the home for your plants, you are literally throwing them down the hole.
- Be sure to know the growth habits, year-round colors, mature sizes, and sun/soil/water requirements of the plants you select to maximize their potential in your landscape.
- Pay attention to the sun. Where does it shine at what times of the year? When and where do you have shade and for how long?
- Do not dig without knowing what lies beneath you! Be sure to ask the builder or previous owner of your new home the location of sewage or septic lines. The gas, electric, and cable companies will locate their underground lines when called.
- Remember that hardscapes (stone walls, paved paths, etc.) are as much a part of the landscape as plants, so budget and plan for them.

When starting your new landscape, discover the place first and feel its sense. Give your new relationship time to develop a bit, and keep in mind that your yard is not meant to be static. Nor is it meant to be daunting. Make it suit your tastes, resources, and time. Think of it like one of those storybooks that allows you to pick the next frame of the plot—the characters and places you know (with some surprises to follow), the story line and ending you don't. Move your plants if you don't like where they are; most can be moved pretty easily during the first two years. Add new plants as your tastes, interests, and landscape needs metamorphose. Change your design; add walkways, benches, fountains, sculpture, or change out beds through the seasons. Be fluid.

Become a partner with your landscape; let it evolve with you. Be patient, be aware, and you'll know what to do.

IT'S A MATTER OF FACT

The abstract of a 2005 study of the economic impacts of the green industry in the United States (see Hall, Hodges, and Haydu in the bibliography) says: "The U.S. environmental horticulture industry, also known as the 'Green Industry,' is comprised of wholesale nursery and sod growers; landscape architects, designers/builders, contractors and maintenance firms; retail garden centers, home centers and mass merchandisers with lawn and garden departments; and marketing intermediaries such as brokers and horticultural distribution centers (re-wholesalers). Environmental horticulture is one of the fastest growing segments of the nation's agricultural economy. . . . Economic impacts for the U.S. Green Industry in 2002 were estimated at $147.8 billion (Bn) in output, 1,964,339 jobs, $95.1 Bn in value added, $64.3 Bn in labor income, and $6.9 Bn in indirect business taxes, with these values expressed in 2004 dollars."

LOCATING LANDSCAPERS

MOST FOLKS NEED HELP with their landscaping—from design plans to installation to maintenance. Numerous individuals and companies are in the business to help. The question becomes: who do you use for what? Here's an overview of who does what. Check credentials and ask for references when hiring anyone to work in your yard.

Landscape architects are professionals who have gone to school, earned a degree, and passed an examination for licensure; they draw magnificent, blue-lined plans and affix their seal. You should enlist the help of one *at the very beginning* of the planning stages of a building job. They are trained to plot out houses and structures, patios, driveways, walkways, and other hardscaping on a building site. They correct drainage problems and design the lay of the land to suit its intended use with visual appeal. They also create planting areas within the site design, sometimes specifically to incorporate mature trees and established plantings; but the horticultural aspect of their work is not their primary function, as most folks think.

We regularly have customers come to our nursery with designs by landscape architects in hand. The creativity is often remarkable, but the plant selection is sometimes difficult to fulfill. Many of the plans specify plants that don't grow in this area, plants that will grow much too big for the location given, plants that need sun when, in fact, they will be in shade (and vice versa), and plants that are unavailable in the market (usually because they're difficult or impossible to grow in this area). Unfortunately, it seems these professionals don't learn enough, or perhaps concern themselves enough, about the plants they suggest for ornamenting the Earth. Because of this often encountered deficiency, my husband says, "Calling a landscape architect to select plantings for your yard is like calling an architect to select room colors, window treatments, and furniture for your house." That opinion might be a bit harsh, but there's a good deal of truth to his comparison—in our experience. We are hoping that our daughter, who is studying landscape architecture at the University of Georgia, has heard our criticism enough that she will always diligently investigate the plants she proposes in her plans. Because that's what it takes—the detailed attention that a landscape architect gives to the architectural and engineering criteria of a job must be equally applied to the plant selection.

So if you choose to use a landscape architect to help plan your plantings, be sure she has the requisite plant knowledge. If you already have a landscape architect's renderings, go to a nursery and check on the plants specified: Are they to your liking? Will they grow where placed in the plan? Are they even available? Don't feel bound by the plans. Make appropriate substitutions if necessary.

Nursery professionals also provide design services. Sometimes they come on site and charge for their plans. Sometimes they provide those services for free, or fee, if you go to their nursery and provide pictures, measurements, and other helpful information, such as where the sun rises and sets and where the tall trees that offer shade are. Keep in mind that these plans, often sketched on plain or grid paper, are done by people who know—must know—about the cultural requirements and growth habits of the plants. They also know what's available, particularly in their nursery.

Landscapers provide all kinds of services. Most design a plan, on paper or not, and install the plants for you. Some understand drainage and have the machinery needed to move large quantities of dirt for changing the contours of the earth. Many don't have the equipment or knowledge required, however, and simply install plants in the existing setting. Some know the cultural requirements of the plants they select, but some don't.

Irrigation contractors design and install irrigation systems. The process is a science and requires knowledge of water flows, equipment capacities, and the like. Although many landscapers also provide irrigation services, they may or may not be sufficiently qualified.

Yard maintenance individuals and companies are often known as "mow, blow, and go" folks. They mow your grass, blow clippings and debris off the walks, and go on down the road. Generally, they don't have the knowledge or equipment to do anything else. However, there are many companies that provide maintenance services *and* landscaping.

Lawn installation and maintenance businesses are just that, and no more. They deal with your turf grass, particularly chemical application.

There are several professional organizations in Georgia with landscaper members. The Georgia Green Industry Association (GGIA) and the Metro Atlanta Landscape and Turf Association (MALTA) have extensive memberships and are a good source for finding the people you need. You can find them on the Web.

LESSON 28 ⌇ March 26–April 1
Spring Flowers

If we could see the miracle of a single flower clearly,
our whole life would change.

—Siddhartha Gautama (ca. 563–483 B.C.)
Founder of Buddhism

Spring-Flowering Trees and Shrubs with Flair

As I've indicated earlier, one of my goals in writing this book is to introduce the novice gardener or gardening transplant to the most basic plant material and landscape culture for the Piedmont area of the South. By necessity, that means discussing plants considered common—the bread and butter kind. Unfortunately, it also means that most of my topics do not include discussions of many of the sensational, newly developed cultivars, "rediscovered" heirloom plants, and plants that simply take a backseat in nursery production and consumer awareness.

Michael A. Dirr, retired professor of horticulture at the University of Georgia and author of *the* bible of woody ornamentals, *Manual of Woody Landscape Plants: Their Identification, Ornamental Characteristics, Culture, Propagation and Uses*, often remarks about this confining and disappointing lack of knowledge and use of the multitude of landscape plants. The size of his book alone speaks to the breadth of the ornamental plant class; it deals only with woody plants and leaves the similarly vast subject of herbaceous plants for other horticultural authorities like Allan Armitage, also of the University of Georgia. Both authorities work tirelessly and selflessly to cultivate new plant introductions with improved qualities and to educate green industry professionals and the public about them.

As much as I want to depart from discussion of the common varieties, I find it difficult to explain our Southern landscape by excluding them, so I want to mention a few of the spring-flowering trees and shrubs that offer unique and provocative additions to the landscape.

Common Smoketree (*Cotinus coggygria*): One of the most interesting plants in late spring/summer, this 10- to 15-foot shrub (hence a "tree" in many minds) looks as if it is enclosed in smoke when covered with its hairs (pubescence), which go through several color changes, including a smoky pink. The purple-leaf varieties have purplish hairs. This shrub has an upright, but spreading, loose and open habit. Leaves may be medium blue-green in summer and yellowish red-purple in fall.

Pink Chinese Fringe-flower (*Loropetalum chinense* var. *rubrum*): These evergreen shrubs that are 6- to 10-feet tall and wide bloom profusely in the spring with flowers that look like the strappy tassels that adorned our bicycle handles when I was a child. The pink or fuchsia-pink flowers appear again in the fall, although not as heavily as in spring. The leaves are reddish purple to maroon. The fast-growing shrub/tree tolerates sun or shade. There is also white-flowering loropetalum with green leaves.

Grancy Gray-beard or White Fringetree (*Chionanthus virginicus*): Another large shrub/small tree, this gem has large panicles that look like white shredded fleece cascading from the stem. It is relatively slow growing and has variable habits, from open and spreading to bushy and full.

Shasta viburnum (*Viburnum plicatum*): This horizontally branched shrub grows quite wide (10–12 feet), stating its place in the landscape, especially in the spring when its pure white flowers line the branches. The profuse flowering is exceptional.

Contorted European Filbert or Harry Lauder's Walkingstick (*Corylus avellana* 'Contorta'): With curled and twisted stems, this shrub grows 8–10 feet. Its likewise twisted leaves and spring catkins (long, earring-like dangles) lend additional attraction to this most unusual shrub. The contorted stems make this specimen spectacular in the winter landscape. Every customer who passes one of these in our nursery stops and comments on its beauty and unusual character, as do nursery professionals at trade shows when we display one in our booth.

Snow Fountains Cherry (*Prunus* × '*Snofozam*'): This is a gracefully weeping tree with fine branching. It is easily pruned to change its exquisite cascading character; the stem can be trained in an irregular, random spiral, resulting in an exquisite, contorted form. Foliage is small and dark green, turning golden to orange in fall. White flowers adorn this 12-foot by 12-foot spectacle in the spring, highlighting the flow of the branches.

Louisa Crabapple (*Malus* 'Louisa'): This weeping crabapple grows to 15 feet by 15 feet. It has dark green glossy foliage with true pink flowers, and the fruit is yellow. Disease resistance is good.

Weeping Yoshino Cherry (*Prunus* × *yedoensis* 'Shidare Yoshino'): Gorgeous in the spring, the white with pink-tinged flowers of this graceful small tree dance in the warm breeze, reminding me of pictures of ballerinas that once hung over my sister's bed. Foliage is medium green, turning to yellow in fall. The tree reaches 7 feet in height, with a 10-foot spread. It is more disease resistant than other cherries.

Double Weeping Cherry (*Prunus subhirtella* 'Pendula Plena Rosea'): With its impressive spring floral display of double pink flowers, this is one of the best weeping trees. Its elegant form reaches heights of 25 feet with an equal spread. The dark green foliage turns yellow to bronze in fall.

Multitrunk Crabapples and Cherries: Usually we picture crabapples and cherries with a single trunk. However, they are available as multitrunk trees also. If kept limbed up, their vase-shaped bottom is revealed. For a traditional feel, their spring flowers can't be beat.

All of the trees and shrubs I've mentioned are hardy in this area, grow readily, and add flowering charm in the spring, and their unusual habits and forms ignite the landscape throughout the year. Also showing this spring, and every spring, is the dogwood—yes, we're back to bread and butter with *the* Southern, spring-flowering tree. The most common dogwoods are members of the *Cornus florida*, or flowering dogwood, clan. The native ones dot the understory of woodland landscapes and stretch horizontal branches in a layered effect.

While many native white dogwoods are grown from seed, some are grafted, which permits reproduction and consistency of bloom colors and size as well as leaf color. Pink and red dogwoods are grafted varieties also, budded onto the root of a white dogwood seedling. If the suckers growing off of the rootstock are left alone, the tree will bloom in two colors. But it's best to prune the suckers; otherwise the rootstock plant will eventually overcome the graft.

The list of flowering dogwood cultivars is extensive, but the effect of all of them is the same. They have landscape appeal in all of the seasons: showy spring flowers; rich summer foliage, especially when grown in shaded areas; bright red fall berries; and winter-exposed distinctive spreading branches and alligator-skin bark.

Many of our flowering dogwoods are being killed by dogwood anthracnose, caused by the fungus *Discula destructiva*. To address this problem in the landscape, some folks have discovered and are planting kousa dogwood (*Cornus kousa*). Unlike flowering dogwood, which produces flowers before leaves, kousa dogwood produces leaves before flowers, resulting in a later bloom time. By growing both the *kousa* and *florida* varieties, you will have a longer blooming season.

Both kinds of dogwoods like well-drained, moist, acidic soil. Flowering dogwoods like partial shade best but will perform in the sun if the soil is deeply fertile. Conversely, kousas prefer sun but will still flower abundantly in light to moderate shade. Furthermore, flowering dogwoods will not tolerate dry conditions while kousa dogwoods are more drought tolerant.

There have been several dogwoods in my life that are embedded in my psyche—they're a part of my soul. One is a pink dogwood I gave my husband when we lived in Massachusetts in the 1970s. He planted it right by the stoop of our front door—placed it so neighbors driving up the street that dead-ended at our yard would most certainly see it. That tree is still there, adding Southern flare to that Northern neighborhood. Similarly, a white dogwood grew in the front yard of my childhood home in Atlanta; I climbed it regularly and sat on one particular branch, feeling like I had conquered the world and accomplished great things. The reality is that I was perched only about eight feet up in the mottled canopy. On a drive by that home a few years back, checking for unwanted changes, I saw that my dogwood had been reduced to a stump; a lump sticks in my throat.

IT'S A MATTER OF FACT

In the mid-1900s, there was a massive destruction of dogwoods for their sprays of white blooms. The threat to the Washington, D.C., trees was so profound, the Wild Flower Preservation Society worked to save them from extinction by placing posters on the fronts of city streetcars, urging the public to refuse to cut or buy any. The campaign was successful—no need for legislation in that, of all cities!

I do not know about the health of another flowering dogwood that was in the woods along the banks of the Chattahoochee River where I walked nearly every day during my high school years. It grew on top of a small-mounded hill that was covered in moss and small ferns and had a small boulder implanted on the side. That tree spread its branches over the entire knoll like an open umbrella providing protection—a secure site for me. Those woods are now part of a national park, and although I go to the riverbank still, I have not ventured across the creek to find my friend. I wonder if the log that afforded me crossing is still there—it's been a long, long time. We should keep up with our loved ones while we can.

Dogwood may be a common spring-flowering tree, but it can be just as special as the unusual ones. So plan to use both in your landscape, the common and not-so-common trees. As you drive around this spring, watch for flowering trees that please you, then visit a nursery to find out what they are, and add the kinds you like to your yard. They'll provide color and form for years to come and will refresh your spirit in the spring. They may just charm your life, becoming a part of your being, a part of your landscape.

FLOWERING FACTS

SPRING PROBABLY MAKES YOU think of flowers. But do you know much about them? There are 310,000 or more species of true plants (as opposed to plant-like organisms) in the plant kingdom. The flowering ones are called angiosperms; according to Edward O. Wilson in his book *The Future of Life*, there are about 272,000 of them and perhaps as many as 300,000. The remaining plants are non-flowering gymnosperms. Wilson indicates that about 2,000 new species of flowering plants are added each year to the list published in *Index Kewensis*, the standard reference work for botany, and that as much as five percent of the North American flora has yet to be discovered.

Most green plants have some common characteristics: they make their own food by the process of photosynthesis; they live in or on a substrate (soil is a substrate); and they are not mobile, that is, they can't move themselves around but need assistance from other sources such as birds or the wind.

All flowers have the same basic structural plan, although the blossom form varies enormously. Complete flowers have sepals, petals, stamens, and pistils, while incomplete flowers lack one or more of these parts. Some flowers (perfect) have stamens and pistils, the male and female reproductive parts. Others (imperfect) lack either the stamens or the pistils. Some plants (monoecious) have both flowers with just pistils and flowers with just stamens on them, and therefore they do not need other plants of the same species around for pollination. Oaks are an example. Other plants (dioecious) bear staminate flowers on some plants (male) and pistillate flowers on others plants (female), so there must be at least one of each within pollination range for reproduction. Hollies are an example.

Single flowers have a minimum number of petals for its kind (usually four, five, or six). Double flowers have many more petals and a full appearance. Individual flowers are grouped together into structures called inflorescences, of which there are several types. For example, the inflorescence of a crapemyrtle is called a panicle, while the inflorescence of a dogwood is called a cyme. Some flowers, like those of the magnolia, are called solitary, indicating there's one flower attached with a pedicel to the stem.

LESSON 29 ⌇ April 2–8
Lawns

I spent part of the afternoon trying to decide who, in the absurdist drama of lawn mowing, was Sisyphus. Me? The case could certainly be made. Or was it the grass, pushing up through the soil every week, one layer of cells at a time, only to be cut down and then, perversely, encouraged (with lime, fertilizer, etc.) to start the whole doomed process over again?

—Michael Pollan (b. 1955)
Second Nature: A Gardener's Education

Changing Your Lawn Paradigm Is Preferred

IT'S THAT TIME OF YEAR when most folks think about grass—not ornamental grass or prairie grass, but turf grass—you know, the plant that, when joined with millions of colleagues, will create, one hopes, a lush, verdant carpet of uniform color and texture—a lawn. As one gets out the mower, one ponders the perennial question: how do I achieve this mainstay of pastoral scenes, this progenitor of springtime frolic, this bastion of the western landscape?

First, there are many grasses, and in selecting the variety that best suits your site and desired effect, you need to consider several questions, with your answers leading you to the proper grass for your needs. Is your lawn in sun or shade or both? Does it tend to be wet or dry? Do you like broad- or thin-bladed grass? Do you want it to be naturally long or short, fast or slow growing? Is your lawn frequented by dogs and clambering children, or is it a space for display and ornamentation? Do you prefer a green veneer year-round, or can you live with brown in the winter?

Answer these questions before you purchase your grass. Then check the labels, seek advice, and pray that you select the prime variety to fill all your needs and desires.

So much for basic knowledge—knowing the right questions. While you ponder the questions, but before entering into or continuing to maintain your codependent relationship with your lawn, know that it will require lots of work—sweat for the hardy, perspiration for the more genteel. Soil preparation, seeding, fertilizing, liming, mowing, aerating, mowing, mowing, dethatching, mowing, mowing—oh, and watering. And edging. And reseeding. And weed control. And pest control. And mowing—ear-rattling, brain-busting, mowing.

What about those bills? No big deal, really. You can pay the store for a mower, gas, fertilizer, lime, pre-emergent, post-emergent, herbicide, and fungicide; and *you* can sweat. *Or* you can pay a lawn maintenance company for these items and *they* can sweat. Either way, add the cost of your public water or the cost of electric power for your private well pump, and the bottom line is essentially the same—time, money, and energy, all expended on a risky race for ofttimes environmentally harmful turf. Why? Why anchor your landscape on such a costly, high-maintenance element?

Maybe it's time to change your lawn paradigm—to minimize and functionalize it. Decrease your lawn size, making it a small, manageable, open space to complement the rest of the landscape rather than dominate it. If that's not practical due to children or other activities, create separate lawn spaces in your yard with different functions and different grasses, then select and maintain the grasses accordingly.

A landscape design that includes perennial ground covers and connecting beds will eliminate much unneeded lawn space while preventing soil erosion and greatly enhancing the interest, texture, and beauty of your yard. Grassed areas that abut beds with rounded edges will simplify mowing since the design will eliminate sharp corners that require the best in mower finesse. And isolated trees and shrubs, a/k/a forlorn flora, when grouped together in islands and joined with mulch or a ground cover (eliminating even more unnecessary lawn), will no longer be subject to the ravages of mower blades. Most important, reduced grass areas also reduce water usage—grass is a water hog.

Now that your consciousness has been raised and you're contemplating your new awareness and willingness to act, go ahead and prepare your lawn mower. It's time. Be sure the blades are sharp since dull blades rip and shred the grass, leaving it more susceptible to pests and diseases.

IT'S A MATTER OF FACT

In Michael Pollan's must-read book about our food chain and choices, *The Omnivore's Dilemma: A Natural History of Four Meals*, he says that "the existential challenge facing grasses in all but the most arid regions is how to successfully compete against trees for territory and sunlight. The evolutionary strategy they hit upon was to make their leaves nourishing and tasty to animals who in turn are nourishing and tasty to us, the big-brained creature best equipped to vanquish the trees on their behalf. . . .[The grasses] developed a deep root system and a ground-hugging crown that in many cases puts out runners, allowing [them] to recover quickly from fire and to reproduce even when grazers (or lawnmowers) prevent them from ever flowering and going to seed. (I used to think we were dominating the grass whenever we mowed the lawn, but in fact we're playing right into its strategy for world domination, by helping it outcompete the shrubs and trees.)"

Whether you will be mowing a large or small area of grass— have you changed your paradigm yet?—you will undoubtedly want to know how to create and maintain it.

- Prepare the lawn area thoroughly before planting, pulverizing the soil and tilling in amendments before broadcasting seeds and fertilizer. If you take the time and effort the first time, you should not have to redo this initial planting (unless you fail to maintain your lawn).
- Plant warm-season turfgrasses starting in late March/ early April and continuing through the summer for lawns that will be green during spring, summer, and fall until frost. This group includes common bermudagrass, zoysiagrass, centipedegrass, and St. Augustinegrass.
- Plant cool-season turfgrasses during March/early April after the danger of hard freezes has passed. These grasses grow best during spring and fall and include bluegrass

and tall fescue. Note, however, that these grasses are ideally planted in the fall. If you plant them in the spring, you will probably have to reseed in the fall since they will not become established well enough before the summer heat. Plant annual ryegrasses, which are used to overseed for green lawns in the winter, September through November.

- Lay sod lawns anytime except when grass is going into or coming out of dormancy. Some hybrid grasses are available in sod form only. Before laying sod, be sure to properly prepare the ground, which requires tedious leveling, raking to remove rocks, and rolling.
- Make the last application of fertilizer to cool-season grasses during March or April. Start fertilization again in the fall. Do not fertilize these grasses in the summer.
- Make the first application of fertilizer to warm-season grasses during March or April, continuing a fertilization program through July.
- Time successive fertilizer applications depending upon the fertilizer used. Slow-release fertilizers give a more even nitrogen release, making the lawn grow more consistently and uniformly.
- Apply pre-emergents for weed control now, *if* the temperature has not reached a steady 65°F or higher. Read the label to be sure it's what you need.
- Apply some post-emergents now, *if* the temperatures are above 65°F but below 85°F. Again, read the label.
- On your first mowing run, set the blades low. This will allow more sunlight to warm the soil and encourage warm-season grass growth. It also will help clean out some old, dead growth.
- After that first mower run, raise the blades—to encourage longer grass to shade the soil and prevent moisture loss. Also, longer grass will develop deeper roots to withstand drought and fight weeds.
- Lime the lawn if necessary to reach the proper pH for your grass selection so it will absorb nutrients and grow properly. Since lime is cheap, don't skimp.

- Water the lawn if there hasn't been significant rainfall in a week. Be sure the sprinkler provides even coverage over the complete lawn, moving the device around if the area is too large for the spray spread. (If this is the case, shame on you and see the beginning of this lesson.) Watering should be thorough, with the water reaching deep to the roots rather than merely wetting the surface.
- Watch for diseases and damaging insects. Fungus diseases are common when we have a prolonged cool, moist spring. Consult your local Cooperative Extension Service agent for diagnosis of grass ailments and recommended chemical control.

Did I say *chemical* control? I guess that puts me right back where I was earlier. As you may have detected, while I am not a fan of massive, manicured lawns, I do think perfected lawns have a place in the landscape, on a small scale. But I hope you will consider the dangers lawns pose to you, your family, your pets, and our environment. The constant application of non-organic fertilizers, herbicides, fungicides, and pesticides saturates the soil with these chemicals that leach into surrounding areas and underground water supplies. They also lie quietly on your lawn, waiting for children and pets to roll all over them, leaving residues on clothes, bodies, and hands. They can be toxic.

There are some organic alternatives to familiar lawn care products. There are some design alternatives for the landscape to minimize manicured lawn space. There are some low-maintenance ground cover alternatives to the high-maintenance grasses. And there are varying attitudes about lawns. Sally [Wasowski's] Axiom (from her *Requiem for a Lawnmower*) says it all: "The more boring the front yard, the greater the need for upkeep and maintenance."

DISEASES, PESTS, AND WEEDS

EVERY LAWN HAS THEM—diseases, pests, and weeds. In response, most folks apply chemicals—with labels that say things like "Always wear protective clothing when applying . . . DANGER!!! . . . Keep away from children, pets, and all other living things . . . except those you intend to harm." I made that last part up, but you get the picture,

I'm sure. Before your next chemical application, think about trying organic measures or applicants—and read this lesson about lawns again. But if you must proceed, at least read the label and follow the directions, and be sure you know what you're trying to kill. Just as the maintenance of a manicured lawn is daunting, so are the diseases, pests, and weeds that plague them. Here are some common ailments that your local Cooperative Extension Service agent can help you identify:

Diseases: brown patch, dollar spot, pythium blight, gray leaf spot, fairy ring, centipede decline.

Pests: ground pearls, mole crickets, white grubs, billbugs, spittlebugs, chinch bugs, sod webworms, armyworms, cutworms. Some pests don't damage the lawn but are attracted to it and are a nuisance: cicada killer wasp, earwigs, millipedes, centipedes, sowbugs, and pillbugs.

Weeds: black medic, creeping buttercup, carpetweed, common chickweed, mouse-ear chickweed, white clover, common crabgrass, silver crabgrass, dandelion, curly dock, henbit, pennywort, knotweed, nutsedge, amallow, oxalis, purslane, spurge, thistle, veronica (speedwell), broad-leaved plantain, quack grass, shepherd's purse, red sorrel, tree saplings.

And then there's moss and algae. Moss, although pesky in a lawn, can be a cushiony, enticing ground cover itself, especially in pathways. Consider the possibilities before trying to destroy it.

We used to have goats at the Loganville farm to "mow" areas overgrown with kudzu, privet, thorny vines, and other undesirables. We enjoy cows, a/k/a grazers, at our Madison County farm.

LESSON 30 ∽ April 9–15
Herbs

*How to use these [herbal] remedies is ancient knowledge, something we
carry in our cellular memory whether we are conscious of it or not. . . . I
can assure you that the capacity to experience a healing relationship with
medicinal plants is still alive in most everyone, even people who've never
known how it feels to be healed by a plant.*

—Patricia Kyritsi Howell
Medicinal Plants of the Southern Appalachians

Herbs Are Helpful and Healing

YOU DON'T HAVE TO BE into natural healing to appreciate herbs,
those herbaceous plants that are valued for their medicinal purposes, flavors, and fragrances. Man has used them since kingdom
come for medicines, teas, seasonings, dyes, cosmetics, fragrances,
crafts, botanical pesticides, and ornamentation in the garden. Even
if you don't care about using freshly cut herbs in your dinner for
flavor or in your bathroom for naturally sweetened air, you should
seriously consider using them in your landscape.

Many herbs will ornament your yard with varying interests—
teeming with textures, colors, and fragrances. Some, like lavender,
Russian sage, and yarrow, have colorful flowers, while others, like
artemisia, purple basil, and woolly thyme, have colorful foliage.
Creeping thyme, winter savory, and parsley are low growing and
make ideal edging plants, rock wall tuck-aways, and stone walkway fillers. Mexican bush sage, bee balm, and fennel, on the other
hand, are taller and give some vertical scale to the garden. Several
herbs, like artemisia, germander, and winter savory, are evergreen
and provide beauty year-round.

Herbs are ideal plants for containers and isolated areas in your garden. You can make unique designs such as knot gardens with them; mix them in beds with annuals and perennials, each enhancing the beauty of the other; and hang them in baskets. Most pleasing, you can place fragrant herbs in strategic areas—near benches and walkways where brushing against them will release their scent.

Some herbs are perennials, coming back year after year, while others are annuals, completing a life cycle and dying after one year's growth. The basic principles and cultivation practices that apply to all plants—planting, mulching, fertilizing, pruning, and general care—apply equally to herbs. The main difference between herbs and other ornamental plants is in their harvest. Unless you're in the nursery business like me, you won't be harvesting your trees and shrubs, but you may be harvesting your herbs for culinary, medicinal, aromatic, or craft purposes.

IT'S A MATTER OF FACT

Traditional herbalism emphasizes preventive medicine—keeping people from getting sick rather than just healing people once they are sick. In fact, in ancient China, herbal doctors had to keep people well to get paid.

If you are interested in cultivating herbs for more than ornamentation, I highly suggest you purchase a book devoted to them. Instruction about their uses and harvest techniques will be helpful, as will the basic cultural and descriptive information. In the meantime, here are a few hints:

- Plant herbs where they will receive at least six hours of direct sun each day. In our climate, try to find a location where they will be partially shaded from the hot afternoon sun. Also choose a site where there is some protection from damaging wind.
- Provide excellent drainage for your herbs. In other words, you must properly prepare the bed—pulverizing the tough clay soil into little bits and adding organic matter to loosen the soil and provide aeration and drainage routes. Gently sloping areas are choice sites, as are raised beds and terraces.

- Amend the soil to make it close to a neutral pH. In our area you will probably have to add lime to sweeten the acidity.
- Keep herbs away from structures and spaced out enough to provide good air circulation, which will help prevent some diseases.
- To conserve moisture, use mulch around herbs, being sure to keep it several inches away from the crown.
- Water herbs thoroughly before planting. Water at least one inch each week—all at one time—during the growing season. Water more often—but deeply—during severe heat and drought.
- Use an all-purpose, slow-release fertilizer sparingly— when planting, after severe harvesting, and again each spring.
- Prune to remove dead or diseased stems, to rejuvenate in the spring, and to cause more blooming. Regular harvesting for use can serve the purpose.
- Completely harvest summer annual herbs and warm-weather perennial herbs in late summer or early fall. Continue to clip small amounts of some herbs like rosemary and thyme throughout the winter, but be careful not to take too much off since you don't want to encourage new growth during the cold months.
- Get rid of dead leaves, stems, and flower stalks from around perennial herbs after harvest to prevent diseases and insects. Add some mulch in November/December for winter protection.

Again, these principles are the same ones that apply to all landscape ornamentals. Keeping that in mind, there's no reason not to include herbs in your landscape design. So consider them when you are selecting your plants this year. They will add a special dimension to your landscape yet will not require any special treatment—other than the sensational pleasures of harvest, if you so choose. And what a fulfilling choice that can be since, by using the herbs from your garden for your bodily pleasures and needs, you will physically integrate your outdoor landscape with your internal one.

A cautionary note:
Before using any herb for medicinal purposes, consult your doctor, an herbal practitioner, or an authoritative book. Improper herbal use and combining herbs with some conventional medications can be dangerous to your health.

SPICES, HERBS, AND THE MARCH OF HISTORY

FROM TIME IMMEMORIAL, spices and herbs have been a part of civilization, helping shape the course of history. They led to the establishment of trade routes, the development of language, the conquering of lands and people, the outbreak of wars, and the realignment of social, political, and economic cultures.

As early as 1485 B.C., ships sailed the Nile River from Egypt to East Africa to collect myrrh trees for Queen Hatshepsut's terrace gardens. Around 1000 B.C., the camel, which carried far greater weight than the donkey it replaced, advanced overland travel, expanding trade throughout Arabia, Egypt, and the Middle East, and an "incense route" flowed between southern Arabia and the markets of Syria and Egypt. Followers of Mohammed, founder of Islam and a spice merchant, built the first spice monopoly while spreading Islam into northern Africa and Spain during the seventh century A.D. The Muslims captured Syria, Persia, and Basra, a thriving spice port that traded with India, Arabia, Persia, and Turkey. Constantinople, too, became a prosperous spice port.

When returning to Europe from the Holy Lands in the eleventh, twelfth, and thirteenth centuries, the Crusaders carried the exotic spices and scents of the "infidels" of the East, introducing seductive pleasures forbidden in those European Dark Ages. Then, in 1271, Marco Polo began a 24-year journey to the Near East and Orient, visiting the courts of Kublai Khan in China. He chronicled his travels, further awakening Europeans to the mysteries and treasures to be found there. He and other Italian explorers established trade links with China and India and set the stage for an explosion in the demand for spices and herbs (drugs) in the Mediterranean. Venice became a great commercial power, trading in the aromatic riches that helped preserve and improve the taste of food. Led by the Portuguese, the Age of Discovery followed with often perilous searches on the high seas for the riches of the world and the fastest routes to them. Christopher Columbus happened upon the "New World" (the

West Indies) in 1492 after Ferdinand and Isabelle of Spain financed his trip to attempt to reach the East Indies by sailing west.

Then British colonization capitalized on the natural resources of the New World and took advantage of its native and imported inhabitants. The Boston Tea Party (a symbolic revolt involving the critical tea commodity) occurred in 1773, followed by the colonial war for independence. Tobacco became a major crop in the new nation and continues to this day to play a major economic and political role. The trade in marijuana (hemp) also blossomed in the Americas as did that of cocaine, which has become a dictate of many national and international political, economic, and social decisions and threatens to be the demise of government control of safety and security and the rise of lawlessness in many areas.

All of this history—the exploration and the turmoil—for the aroma, the headiness, the allure, and the high of spices and herbs.

John and I love to visit botanical gardens, and when the kids were younger we took them to many. Our favorite by far is Callaway Gardens in Pine Mountain, Georgia. We spent untold numbers of days there over a period of many years. We RV'd at nearby F.D.R. State Park and drove to the gardens each day. We rode our bikes throughout the meandering trails, crossed the lake on the ferry, and stopped at each point of interest. James even learned to ride his bike there on a lawn near the dock. During the summer, the kids loved spending time at Robin Lake. And we all enjoyed the afternoon performances of the Florida State University Flying High Circus acrobats under the big tent. Here, Cat enjoys a rest at the conservatory during our spring break visit in 1999. She and James played in a tennis tournament at the gardens that week.

LESSON 31 ~ April 16–22
Shopping and Planting

If the environment is suitable, suitable trees will grow there.
If it is not, they won't.
—Bernd Heinrich (b. 1940)
The Trees in My Forest

Planting Plants Properly Is Prudent

IF YOU'RE LIKE MOST SOUTHERN gardeners, homeowners, and others interested in making their surroundings on this spaceship Earth more aesthetically pleasing, then you're probably in the midst of spring planting. Whether planting trees and shrubs, perennials, or herbs and annuals, you can't just stick them in a hole and expect them to thrive. In this sector of the ship, the clay soil retains water like a dam, chokes oxygen flow, and confines root growth. Even sandy soils and loamy soils have their own growth-defeating characteristics. And all soils in developed areas, in places that previously have been cultivated, and in spots subject to human activity are most likely in need of help so they can sustain healthy growth.

Whether you choose to prepare an entire bed for multiple plantings or a single hole for one plant, the first step in planting plants properly is preparing the ground. The goal is to help the soil by improving its drainage, nutrition and nutrient availability, structure and aeration, and pH. Now, I know I've already discussed bed preparation in Lesson 5, but it is so important, I want to talk about it again briefly here.

Creating beds rather than single holes for your plantings is best. Beds come in all sizes, shapes, and areas: a wide girth around the foundation of the house; peninsulas or islands in the middle of the lawn; borders along walkways, driveways, and boundary lines;

and any other creation that claims space exclusively for non-turf plantings. The trick is to prepare the *entire* bed before planting—tilling and pulverizing the soil as much as possible in the well-defined area surrounding the plantings.

For small beds, use a shovel and wide-toothed rake to break up the soil as finely and as deeply as possible; for large beds, use a tiller or plow. After you plow or till, cross-plow or till to a depth of 10–12 inches, breaking up clumps of clay. Don't stop until the soil is as pulverized as you can get it.

Add 3–6 inches of compost or soil conditioner on top of the tilled area and plow or till it in until there is a uniform mixture in the bed. If the bed is to have a section just for annuals, you may want to add other amendments to these areas for better nutrition. Also, this is a good opportunity to mix in fertilizer and lime to adjust for nutrient deficiencies or to correct pH levels in the bed. (See Lesson 5 about bed preparation and Lesson 6 about soil nutrition and testing.)

When you've finished chopping, churning, and mixing, the bed will be several inches higher than when you started. You can lightly roll the bed, but simply working in it usually packs it sufficiently.

Now it's time to plant—*easily* since you've properly prepared. When planting a plant grown in a container, gently nudge it out. Do not pull on the plant to remove it. Instead, turn it almost upside down and jostle it until it breaks free. If it still won't come out, run a knife around the inside edge of the container as you would to release a stubborn cake from its pan. Let the plant slide out while you take hold where the trunk meets the soil. It's okay, but not always necessary to cut any roots dangling from the pot's drainage holes.

Before planting, gently break up the soil around the roots, enough to loosen the root mass. Then dig a hole slightly larger than the root mass and place the plant in the hole, making sure the top of the root mass is level or higher (but not lower than) the surface of the bed.

When planting balled-and-burlapped trees or shrubs, cut the burlap in several places along the sides and bottom of the root-ball to allow the roots to grow through with more ease. Do not take real burlap off the root-ball since it holds the soil around the roots while you're planting, but if your plant has a burlap substitute (plastic, for instance), take it off completely before planting since it will not decompose. Dig a hole in the well-prepared bed and gently place the plant in it, again being sure that the top of the root-ball is level with, or slightly higher than the surface of the bed. Loosen, cut, or unwrap the twine or rope from around the trunk of the plant after it is in the hole but before filling the hole with loose soil. Better yet, leave the strapping in place (except right around the trunk) and, in one year, come back, cut it, and pull it out. This method will help keep the root-ball intact better, and if you have properly prepared the bed, you should not have any trouble pulling the strapping out.

IT'S A MATTER OF FACT

Plants that are native to a particular soil and climate need less water, fertilizer, and chemical pesticides than nonnative plants. Allan Armitage, in his book, *Armitage's Native Plants for North American Gardens*, says that "many of our natives have evolved large taproots for survival or small leaves to conserve water. Overwatering may be a problem with plants that are drought-tolerant, as many of our natives are. . . . They do not want or need great handfuls of fertilizer, and they benefit from vigorous pruning when they begin to look weedy." Native plants also may support 15–50 times more species of wildlife than nonnatives do.

If the situation demands that you plant a tree or shrub in a single hole rather than in a bed, the work will be more difficult. Dig an irregularly shaped hole that is deeper than the plant's root mass and at least twice its width. Use a sharp shovel to gouge the sides of the hole as much as possible, to break up the natural clay barrier that will keep roots simply circling the hole rather than breaking out. Chop up the dirt taken out of the hole and push some of the crumbs back in until it is at a level to support the plant at the proper height. Put the plant in the hole and shovel in the remaining soil (but no amendments, unless the plants are very shallow rooted like ericaceous ones are), compacting it to fill the hole. Make a berm of soil about 4–5 inches high at the perimeter of the planting area to help direct water to the roots. (See Lesson 43 for the proper planting of ericaceous plants.)

Treat bare-root plants the same as containerized and balled-and-burlapped ones, with the following exceptions: You'll have to build up the loosened, replaced soil in the bottom of the hole to a higher level than with the other kinds. And, after placing the bare-root plant in the hole on top of the built-up cone of soil, you should fill the hole with soil and water and then gently pull the bare-root plant up and down to allow for settling and repositioning on the built-up soil.

Water new plantings thoroughly and deeply; then add extra soil if necessary due to air pocket elimination and settling. Lay mulch 2–3 inches deep in the beds (or around single plantings) to retain moisture. Be sure the mulch does not ride up on the plants; leave some space around their bases.

If your newly planted tree has a trunk that's more than one inch in diameter or is over six feet tall, stake it for the first year. When running wire over the lowermost scaffold branches, use rubber hose around the wire—to protect the tree from injury. Use at least three *long* stakes, angling their tops away from the tree to prevent them from being pulled up when the wind sways the tree.

Planting herbaceous perennials, annuals, and herbs grown in pots or flats (cell-packs) requires the same care as planting woody trees and shrubs. The principles are the same, just on a smaller scale. The benefits of bed planting, rather than single-hole planting, are even more profound for these smaller plants. Be especially careful when removing these tender plants from their containers. Using a round-edged knife or spatula is helpful in loosening the root system away from the container sides, as well as for cutting divisions before planting.

If you take the time to plant your plants carefully, you should find that your prudence will pay off. Congratulate yourself for spending the time and making the effort since your plants' chances of survival and enhanced performance are greatly increased. And remember the old adage: "First they sleep, second they creep, and then they leap." In other words, generally it takes plants a couple of years to establish solid root systems to support substantial growth.

ON PLANT SHOPPING

PLANTS ARE NOT LIKE TOWELS, games, tools, or garments sitting on a store shelf. They change each day—growing into a different product. Most are not sold by brand name, and they do not have set sizes. Yes, a plant may come in a 5-gallon container, but how tall, wide, or full is it? How is the foliage—lustrous green or sickly yellow? How is the root system—rotting brown or healthy white, strangled or firmly established? Has the plant been grown locally, or is it recently imported from distant and different climates— Florida, Texas, or Oregon, for instance?

Buying plants requires looking at them. You can call plant dealers all day long and do "comparison pricing," but in the plant world, comparison pricing is not the same as "comparison shopping." You have to literally shop, in person, to see the plants—and enjoy a pleasant outing in the fresh air.

Buying close to the plant's source—buying direct from a local grower—is best since you can be assured that the plant is acclimated to your locale, giving it a better chance of survival in your yard. Local garden centers may or may not be good sources. Those that sell everything from plants to patio furniture buy most of their ready-to-sell plants from someone else, hoping to sell them quickly and not intending to grow them out. Some garden centers buy much of their stock from local nurseries; some buy lots from far away places. Mass merchandisers and discount stores with garden centers usually buy their plants from wherever they can get them the cheapest with their bulk-for-multi-stores discount buying; local growers are generally not their source. Because these retailers don't grow the plants out either, plant care at the facilities is minimal at best, and often abusive—black pots sitting on black asphalt, soaking up the heat and damaging the roots, for instance.

Be aware that some plants just don't do very well in containers since they're aching to get out of the confinement and be placed in some roomy soil. So they may not look particularly good when you see them in a nursery. If you spot a plant that you like but that looks somewhat dreary, ask the nursery professional about the

We enjoy seeing customers arrive at the nursery in pickup trucks or pulling a trailer since it usually means they'll be taking home some of our larger stock or at least lots of our smaller plants. Our customer service building is in the foreground, and the shop and office building is in the background in this photo taken in 2000.

vitality of that particular species growing in containers and ask her to assist you in checking the roots. If they are healthy looking—with white or light-colored ends in most cases—and don't smell rotten, you've probably got a winner.

One final, and critical, note: Be prepared for transporting your plants home. Try not to cram them into the car, breaking stems and injuring them. Rather, enlist a larger vehicle if possible—SUVs do have their advantages. If you have an open vehicle like a pickup truck, lay the plants down (unless they are Japanese maples, which can't endure the stress on their outstretched fine branches) and cover them with a tarp before going down the road. It's worth the extra expense to protect your newly purchased plants since excessive wind on uncovered ones will cause windburn and leaf removal that can be devastating to them just as a windy-day or convertible-ride whipping of your hair results in unhealthy split ends and shedding. Also, be sure you have a means for getting heavy plants out of your vehicle, because dropping them or otherwise jarring them can cause them irreparable damage. Have some help planned, whether human muscles or machinery. But if you can't manage these tasks, then pay to have the nursery deliver the plants to you, hire someone to get them to your house and unloaded, or engage a landscaper to do the job.

LESSON 32 ᦇ April 23–29
Perennials

To analyze the charm of flowers is like dissecting music; it is one of those things which it is far better to enjoy than to attempt fully to understand.

—Henry Theodore Tuckerman (1813–1871)
Godey's Lady's Book

Perennials Proliferate in Sun or Shade

OUR LANDSCAPES ARE DIVERSE, each having its own unique character. Like a person, a landscape's quality results from its composition—the combination of its elements and their arrangement. Just as people have honesty, integrity, humor, intelligence, greed, sloth, and the like, landscapes have color, texture, scale, proportion, dimension, and so forth. The most desirable landscapes have some essential elements around which other elements are arranged in complementary fashion.

Since there are many ingredients—of the plant world—available for landscaping, we should use as many of them as possible, so long as they work to make the landscape whole. Some, like herbaceous perennials (particularly those that flower), are essential for inclusion. They are plants that grow more than two years and indefinitely year after year but that have fleshy, soft tissue that usually dies to the ground each winter. They make great fillers for tight spaces, combine well with many other plants (annuals, shrubs, and tropicals) for added interest in the landscape, and dramatically contribute to the continuing seasonal metamorphosis in your yard. They are the least expensive assets in your garden. They grow and grow and grow, and then you divide and conquer—replanting those divisions in other places, or giving them to a friend. Either way, you are always reaping dividends from your investment. (See Lesson 9 on dividing perennials.)

Perennials that love shade offer a superb alternative to an attempted lawn in shade. The fairy-tale image of lusciously cool, green grass waving gently in the hot summer breeze, tall trees towering above, lovers and lazies alike underneath is just that, a fairy tale. Such lawns don't exist, at least not without untold investments in time, energy, and money—repeatedly. (See Lesson 29 on lawns.) Turf grasses simply don't do exceptionally well in shade. So any illusions you may have of creating a paradise of pleasant pastures under your shade trees should be replaced with images of a perennial paradise. You may not want to lie down atop your perennials, but a low-lying hammock, a stone, or a stump may suffice for repose while enjoying the coolness of your anything-but-boring shady spot.

SHADE-LOVING PERENNIALS

The list of shade-loving perennials is long, but I have selected a few of the easy to grow and maintain, enduring favorites. They have varying colors, bloom times, heights, and characteristics.

Astilbe: This plant, often called false spirea, comes in many sizes and colors: red, white, pink, purple, and lavender. The plume-like flowers are spectacular and range in size from a few inches to 4–5 feet; the delicate leaves provide contrast to other shade lovers like hosta. While most varieties have dark green foliage and green stems, the red-flowered varieties have a red tint to both the stems and foliage. To maintain healthy looking foliage, *Astilbe* needs plenty of moisture during dry periods.

Chrysogonum virginianum: Green and gold is an American native with daisy-like flowers that bloom in the spring. It serves nicely as a ground cover with its relatively low-growing (about 6 inches) habit. The bright gold-yellow flowers lighten a shady area and contrast nicely with the deep green foliage.

Heuchera: Coral bells, or alumroot, is a charming, large-foliage evergreen perennial that enjoys shade and plenty of moisture. There are green-leafed varieties as well as bronze and purple-leafed ones. The maple-like leaves stand 6–12 inches above the ground, creating a mound of texture and color. Spring flowers on tall stems are small but lovely and should be removed soon after blooming.

Many cultivars have been developed, including some that bloom in the fall.

Lamium galeobdolon: Yellow archangel acts as a ground cover with its long shoots that grow rapidly. The silver-variegated-leaf varieties lend themselves nicely to shady areas where they brighten the floor. Yellow flowers emerge above the fuzzy foliage on this plant that divides easily and hardily. Despite its fine qualities, it *is* aggressive. Do not plant it in small areas where control will be difficult.

Iris cristata: Crested iris is a dwarf variety that grows best in partial shade. An early-spring bloomer, the blue flowers have yellow crests and stand on 4- to 6-inch-tall stems. The plants multiply and create an oasis of gorgeous color in the shade garden just as they do in their native wooded habitats in the Southeastern United States.

SUN-LOVING PERENNIALS

There are also many perennials that prefer proliferating in the sun, and they too vary in color, bloom time, height, and characteristics.

Achillea: Yarrow is a low-maintenance perennial with a wide range of flower colors among its numerous cultivars and hybrids. The fernleaf (*A. filipendulina*) varieties grow 3- to 4-feet tall as does the ever-popular hybrid 'Coronation Gold', which remains tall yet compact. Some hybrids grow shorter, and some like *A. millefolium* spread rapidly, growing together and forming a mat. Cultivars vary in effect: 'Paprika' has dazzling red and yellow flowers; 'Summer Pastels' has a calming combination of lavender, rose, pink, orange, and salmon flowers; and 'Terra Cotta' has an earthy, subdued feel. Although it sometimes can be too hot for yarrow—stems may weaken if night temperatures stay above 70°F—these plants will survive our Southern climate. They make handsome cut and dried arrangements but should be harvested early in the season, before the warmer weather affects the stems.

Liatris: Gayfeather (Blazing Star) is a common, yet unusual perennial in that its spired flowers open from the top down. The strap-like foliage radiates from tall, thick stems that bear lavender-purple to white flowers, depending upon the species. The summer flowers are good for cutting, and the plant is easily divided in the fall. It is drought tolerant.

Rudbeckia: The coneflower genus includes the native golden yellow–petalled black-eyed Susan (*R. birta*) that is an annual—sometimes biennial or perennial—that reseeds itself easily. The perennial forms of *Rudbeckia* also have golden yellow colors, with the cultivar 'Goldsturm' (*Rudbeckia fulgida* var. *sullivantii* 'Goldsturm') being the most popular and prolific in American gardens. Its petals are deep yellow and surround a dark brown cone, rising above dark green foliage. *Rudbeckia* spreads easily, creating beds of relatively tall color. The various species of the genera *Coreopsis* (tickseed) and *Echinacea* (coneflower) have somewhat similar looking flowers.

Butterflies congregate around *Echinacea purpurea* (purple coneflower) just as they do many other sun-loving perennials. I took this picture at the State Botanical Garden of Georgia in Athens many years ago.

Gaillardia: Blanketflower is a plant whose flowers look rough and tough to me, speaking to their foolproof, easy-to-grow character. They make me think of chrysanthemums, despite the multicolored summer flowers. Although they are perennials, they do not persist after several years. The dwarf cultivar 'Goblin' is a good performer in this area.

Chrysanthemum × morifolium: Hardy mum is the favorite fall-flowering perennial for the garden. Most people buy them in the season and enjoy them in pots while they are in bloom but never plant them for future years of pleasure. Plant yours and heed the following tips. Mums may flower in spring—don't let them. Instead, pinch back the buds and stems, and keep pinching them back until about mid-July, keeping the plant at about 6- to 8-inches tall. This practice will keep the plants from becoming gangly and will allow for maximum flower production and remarkable fall color.

IT'S A MATTER OF FACT

Hildegard von Bingen (1098–1179), an abbess in a Benedictine monastery in medieval Germany, wrote in her first book, *Scivias* (Know the Ways of the Lord), about *viriditas*, the "greening power" found in the lushness of Earth. She believed a connection existed between creativity and this greening power: "Greening love hastens to the aid of all. With the passion of heavenly yearning, people who breathe this dew produce rich fruit." She believed that all creatures were green and vital in the beginning; that the Virgin Mary was the greenest persona of all; and that Jesus himself was the green figure who later came to Earth.

There are literally hundreds and hundreds of perennials. I have intentionally omitted many favorites from this list because I have given them special treatment in some other part of this book, and because there just simply isn't enough room to discuss any more than I have.

It's easy to find pictures of perennials and descriptions of their cultural requirements. I suggest you look through books and visit nurseries to decide which ones you like. Culturally, the biggest issue is whether your choices like sun or shade. Also, the planting spot must be moist but well drained. (Many perennials die from soil that remains too wet in the winter.) Beyond that, the basic cultural practices are indicated: well-prepared, loose, aerated soil; about three inches of mulch; transplants planted no lower than they were in the pot; divisions planted with the crown at or just below the soil surface; hand weeding to prevent pulling up the small plants; 2–3 fertilizations during the growing season; staking if top heavy; deadheading to promote vigorous growth and additional flowering (although not necessary on all perennials, especially on some newer cultivars bred specifically to eliminate this maintenance); dead foliage and stem removal in the fall; and fall or spring division when cramping occurs (every 2–3 years).

Try different colors of one perennial kind; mix them in the same beds; and try combining them with annuals, bulbs, shrubs, and tropicals. The possibilities are endless and the rewards absolute.

COLOR IN THE GARDEN

WHETHER YOU HAVE A YARD that you find a chore to maintain, or a garden that embraces the artistry of nature and the passion of your soul, you are surrounded with color. It may all be green, or it may be a rainbow of colors. Either way, the light plays with it in different ways at different times of the day, changing the tones from sunrise to sunset. The colors in the garden, singly and in combination with others, through all their permutations throughout the day and year, affect your moods and emotions.

Christopher Forrest McDowell and Tricia Clark-McDowell, in their exceptionally delightful book *The Sanctuary Garden: Creating a Place of Refuge in Your Yard or Garden*, talk about allowing your soul to speak through color and lighting in your landscape and how using the language of color in our gardens allows us to reveal our personalities and to heal and grow our hearts and souls as well as our bodies. They explain in detail the therapeutic and spiritual values of the colors, and I have summarized them using, by necessity, many of the authors' descriptive phrases.

Red: This aggressive, rather masculine color can represent or stimulate courage, activity, movement, and passionate love. Too much red may make a garden seem too small, while an overabundance can be too exciting and energizing. Red helps fight depression, lethargy, or lack of motivation.

Orange: A positive and energizing color, orange has an encouraging effect. Although it can become overpowering, it can be very refreshing in small doses. When people are discouraged, a view of orange flowers or an orange sunset may be just the prescription for the willpower and energy to overcome their fears and frustrations.

Yellow: This bright and cheerful, warm and stimulating color is the color of wisdom, knowledge, and clear thinking. Creative, enthusiastic, somewhat aggressive people tend to like this color of the sun. It stimulates the nerves and brain and has a harmonizing effect.

Blue (Indigo): Blue is a "symbol of infinity and the heavens," and the blue *chakra* (a power center in the body) is "the doorway to the spirit." Calmness, sincerity, and honesty are associated with it. People who favor blue tend to be satisfied with their achievements, meticulous, and stable. Blue is restful to the eye and can make a garden look bigger. Too much blue can cause depression, fatigue, or passivity.

Purple (Violet): It is the color of love and the symbol of royalty, contemplation, and spirit. Cheerful, lighthearted people who are interested in the unusual tend to like purple. When combined with its sister blue, these colors evoke "restful spaciousness, and seem to stimulate the opening of the heart on a more noble or spiritual level."

Green: The predominant and most powerful of the garden colors, green yields hope, peace, and healing. It bridges cool colors to warm colors and "symbolizes the connection between the vitality of our physical body and the quietude of our soul, via the heart." It is "the cornerstone of the Sanctuary Garden." Humans see more shades of green than any other color.

White: A combination of all colors, white is pure and can offer a sense of peace and tranquility. Pure heart and soul, pure thoughts and actions may arise from association with this complete color.

As the McDowells say: "It takes time and devotion to learn the language of color and lighting in the garden. Your tastes are sure to change over time, reflecting your inner evolution. . . . Perhaps your greatest insight will be that this glorious exploration of light and color and their interrelationship is really meant to illuminate the many facets of your being and personality."

LESSON 33 ᪥ April 30–May 6
Vegetables and Agriculture

*Organic gardeners have learned to mimic nature's own methods of building
fertility in the soil, controlling insect populations and disease, recycling
nutrients. But the practices we call "organic" are not themselves "natural,"
any more than the bird call of a hunter is natural. They are more like
man-made analogues of natural processes.*

—Michael Pollan (b. 1955)
Second Nature: A Gardener's Education

Growing Vegetables Is a Venerable Vocation

To me, gardening means creating a unique spot of beauty on this
Earth using ornamental plants. But to many people gardening means
growing vegetables. Creating *physical* sustenance for man and animal
by using the nourishing elements of Mother Earth probably is, in
fact, cultivation at its best. Ornamental gardening, although beneficial for the health of the Earth if practiced properly, tends toward the
spiritual sustenance of man and is an activity more easily pursued by
those who do not need to concern themselves with the whereabouts
of their next meal.

I'm not going to pretend to know much about vegetable gardening. I don't. I remember growing a few anemic-looking carrots with
my mother one year and promptly giving up the avocation, until
I met my husband. He and I had a rather nice garden for several
years in Massachusetts. One year in August when it rained all day,
we picked the tomatoes and gathered the cukes, canned and pickled
until dark, and lined our pantry in red and green. What a great feeling at the end of the day, and what a feast of harvest we had all winter.
(The short-brine pickles that we put in a crock were gone before the
end of the week, after a few friends dropped by and had their fill.)

After that satisfying activity, however, and a vegie garden our first year or so in Georgia, we didn't have one for many, many years since we found that growing our nursery and children absorbed more time than we had to grow our vegetables. But every once in a while, in an effort to teach our children the importance of knowing how to grow ones own food, we grew a small selection of our favorite vegetables in 25-gallon tubs filled with rich potting soil and mushroom compost. Now we've come full circle, the kids are gone, and we have more time on our hands—sort of. So this year, 2008, I grew delicious tomatoes in large clay pots in the North Carolina mountains. My only effort was planting and staking them, occasionally adding twine for additional support as they grew. And I did have to water, especially because of the drought conditions. I have learned that, for me in my circumstances, container vegetable gardening is easier and kept in reasonable proportions than ground growing.

I think that probably the biggest mistake folks make when planting a vegetable garden is they make it too big for their circumstances and needs. Yes, it's gratifying to give away vegetables to family and friends, but it's often done in desperation and guilt—wouldn't want to waste that food, much less all the sweat and backache generated by growing it. So my first piece of advice: plant a garden that's truly manageable for you. It takes very little space to grow enough vegetables for a family of four and takes only a bit more if you intend to can or freeze.

Second, start to think about your vegetable gardening year-round. Begin to prepare your plot (unless you use a container garden) in November/December, tilling in compost, manure, and other organic matter. Planning your garden and ordering seeds in January leads to planting seed boxes in February (if you choose this route) and planting early vegetables like carrots, radishes, and turnips. March calls for second plantings of early-season, fast-maturing vegetables, and April is the time to plant warm-season vegetables like lima beans, cucumbers, tomatoes, etc., after the danger of frost has passed. Things really start to grow in May; additional plantings can be done, water becomes critical, and insects start their onslaught. You can start harvesting in June and continue to savor your summer vegetables in July, when you also should start planning your fall garden. Watch your "no-later-than" dates in August for plantings of beans, Irish potatoes, cucumbers, and squash, and prepare the soil for cool-season crops. Plant

IT'S A MATTER OF FACT

In 1904–05, the first Boys' Corn Club in the nation was formed in Newton County, Georgia, by G. C. "Claud" Adams, an educator who was instrumental in building the first consolidated school in the South, and my great-granduncle (that's my great-grandfather's brother). When the boll weevil was advancing toward Georgia, threatening to wipe out its primary crop, cotton, and "New South" proponents were urging crop diversification for economic reasons, the clubs were organized to devote attention to increasing corn yields per acre and to giving rural and semi-rural youth training in farming. The state Department of Education and University of Georgia helped promote the corn clubs—the predecessors of the present-day 4-H clubs—to encourage the state's youth to continue farming and for youth development. The success of the clubs quickly gained national attention, encouraging the formation of similar organizations throughout the country as well as the formation of the girls' tomato canning clubs.

In 1915, in a move to stimulate the food crops and livestock industry in Georgia (because of the tight cotton market), a regular agricultural fair that was bigger and truly statewide in draw than those previously held was created, and the first two Southeastern Fair buildings at the Lakewood fairgrounds south of Atlanta proper were erected, primarily to house the corn club exhibits and competitions.

Adams became a Georgia state legislator and member of the committee on education and agriculture in 1926. In 1932 he succeeded Eugene Talmadge, who was running for governor and took office in 1933, as Georgia's commissioner of agriculture.

cabbages, carrots, spinach, onions, or other similar vegetables in September/October while harvesting green peppers and tomatoes. And there you are, back at November/December, ready to prepare for another round.

I highly recommend you visit your local Cooperative Extension Service and ask for booklets and brochures about vegetable gardening. If you haven't familiarized yourself with this tax-dollar funded organization, you should. They have a wealth of information, and their mission is to educate and assist the public in all manner of agriculture. If your plants (vegetable or ornamental) have insects or diseases that you cannot identify, they probably can. For a small fee, they will test your soil, providing you with an analysis of its pH, nitrogen, phosphorus, and potassium. And they can answer many questions you may have about cultivation.

Vegetable gardening is a venerable vocation that speaks to the very heart of man's relationship with the Earth. It is incredibly satisfying to sit down to a meal that you grew, that you manufactured from the soil yourself. And the taste . . . oh the taste!

The Adams brothers. Standing left to right: Lee Hurst, William A. "Billy," Newton Columbus, **George Claud** (Georgia Commissioner of Agriculture), Dillard Joseph. Sitting left to right: John Hurst (my great-grandfather and a Georgia legislator), Charles "Charlie," Homer Bellflower, James Monroe, Silvester Hendricks "Doc." Note the hats in the vine. I suspect this picture was taken at the Adams homestead in the Dixie community of Newton County, Georgia.

The Development of Agriculture

UNTIL 10,000 YEARS AGO, human beings hunted and gathered their food; they didn't cultivate and grow it. They were nomadic, moving from place to place to find wild animals and plants to eat. But something changed, and they began planting seeds, growing their food, and settling in one spot. By so doing, they set in motion the most profound revolution in human—and Earth—history. With the development of agriculture came the development of civilization and an unleashing of human creativity, resulting in philosophy, science, art, music, and literature, activities unique to the species.

Humans did not adopt agriculture simultaneously in all areas of the world. In fact, there's no clear answer for why they adopted it at all. But there are numerous theories, many laid out by Otto and Dorothy Solbrig in their book *So Shall You Reap: Farming and Crops in Human Affairs* and partially summarized below.

One theory says that the population increased where the hunting and gathering territory could not expand and planting became an option to meet the increased demands for food. Another theory says that agriculture was adopted in response to a drying trend that reduced fruits, seeds, and game available for food. The idea is that people then moved to riverine areas like the Euphrates and Nile. The resulting concentration of people then required augmentation of the diet since there was not enough food readily available from the wild.

One theory—my favorite—is called the "rubbish-heap hypothesis." According to it, people dumped their refuse outside their dwellings, and plants began to grow in the disturbed areas. Finding it more convenient to gather their food at their "doorstep," these early farmers collected the seeds, scratched the ground, and sowed them for future crops.

Some theorize that agriculture began as a way to produce surplus food to feed those whose time was spent making tools and pottery (relatively new occupations for humans) rather than hunting and gathering. Another theory suggests that trading seed for toolmaking materials emerged, as evidenced by early agricultural settlements situated along ancient trade routes.

Did the retreat of the glaciers and resulting changes in vegetation and scarcity of certain large mammals like bison lead to a need for agriculture? Did an increase in population necessitate it? Or did the production of crops lead to an increase in population? The questions go on, and the theories continue. We probably won't ever know precisely what caused humans to engage in agriculture. And we probably won't ever know if one presumed cause was actually an effect, since our timelines are fuzzy, our evidence inexact.

But we do know that agriculture—the growing of crops— slowly evolved, supplementing and eventually replacing hunting and gathering as a source of food, in most areas of the world. The herding and domesticating of animals such as pigs, goats, and sheep—made possible by the sedentary agricultural lifestyle— accompanied the growth of agriculture and became another means of food production.

As agriculture grew, populations increased; societies formed; governments emerged; civilizations blossomed; and knowledge, creativity, exploration, and scientific innovation soared. But not without problems: We find ourselves in an industrial and technological world that has raped the forests and other ecosystems, to plant crops; a world that has polluted its air, water, and soil; a world that relies upon fertilizer-driven, pesticide-riddled plants and hormone-hyped animals for food; and a world that's over-populated and cannot feed all of its inhabitants.

Organic agriculture is a way to combat the ravages of industrial agriculture. It is a sustainable method of production of foods and fibers and seeks to restore, promote, enhance, and maintain biodiversity and biological cycles, particularly soil fertility. To that end, it incorporates various techniques such as crop rotation, biological (non-synthetic) weed and pest control, limited or no use of growth regulators and livestock feed additives, use of compost and green manure, and recycling of farm-produced organic materials. In 2008 in Georgia—a word meaning farming in Greek—organic agriculture comprised 1,800 certified acres, although there may be more organic acreage that has not been counted because it is not certified by the government. Nevertheless, there are 10.8 million acres of agricultural land in the state.

LESSON 34 ∽ May 7–13
Mother's Day Flowers

We must learn to look on plants not as mere points of colour, but as old friends on whose coming we can rely, and who, returning with the recurring seasons, bring back with them pleasant memories of past years.

—Henry Bright (1724–1803)
The English Flower Garden

Mother's Day Memories Persist with Plants

MOTHER'S DAY, AN OFFICIALLY designated holiday resulting from the love and dedication of one woman for her mother, was started in 1907 when Philadelphian Anna Jarvis's mother died. Anna thought one day each year should be dedicated to mothers, so she held a memorial service and asked those attending to wear white carnations. Within seven years, Anna had convinced Congress to proclaim a national day for such a tribute.

Anna's notion to wear white carnations was not a novel one. William McKinley, one of our assassinated presidents, always wore a carnation in honor of his mother and was, himself, remembered by citizens who donned the slightly fragrant flower.

Today I see people wearing ribbons or plastic bracelets for different causes, and an occasional green carnation on St. Patrick's Day, but I rarely witness the Mother's Day wearing of carnations— red for living mothers and white for those deceased. I do, however, fondly remember the tradition, modified during my childhood by convenience and beauty. We had peony "bushes" in a turn-of-the-century, brick-lined, formal rose garden that had since become a mixed use, whatever-will-grow arena centered around a birdbath. The peonies did grow, and they were laden with drooping pink and white blooms on Mother's Day.

It seems that Mother's Day was always sunny and blissful and, in some respects, carried an exciting aura superior to that of Easter Sunday. We dressed in our best: patent leather shoes, frilly dresses, white gloves, and prissy pocketbooks. We—usually my mother and I—visited the garden and selected the whitest peonies for each of our five family members. Although the flowers always had a tinge of pink on portions of the petals, they nevertheless served the purpose for my mother, father, sister, brother, and me, since we all had living mothers.

On our return to the house, we shook the beaded dew from our shoes and the prodigious flowers. We pinned the blossoms to our breasts, ofttimes a disagreeable affair when knuckles poked collarbones and long, pearl-headed pins pricked our defenseless flesh. Then we glanced in the mirror at our bedecked frocks; the sweet and tender yet musky, rose-like fragrance wafted to my head; and any discomfort was quickly assuaged.

Gussied up and ready to go, we attended Sunday school and proclaimed our love for and dedication to our mothers. More often than not, we skipped church to make Sunday dinner at Granny's fifty miles away. One could not delay the noon-hour feast that was laboriously and lovingly prepared by the matriarch of our Southern family. After presenting a bouquet of peonies to our perennial hostess, we sat down to a spread of ham, fatback-cooked vegetables, corn bread, iced tea, and desserts aplenty. We enjoyed the afternoon and the simple and comfortable pleasure of home, my grandmother's home, my father's mother's home.

Our peonies are long since gone; subsequent owners chose to replace the garden with a swimming pool. My blessed grand-mother spent her last years away from her home and passed on at the age of 102. And our extended family gatherings are now confined to weddings and funerals. The traditions have not been kept, but my memories still linger.

Life does goes on, and my traditions and memories are not everyone's traditions and memories, so over the years my family—my children, husband, and I—have created new traditions, for new memories. We've not worn peonies or carnations, rarely visited church, and only sometimes visited our children's grandmothers.

The tradition of gettin' gussied up for special Sundays continued
with my children. Cat was all ready to meet with family and
share a Southern meal on this spring day in 1990.

But we gather at our home for Mother's Day, and the celebration
of my birthday, which is the same week. My daughter picks a magnificent floral bouquet from the yard and nursery to fill our dining
room with my favorite gift, my husband cooks a delicious meal,
my son enjoys relaxing on his couch, and I try to do nothing other
than enjoy having my family together. That may not seem much of
a tradition to you, but it is. We do it year after year. It has become
expected.

I'd like to suggest an outstanding Mother's Day tradition for those looking for some anchorage for the present and some rigging in the future. Each year, give your mother a living plant, or honor your deceased mother in a similar fashion. A flowering tree, shrub, or perennial planted in the yard will provide lasting memories and year-round pleasure. It will tie the present, which becomes the past, to the future, which becomes the present. Think of the significance of celebrating your mother's nurturing spirit by planting in the soil of our nurturing Mother Earth.

Peonies played an important part in the Mother's Day of my childhood; they are the focal point for my memories of a special time gone by. And so it is with plants and flowers. There's potent sentiment in a gift of plants that will remind you, and your mother, of your bonding love each time you see or smell them for years to come.

Honor the eternal, maternal spirit this Mother's Day. Give live, flowering plants and enhance the landscape with powerful emotion and nurturing love.

PEONY POINTERS

MOST OF THE PEONIES seen in our North American gardens are herbaceous, and they die back to the ground in the winter but return year after year, acting as perennials. The woody "tree peonies" that do not die back to the ground in the winter actually are more like shrubs, reaching heights of only about four feet.

Peonies love cold weather, requiring a certain number of chilling hours (below 40°F) to break dormancy in the spring and flower. To assure blooms, select early- to midseason-blooming varieties for the more southern climates. Single- and

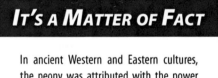

IT'S A MATTER OF FACT

In ancient Western and Eastern cultures, the peony was attributed with the power to cure various ills. It got its name from the pre-Apollonian physician of the gods, Paeon. An undisturbed peony can live for a century or more with its immense blooms. It truly deserves our joyous song of praise and thanksgiving, otherwise known as a paean.

Japanese-flowering forms generally perform better in the warmer zones than the semi-double- and double-flowering types.

Peonies prefer full sun, well-drained soil, lots of water, and moderate fertilization. Failed flowering may be a sign of planting too deep (the eyes are more than three inches below ground), clumps that are too large (divide after 3–10 years, but not too often, leaving three eyes per division), too much nitrogen (cut back on fertilization), or not enough sun (perennial varieties like full sun, while tree forms like partial shade in the more southern zones). Flowering problems may also be due to thrip invasion, botrytis disease, late frost, too much rain (or water logging due to heavy clay soils that have not been properly prepared for adequate drainage), undernourishment due to lack of fertilization, or weather that's just too hot.

Mother's Day at Granny's, 1993. Back row left to right: John's father, Gramp (John J. Dunleavy, Sr.), John, me, John's mother (Mae Dunleavy), Dad (John T. Godwin). Front row left to right: James, Cat, Granny (Georgia Ann Adams Godwin). This was Granny's last Mother's Day at her house before going to an assisted living facility down the street. She was 96 years old. John's parents had recently moved from Massachusetts to live at our farm. I think my mother took the picture.

LESSON 35 ∽ May 14–20
Favorite Plants and Plant Sellers

Ah, everything has changed since I was a girl, except my flowers.
—*Journal of Horticulture and Cottage Garden,*
October 13, 1863

Favorite Plants Are Friends Forever

THERE ARE OVER 310,000 known plants on this Earth, all unique in one way or another. They range from the miniature mosses to the statuesque giant sequoias, the leafless cacti to the frilly ferns, the green turfgrass to the colorful primrose, the vaguely odored oak tree to the sweetly scented magnolia. As I grow in my appreciation of plants, I find that there aren't any I don't like—some attribute always intrigues me. And there are many I would love to see up close and personal, not just in a book. So I hope to one day "retire" to that venture, seeking out strange new worlds and new civilizations of plants, on Earth.

But back to the present, and past. I've experienced many plants—plants that have been a part of my life in one fashion or another. Some hold memories of people, places, or events, some evoke emotions speakable and otherwise, some lift my mood, and some calm my nerves. Some are just plain pretty, in whole or in part, and some are just plain fascinating. Most I want to caress. Some I do.

When I started to list my favorite plants, I could not stop; the list kept growing. So I decided to mention just a very small sampling of them, in no particular order, with a simple reason for my fondness. I have intentionally used the names as I know the plants, and have added the botanical or common name as I think necessary for clarification of identification.

Sourwood tree: The wildness and finger-like, white flowers that extend over the fall foliage like a delicate hand draped on top of a red-adorned purse.

'Thunberg' Spirea shrub: The wispy, tiny, fine-textured leaves that contrast in color and texture with almost everything around it in the landscape; the daintiness of the misty flowers.

Osmanthus fragrans **shrub** (fragrant tea olive): The surprising, strong, sweet fragrance in the fall, which remains sporadically throughout the winter and beyond.

Veronica (speedwell): The thin, spike-like flowers that shoot toward the heavens.

Loosestrife (*Lysimachia clethroides*): The gooseneck-like white inflorescences that are, as a group, animation at its best (despite its invasive qualities and need for defined space).

Leatherleaf Mahonia shrub: The contrast between the coarse, clumsy structure and the late winter, lemon-yellow flowers that rise above the big blue clusters of berries.

'Merritt's Beauty' Hydrangea: The deep-purplish (because of my soil), large mophead blooms.

Helleborus orientalis (Lenten rose): The mid- to late winter and spring-blooming, demurely colored, bell-shaped flowers that shyly face the ground, hiding their sweet faces.

Pansies and Violets: The smiling, upright faces in the dead of winter.

Knock Out® roses: Their persistent, bright blooming from spring until frost and their essentially maintenance-free ease of growing.

Glossy Abelia shrub: The tiny, light-colored, fragrant flowers that attract butterflies and bees to this summer-to-fall flowering, high, evergreen bush that makes a good hedge of movement.

White Oak tree: The soft curves of the leaf lobes and the scaly white-gray bark. The grand stretch to graceful heights.

Holly Fern: The boldness of the leathery, glossy-green evergreen leaves and the golden-brown furry fiddleheads.

Maidenhair Fern: The softness of the leaves and the sense of primordial time.

'Stella de Oro' and 'Supreme' Daylilies: The persistent blooming throughout the summer and into fall in their orange and yellow colors, respectively, at their rather low height.

'Greenleaf' American Holly: The substantial appearance and hardy habit.

Lusterleaf Holly (*Ilex latifolia*): Its Southern magnolia–like look and its dark green leaves that remain so throughout the year and red berries that virtually encircle the stems.

Spider Lily (*Lycoris radiata*): Its tall leafless stalks that appear in the fall overnight—or so it seems—with exotic-looking red flowers, and the fact that you forget exactly where they are until they suddenly emerge and bloom.

IT'S A MATTER OF FACT

When the 1996 Olympic soccer games were slated for Athens, the privet hedges that lined the Sanford Stadium football field at the University of Georgia had to be removed. The football games had been played "Between the Hedges" for decades, and the fans could not bear to see them gone. So, in a stroke of genius (and marketing savvy), cuttings were taken of the hedges before they were destroyed, and new bushes were grown at a local nursery to replace the hedge after the Olympics left town. Plus, fans were able to buy some UGA privet in containers.

Purple Fountain Grass: The sun- and wind-catching, soft, reddish purple flowers on shoots that arch over its narrow purple leaves.

Aucuba shrub: The ability of the variegated varieties to shine in the shade; the huge, bright red berries on the green varieties; and the long-lasting leaves, when placed in water, for indoor enjoyment.

Gardenia: The exceptionally strong, sweet fragrance that persists for months.

Tiger Lily: The tall, regal stalks that support bending heads of bright color on petals that open themselves to the world.

Swamp Sunflower: The rich yellow on tall stalks that bloom against the fall blue skies.

Vitex: The straight shoots of flowers that reach to the sky from the vase-shaped bush, basking in the summer sun and enticing flighted visitors.

Florida Leucothoe, Dog-hobble (*Agarista populifolia*): The reminder of the wildness of the mountains that I so love to visit.

Lady Banks' Rose: The tender yellow sweetness wrapped in memories of a childhood friendship, a farm sadly sold, and my parents' last home.

'Shasta' Viburnum: The wonder of this large shrub that provides a massive burst of snow-white in spring, flocking birds in summer, brilliant wine-red dancing in the fall winds, and horizontal branching displaying in winter.

Caladium: The large leaves that bob like a dashboard doll with the push of the slightest breeze.

If I don't stop now, I never will, as there is no stopping point; my list goes on and on and on. I know I've omitted some favorites, and I can't order those listed by preferential status. There are just too many plants that speak to me, each in their special way. To attempt to compare them is virtually impossible. So, once again, I have kept to the basics (of my favorites), leaving you to explore the wealth of color, texture, form, and function available in the burgeoning number of new cultivars of all kinds of plants.

I hope that those you come to love will be as my favorites have been to me, sharing a special time or place in my life. We have connected through some experience, and so our spirits have united. Some instances that have initiated or sealed our relationships come to mind:

- Every winter I sat in my mother's den, looking at the cheerful green aucuba cuttings as they rooted out through the season in wait for spring planting.
- One gorgeous fall day I took brilliantly colored photographs of the swamp sunflowers by our nursery.
- I regularly travel by a 15-foot-tall osmanthus that reputedly came from the Augusta National Golf Club and that

now lives next to a parking lot in Athens—it welcomes me as I stride by, and perfumes my passage each fall.

- Annually I visit the State Botanical Garden of Georgia in the middle of winter to speak to the nodding Lenten roses.
- I used to admire the waving purple fountain grass that greeted me and my children to Memorial Park in Athens in the fall, when we visited to enjoy the playground and the warm air chilled by autumn breezes.
- I "cooled off" by watching the busily populated-with-bees abelia hedge while I sat next to it one hot fall day during a rush-hour traffic standstill in Atlanta.

The list of memories, pleasures, and connections made grows continuously.

What are your favorite plants? Incorporate them into your landscape if you can. You will be adding a part of yourself—your spirit—to your yard, making that landscape more whole. And, with that wholeness and reminder of things you love in daily sight, your spirit will also be made whole, and will grow.

ON NURSERIES AND OTHER PLANT SELLERS

WHEN BUYING A PLANT from a nursery, garden center, or mass merchandiser, you're buying a product. It hasn't been manufactured like a car, television, or piece of clothing—components bolted, glued, sewn, or stapled together to finished form. Rather, it's a living product that continues to grow each day, changing character, shape, form, and size. It's a product that needs continuous care.

Mass merchandisers and many garden centers that sell not only plants, but also tools, seeds, chemicals, patio furniture, grills, garden sculpture, knickknacks, etc., are like retail stores that buy all of their finished products from a manufacturer, set them on display, and count on a sale within a fixed time. They water the plants to maintain them, but otherwise provide them very little care. Depending upon a fast turnover, they don't want to be in the business of fertilizing, pruning, potting up, and otherwise caring for plants as they grow. Nurseries, on the other hand, are the manufacturers themselves. They start with small plants and grow them to a healthy size, whatever that size might be to suit the various demands of their customers—mass merchandisers, garden centers, landscapers, builders, or homeowners (if the nursery chooses to sell direct to the public).

Nurseries tend to have a niche and specialize in certain kinds or sizes of plants. Some grow only annuals or herbs, and some limit their production to containerized perennials. Some grow only containerized trees and shrubs or only field-grown, balled-and-burlapped specimens. Some grow only one crop—cacti or roses, for instance—while some grow a multitude of species. Some sell only wholesale to other nurseries, garden centers, mass merchandisers, and landscapers, but some sell to the public as well.

Nurseries that grow plants that are not hardy to their winters—like summer-flowering annuals, tropicals, poinsettias, and some cacti—have to grow them in greenhouses that are heated during the cold months. Nurseries that grow containerized trees and shrubs have a bit more flexibility in their production facilities, but they must have irrigation to water regularly, since potted plants dry out quite rapidly. If a plant outgrows its pot before it is sold, the nursery can put it in a larger container (bump it up), creating another, larger product with a higher price. Field-grown plants are the most tolerant nursery stock. Other than newly planted trees and shrubs, field-grown plants do not require as much irrigation as containerized ones, although the more water they get, the faster they will grow, the quicker their growing to digging time will be, and the faster the nursery will get a return on its investment.

The nursery industry is just like any other, with manufacturers, distributors, and consumers. However, the product, a plant, is distinctive since it changes as each day passes and must be cared for constantly, or it may perish. Furthermore, if it doesn't sell or hasn't perished and continues to grow, it then becomes a new and larger product. It's living inventory.

LESSON 36 ⌇ May 21–27
Wildflowers and Drugs

When we try to pick out anything by itself, we find it hitched
to everything else in the Universe.

—John Muir (1838–1914)
My First Summer in the Sierra

It's a Wonderful World of Wildflowers

WHEN I THINK OF WILDFLOWERS I think of open meadows spar-
kling in the sun, a profusion of colors held together by green, a
breeze gently swaying the tallest flowers. I think of Dorothy in her
field of poppies, and the Von Trapps in their hills that are alive with
the sound of music. Those are my most instinctive, first thoughts—
when I think of wildflowers.

But I quickly think, too, of the Confederate Daisy, or Stone
Mountain Yellow Daisy, that grows on the granite monadnock of
the same name. Claim is made that *Helianthus porteri*, formerly
known as *Viguiera porteri*, grows only within a 60-mile radius
of the mountain, but I fear that not to be the case as there are a
few reported populations in surrounding states. Nevertheless,
the annual is very rare, and because I believe to this day that we
had some growing around some granite outcrops at our farm in
Loganville, just 15 miles or so from Stone Mountain, I feel quite
privileged.

My next thoughts of wildflowers take me to the woods where
I witness fragile shoots of blooms that peek through the decaying
mulch of leaves and needles. These flowers differ in my mind from
the meadow ones—shy rather than outspoken.

But when I decided to say a few words about wildflowers I
found I did not know what the term meant, really. So I went to

the experts—and found the answer to my quandary as clear as mud. Books dedicated to the subject of wildflowers describe the relatively short, generally fragile, delicate plants with flowers that entice us to pick them. But many wildflower books also discuss various trees, shrubs, and vines. The thought behind the inclusion of this wide range of plants in the definition of wildflower is that any angiosperm (flowering plant) that grows naturally from seeds developed in its ovaries—without cultivation or human intervention—is "wild."

I prefer to follow those who disregard the trees, shrubs, and vines, and include in the term wildflowers only herbaceous (fleshy-as opposed to woody-stemmed) plants. Wildflowers belong in one of two groups: native or alien (exotic). Native wildflowers evolved in the very habitat in which they live today. Aliens, on the other hand, were originally introduced accidentally or purposely from Europe, Asia, or elsewhere and grow especially well in soils and conditions that are common to their native lands. They include the flowers we see on roadsides (many due to "beautification" projects); in lawns and gardens (known as weeds, and otherwise known as Emerson's "plant[s] whose virtues have not yet been discovered"); and in many other areas where the soil has been disturbed (railroad beds, quarries, construction sites, etc.).

Wildflowers grow virtually everywhere—in meadows and pastures, forests and woodlands, deserts and rock outcroppings, marshes and bogs, prairies and grasslands, along roads and streams, on cliffs and mountains, and in wetlands. They grow in a spot on Earth that meets all of their needs for survival. If their habitat—native environment—is destroyed, the plants must locate another site for reproduction and continuation of the species. But one of the characteristics of a plant is immobility—it cannot just pick up and go searching for another suitable site in which to live. So unless there has been some seed dispersal and germination at other similar sites that are not filled to capacity (plants won't tolerate overcrowding like humans will), the plant dies. If the destroyed location was unique and there are no other suitable habitats, the species may become extinct—a final testament to the destructive power of agriculture, urbanization, and human disturbance.

Many botanical gardens attempt to rescue endangered plants and create a suitable environment for them. But these institutions are not the answer to habitat loss. A rare species may survive in such a refuge, but it will not there serve its purpose on Earth.

Wildflowers are everywhere. Some we like, and some we consider weeds. James thought these were real pretty and stopped while on his way to see our goats at the Loganville farm in 1987.

Taken out of its natural habitat, a plant's function in the web of life disappears. It's like taking a button off of a skirt and placing it in the pocket. The button is still there, and it's still a button with the potential to perform, but because it's not where it's supposed to be, it's not serving its purpose of holding the garment closed.

Unless it is reattached at the exact spot from which it came, stress will be placed on the skirt material, threads, and other fasteners to the point that they cannot properly perform *their* functions, and eventually the clothing will fail in its purpose, falling open to expose the body beneath. Like the button, a plant must be in its own ecosystem to serve its function in the web of life. Take it out, and the web will start to fail—although the plant may survive elsewhere.

Although botanical gardens cannot fix habitat loss and the unraveling of ecosystems, many *are* exceptional institutions for plant preservation. You too can help preserve various species of wildflowers by planting them in your landscape. Opt for native species and their cultivated hybrids and cultivars, rather than alien species, which are very aggressive and may crowd out the natives. Buy seeds or seed mixes of native species that grow locally— typical commercial "wildflower" seed mixes are really blends of aggressive garden flowers that are capable of naturalizing along roadsides—or buy rooted plants in flats or containers. But never remove a native wildflower from its native habitat to plant in your yard. Furthermore, be sure that those you buy at a nursery have not been propagated from stock taken from the wild; be sure they are nursery-propagated. And be aware, should any suspicion arise, that, on occasion, unscrupulous growers have stolen rare and endangered species from botanical gardens and sold them.

There are additional ways to preserve wildflowers, the easiest of which is to be vigilant of unknown plants found in your yard, practicing caution in your assessment of their constitution. They may be "weeds" to be pulled or wildflowers to be preserved, a sub- jective characterization that may need some expert advice. Also, restrain yourself from picking wildflowers found in the wild since you will be reducing their seed production and possibly harming the more tender varieties.

I've been told since I was a child that I should never pick or move a trillium or lady's slipper since they are special and rare. Now I know that all wildflowers are special and potentially rare, primarily because of human activity. All wildflowers are necessary and all are beautiful. Be responsible in your treatment of them.

The Medicinal Power of Plants

Many people in our culture tend to think of plants merely as ornamentation to enhance the beauty of their landscape or house. Some realize the utilitarian virtues of plants in providing shade, reducing erosion, emitting oxygen for us to breathe, manufacturing food for us to eat and spices for our enjoyment, and providing fibers and wood for the creation of numerous products like clothes and houses. But few appreciate the medicinal qualities of plants and the importance they have had for man throughout history.

Plants are, or become, our narcotics, antihistamines, hormones, and antibiotics. Today, about 40 percent of prescription drugs sold in the United States have at least one ingredient taken from plants; about 80 percent were plant based at some time. Add to these figures the quantity of herbal pills, teas, and concoctions used to prevent or fight any number of pains and ills, and the significance of plants to our lives becomes even more impressive.

Man first started manufacturing synthetic drugs in the twentieth century. They were more cheaply and easily produced than pure herbal medicines, and many scientists thought they would replace the use of medicinal plants. But in the 1970s, as part of the "back to nature" movement, there was resurgence in this country of interest in natural medicines. At the same time, many developing countries wanted to reduce their dependence on expensive imported medicines and began to investigate anew the cultivation and use of traditional medicines with local herbs. The search for the curative properties of plants continues today as we attempt to combat a broader range of diseases and as many disease-inducing bacteria become resistant to our synthetic drugs. And most recently, the move toward a more holistic approach to health care has prompted Western scientists to look at the preventive qualities, not just the curative ones, of plants.

How do scientists know what plants to investigate? Most do *not* follow the Doctrine of Signatures, which taught that "like cures like," because they know, for instance, that a plant with heart-shaped leaves does not necessarily cure heart-related illnesses. However, this avenue of investigation *is* sometimes pursued since some of the ancient claims have been verified; some scientists are stimulated by the reputation of a particular plant in folk medicine, and some are spurred on by known properties of a plant. For example, plants that contain strong toxins are earmarked for research since it is known that plants that kill are often plants that cure.

IT'S A MATTER OF FACT

For ages, people found plants that could cure, heal, dull pain, give energy, induce sleep, and create hallucinations, and some that could *either* cure, kill, or create visions, depending upon the amount taken—a determination best left to the witch doctor. But faith in the proven powers of plants was obscured by ritual and superstition that often looked to the spiritual cause of illness, passed along by oral tradition. It wasn't until the birth of organic chemistry in the nineteenth century that the scientific basis for the curative properties of plants began to emerge, and the magical mystery began to dissolve, at least in Western culture.

There are numerous ailments and diseases that continue without cures. Surely, in this great plan, in this great ecosystem, there lies a cure for all. The question is: will we destroy the magical medicines before we discover their virtues? Indiscriminate collection of plants and destruction of their habitats are seriously undermining our chances of preserving the plants we know or might discover to have medicinal powers. There are tens of thousands of threatened plant species, and the numbers continue to increase. Many will become extinct before we even know they are endangered.

The research is therefore urgent. Our willingness to stand for the preservation of the tropical rain forests, which are home to at least 50 percent of the world's plant species; to protect our local habitats; and to respect all plants, wild or tame, is essential. We can't delegate the job to someone else. *We* have to participate. *We* have to make it happen.

LESSON 37 ✧ May 28–June 3
Annuals

Everybody needs beauty as well as bread, places to play in and pray in,
where nature may heal and cheer and give strength to body and soul alike.

—John Muir (1838–1914)
The Yosemite

Award-Winning Annuals Go Beyond the Usual

IF YOU HAVEN'T YET PULLED your wilting pansies from your beds
and replaced them with summer annuals, it's not too late. But if
you have made the switch and lined your beds with impatiens,
begonias, dusty miller, and other tried-and-true flowers, it's time
you considered adding some variety to your landscape. There
are multitudes of annuals on the market that beg for inclusion in
your yard. Cosmos, coleus, dianthus, lobelia, marigold, hibiscus,
nasturtium, cockscomb, dahlia, salvia, and vinca ring a bell with
most gardeners, but the list goes on and includes many Georgia
Gold Medal Winners—those that have been recognized for their
ease of propagation, seasonal interest, suitability to our area, low
maintenance, and great survivability.

Some of my favorite annuals are any of the Wave® petunias, a
family of five groups of petunias—Wave®, Shock Wave™, Double
Wave®, Easy Wave®, and Tidal Wave®—that will be growing in
Spring 2009 with the introduction of two more varieties. (I've seen
a picture at the official Web site for the plants of the new Easy
Wave® Burgundy Star; it's an exciting flower that's burgundy
with a large bright white star radiating from the center.) Each
Wave® class has distinct characteristics and several varieties. The
first introduction was **'Purple Wave' Petunia** (*Petunia* × *hybrida*
'Purple Wave'), which made the 1996 Gold Medal Winner list. It's

a vigorous grower that creates a carpet of fluorescent color with its rose-purple, velvety-sheened flowers; a single plant forms a dense mat about 6 inches high and will cover 4 square feet by midseason. It's extremely heat tolerant and renews quickly after extended dry periods, and it maintains its fullness and does not become leggy in late season,

Wave® petunias require full sun for optimal performance, and because of their vitality, they need plenty of room to grow and steady nutrition. Plant these winners at 2-foot intervals in well-drained soil with organic amendments and apply liquid fertilizer every two weeks. Or try some in hanging pots and mixed with other annuals and perennials in containers, and you'll see why I, although never much of a petunia fan, rave about the new Waves, like so many other folks.

'New Gold' Lantana (*Lantana camara* 'New Gold'), a 1995 Gold Medal Winner, is another intense creeping or cascading plant. It too prefers full sun and has few pest and disease problems. Once established, it grows rapidly, forming a dense mound 12–18 inches across. It blooms consistently from April until first frost and does not require deadheading.

Plant 'New Gold' 18–24 inches apart. Use accompanying deep blue plants such as *Salvia guaranitica* and *Scaevola aemula* 'Blue Wonder' to complement and enhance lantana's golden yellow color.

The 1997 Gold Medal Winner in the annual category, 'New Wonder' Blue Fan Flower (*Scaevola aemula* 'New Wonder'), was introduced from Australia. It provides a continuous display of small, sky-blue fan-shaped flowers from spring until first frost and has small, medium green leaves that are inconspicuous and become overshadowed by the dime-sized flowers that radiate in clusters from each node. The plant reaches 4–6 inches in height and forms a 12- to 15-inch circular mat of radiating vine-like stems. Plant 'New Wonder' about 18 inches apart since it will spread 3–4 feet by September. It requires full sun with moist, well-drained soil that is high in organic matter, and it tolerates heat well but does not like drought, so watering is essential when rainfall is scarce. 'New Wonder' makes a dramatic statement in the landscape, in planters, or in hanging baskets.

'Homestead Purple' Verbena (*Verbena canadensis* 'Homestead Purple') is another proven Gold Medal Winner (1994) with rich purple flowers that come early and persist throughout the season. Each flower head contains numerous florets, which bloom for up to two weeks. 'Homestead Purple' grows rapidly, spreading to cover banks and other display areas with its carpet-like habit and prolific flowers. It requires full sun, well-drained soil, 2–3 fertilizer applications each season, and may need cutting back when it becomes overgrown. There are two bonuses: this verbena, although an annual, will overwinter in our area, and you'll find many butterflies flitting around this gem of plants.

Prized for their foliage, **sun-loving coleuses** (*Coleus* × *hybridus*) are a new twist on an old favorite. No longer do you need to have shade to enjoy these fast-growing ground or hanging basket fillers that come in multiple colors, ranging from a mix of deep crimson and golden-sunset orange, to deep brick-red with yellow and white margins and chartreuse veins. The names given the cultivars reflect their coloration:

It's a Matter of Fact

Before plastic cell packs were introduced in the early 1960s, seedling annuals were planted in wooden flats, often made from the slats of grape and tomato crates. When sold, the plants were dug out of the flat and wrapped in a piece of newspaper.

Solar Flare, Solar Sunrise, Red Ruffles, Alabama Sunset, Cranberry Salad, and Purple Ducksfoot, for instance. These 2000 Gold Medal Winners grow between 18 and 36 inches tall and wide and will cascade.

The 1999 Gold Medal annual is **'Nova' Penta** (*Pentas lanceolata* 'Nova'), a superb butterfly and hummingbird attractor. Also known as Egyptian starflower, penta thrives in hot, humid conditions, like that of its native habitat, tropical Arabia and east Africa. 'Nova' blooms in clusters of rose-pink flowers, 3–4 inches across, all summer long. One plant may have as many as 10–15 clusters at one time.

Not to be confused with the root crop many love to eat, the 2001 Gold Medal Winner is **Ornamental Sweet Potato** (*Ipomoea* *batatas*). This trailing, vine-like, fast-growing plant reaches 12 inches high with a 10- to 15-foot spread. It likes full sun to partial shade and moist, well-drained soil. 'Blackie' has purple, almost black, foliage, and 'Margarita' has chartreuse foliage. Plant them together or with other annuals for a commanding contrast.

Athens Gem Plectranthus (*Plectranthus* 'Athens Gem'), another foliage annual, was a Gold Medal winner in 1998. It has thick, fuzzy leaves, which are yellow-green in the center with a pure green border and grows 18–24 inches tall and wide in full sun or shade, which is preferred in the late afternoon. When touched, 'Athens Gem' releases a spicy fragrance.

Lady in Red Salvia (*Salvia coccinea* 'Lady in Red') made the 2002 Gold Medal Winner list. Although most salvia is low growing, this one reaches a height of 2–2½ feet. It does not require deadheading like many other salvias, and it will reseed. 'Lady in Red' prefers full sun and afternoon shade.

The 2003 winner, **Mexican Zinnia** (*Zinnia angustifolia* 'Star Series'), is drought, heat, and humidity tolerant, requires little care, and blooms from spring until frost. There's 'Star Gold', 'Star Orange', 'Star White', and 'Starbright Mixture', each name suggesting the daisy-like flower color. The compact plants have narrow leaves, are low-growing mound-shaped, and enjoy full sun and well-drained soils.

The 2004 Gold Medal winner is **Chartreuse Joseph's Coat** (*Alternanthera ficoidea* 'Chartreuse'). It has bright, yellow-green stems and foliage and serves as an excellent ground cover. The compact, mounded plant grows 4–8 inches tall and 6–12 inches wide and makes a good bed edger as well as complement to other plants since it "echos" their colors, making them more vibrant. To keep the plants compact it's best to pinch the terminal shoots periodically; they can also be sheared for a more formal look. Plant these brilliant annuals in full sun for nonstop foliage color from spring until frost.

They call it a begonia on steroids. **Dragon Wing Begonia** (*Begonia* × *hybrida* 'Dragon Wing'), the 2005 winner, is a summer annual that enjoys partial shade. With leaves and flowers larger than other begonias, these monsters grow rapidly to 12–15 inches tall and 15–18 inches wide. The wing-shaped, glossy, dark green leaves serve as a backdrop for the red or pink (depending upon variety) flowers that are borne on stalks. The spent flowers shed naturally, giving room for new ones to appear.

The 2006 Gold Medal winners are of the **Cuphea** species (*Cuphea* spp.). *Cuphea* 'Firecracker Plant', 'Mickey Mouse' (also called 'Tiny Mice' or 'Georgia Scarlet'), and 'Tall Cigar Plant' are three selections of the species that offer spectacular color in the landscape. 'Firecracker Plant' has tubular, scarlet-red flowers edged in black; 'Mickey Mouse' has red and purple flowers that resemble the face of the venerable creature; and 'Tall Cigar Plant' is 3- to 5-feet tall with 2-inch tubular, cigar-shaped blooms that are reddish at the base, yellow in the middle, and green at the top.

Firespike (*Odontonema strictum*) is a vigorous-growing shrub-like annual that blooms with crimson-red tubular-flower spikes from late summer through fall. It has shiny dark green leaves with wavy margins that are 2–3 inches wide and up to 6 inches long. Hummingbirds and butterflies are strongly attracted to the flowers' sweet nectar. Firespike likes full sun to partial shade and moist, well-drained soil and will tolerate periods of limited rainfall. No wonder it earned the 2007 gold medal.

Earlier I mentioned dianthus as an annual commonly, perhaps boringly, used in the landscape. But the 2008 Gold Medal winning **Amazon Dianthus Series** (*Dianthus barbatus* 'Amazon' series) is anything but dull. However, it is a cool-season annual rather than a warm-season one like its predecessor and therefore does not deserve mention in this discussion of summer-flowering annuals. But, having now made that distinction for you, I want to take this opportunity to elaborate on this fine addition to the garden pallette, which I also touch upon in Lesson 4. The dianthus of old, also called Sweet William (*Dianthus barbatus*), was crossed with a Chinese pink (*Dianthus chinensis*) to create the first 'Amazon' series introduction, 'Neon Duo'. Others such as 'Neon Cherry', 'Neon Purple', 'Rose Magic', and 'Bouquet Purple' soon followed. They all have striking variations of flower color, often on the same plant, and attract hummingbirds and butterflies. Plant these annuals in fall for winter and spring color. (See Lesson 45 for a discussion of perennial dianthus.)

That's just a sampling of some exciting, relatively new flowering annuals available in the market to perk up your yard in the summer. So get busy planting new beds, supplementing the ones you already have, or adding some hanging baskets or patio pots to your landscape. Try some Gold Medal annuals that survive easily in Georgia, are simple for you to maintain, and are sure to add brilliance to your surroundings. It only takes one eye-catching area of color in a sea of green to bring a smile to your face—guaranteed.

What Is An Annual?

An annual is a plant that completes its life cycle—seed germination, growing, blossoming, seed setting, and dying—within a year. We usually plant annuals for their flowering characteristics, although some, like coleus, we plant for their spectacular foliage.

Annuals bloom at different times of the year, depending upon the length of the day. In spring, as the days become longer and the nights shorter, "long-day" plants bloom; conversely, as the nights become longer and the days shorter during late summer, "short-day" plants bloom. Some plants are "day-neutral" and bloom whenever they have enough water and sun for flower production. Some plants can tolerate an interruption to the darkness, while others reset their clocks if the slightest light invades the darkness. And, in addition to consecutive hours of darkness, some plants need a certain number of nights before blooming can occur.

Because the leaves of a plant measure darkness, a plant without leaves will not bloom. However, a single leaf exposed to night darkness can be grafted onto a leafless plant, triggering blooming in the new plant—even if the two plants differ in species or blooming category, like short-day and long-day.

LESSON 38 ॐ June 4–10
Summer Plants—The Good and Bad

Everblooming, billowy, blowsy, celestial, cumulus clouds of cerulean blue on
a terrestrial plant . . . am I dreaming or has hydrangea fever taken hold?
—Michael A. Dirr
Hydrangeas for American Gardens

The Hydrangea Puzzle Is Simple to Solve

THE FLOWERS ON THE HYDRANGEA my mother grew in the bed between our drive and house were always a pleasant pale-spring-blue. The enchanting bushes in our neighbor's yard bore dark, almost royal-blue blossoms. And the ones I passed on the way to my grandmother's house were pink. "Mom," I would say, "I want to have pink bushes too."

I don't remember her response. Perhaps I didn't get one. Maybe my mother thought that one day she would buy that pink bush. Or maybe she knew that a new hydrangea, if placed near our existing one, would most likely be blue, regardless of its color at the nursery. Maybe she knew that it was the pH of the soil that determined the hydrangeas' colors. But I didn't, and for years I had no idea.

These fickle hydrangeas are of the species *Hydrangea macrophylla* (French, bigleaf, or garden hydrangea) and are the hydrangeas typically thought of when the name is mentioned. Generally, when they are grown in acidic soil (a pH around 5.5 or below) they bear blue blossoms and when grown in alkaline soil (a pH around 6.5 or above) bear pink flowers. The intensity and hue of the blue or pink increases as the soil becomes more acidic or sweeter.

You can treat the soil to change blossom coloration, but you have to act well before blooming since the hydrangea needs time to adjust. To create pink blossoms, sweeten the soil by applying lime, preferably during the fall or winter months. The more alkaline soil keeps the hydrangea from taking up too much aluminum, the element that promotes blue coloration. To create a blue or bluer blossom, apply sulfur or aluminum sulfate to the soil, encouraging aluminum uptake. If you choose the pink path, don't increase the soil pH too much, since as the pH increases, the hydrangea may experience iron deficiency, resulting in yellowing leaves.

H. macrophylla is the most common hydrangea species and the one most susceptible to colorful whimsy, and, other than the whites, they will change color if the soil pH demands, despite the nursery tag or catalog description. The cultivars in this species will be either hortensia (also known as mophead, with solid, hemispherical masses of color in the heavy flowers) or lacecap (with pinwheel-appearing flowers that have nonshowy centers and showy outer rings).

There are dwarf varieties of *H. macrophyllas*, growing only 18 inches tall and wide, and varieties growing up to 8- to 12-feet tall. Leaf color of these deciduous shrubs varies from lustrous dark green, to golden yellow, to variegated, to light or medium green. Some *H. macrophyllas* have white flowers, and some are remontant (reblooming).

Flowering of *H. macrophyllas* occurs primarily on old wood, so they should be pruned after flowering. Unfortunately, the dry flowers of hydrangea, which will linger throughout the winter if allowed, are just as becoming in the landscape then as during their colorful summer display. But if you want more flowers next year, you can't wait long after flowering to prune, so you'll have to judge your priorities—dried flowers now or more flowers later. Perhaps several bushes in the same area of your yard, with staggering treatment each year, will give you the best of both worlds. *Or* you can now enjoy repeat blooming *H. macrophyllas* like those of the Endless Summer® Collection or Mini Penny™. Their mophead flowers emerge on new and old wood, resulting in repeat blooming from midspring until frost, and pruning can be done any time.

Although my purpose in this lesson is not to introduce you to specific hydrangea cultivars (there are hundreds), I do have to mention a new patent-pending *H. macrophylla* introduction being released in spring 2009: *H. macrophylla* Twist-n-Shout™ is a reblooming lacecap variety with rich rose-pink flowers throughout the summer until first frost. Its stems are pink-red, and the foliage is dark green, turning orange to rose-pink to red-purple in the fall. I recently saw one at a growers' gathering hosted by the breeders of the plant, Plant Introductions of Watkinsville, Georgia, a company started by Mark Griffith, Jeff Beasley, and Michael Dirr, retired professor of horticulture at the University of Georgia. I was immediately impressed with its beauty; it's an extraordinary plant, lively like its name.

Dirr is also the developer of *H. macrophylla* 'Lady in Red', the first patented release from the University of Georgia plant improvement program. It has pinkish white lacecap flowers that turn burgundy-rose through the season. The green foliage turns a rich reddish purple in the fall, while the stems and veins are red throughout the growing season. Dirr has also introduced Mini Penny™, a compact (2–4 feet) reblooming *H. macrophylla* variety that is hardy to Zone 5. (Most *H. macrophyllas* are hardy only to Zone 6.)

There are many other species of hydrangeas and numerous varieties and cultivars. Hydrangea horticulture varies depending upon species, so knowledge of the following groupings most common in the landscape makes hydrangea cultivation easier. For an in-depth discussion of the most commonly used species and varieties of the genus, consult Dirr's *Hydrangeas for American Gardens.*

Hydrangea paniculata (Panicle Hydrangea): This flaky-barked group tends toward an arching, multistemmed tree form. It has summer clusters of white or whitish papery flowers that age to pink and rose shades and then to rust in fall. Flowering occurs on new wood, so this shrub should be pruned in winter or early spring. The fewer canes that are left (perhaps 5–10), the larger the flowers will be. Some may reach up to 12–18 inches in length with 6- to 12-inch bases, weighing down the branches of this 10- to 20-foot-tall bush into a spectacular water-fountain form. The most common panicle cultivars are 'Grandiflora' and 'Tardiva'.

'Chantilly Lace', a cultivar selected by Dirr and Kay Bowman, former director of the Center for Applied Nursery Research in Dearing, Georgia, was an exciting introduction for the nursery industry at the turn of this century. Its strong branches hold the flowers upright, avoiding the excessive drooping common to the species. The white inflorescences are large (9- to 10-inches high and 6- to 7-inches wide), blooming from June into September, turning pink with age, and remaining delightful until November. The leaves are very dark green.

IT'S A MATTER OF FACT

The hydrangea "flower" is most accurately referred to as an inflorescence, each flower head a group of many florets. The overall shape of these floret groupings is either globose (rounded, mophead), panicle (more elongated), or flat-topped corymb (as in the lacecap varieties). If a hydrangea fails to bloom or blooms sparingly, it could be because the flower buds were killed by a late winter cold snap; pruning was done too heavily in the fall, winter, or spring and flower buds were removed; or the plants are in too much shade.

Hydrangea quercifolia (Oakleaf Hydrangea): This is an excellent southern native plant with year-round appeal when placed properly in the landscape. The very coarse, oak-like leaves are a deep green in the summer, changing to shades of red, orangish brown, and purple in fall. If winter remains mild, the leaves may cling until temperatures drop below 20°F. Late-May flowers, 4- to 12-inches long, are white, changing to purplish pink/burgundy-red, and then brown. The cinnamon-brown bark exfoliates and adds to the woodsy appeal of this 4- to 8-foot-high and -wide shrub, which is most appealing in a natural, shaded area. Because flowering occurs on old wood, pruning should be done after the flowers are spent. 'Alice', another Dirr selection, has made great strides in nursery production due to its massive inflorescences, handsome foliage, sun tolerance, and vigorous growth.

Hydrangea arborescens (Smooth Hydrangea): Sometimes known as Hills of Snow hydrangea, this species is native to our Southeastern woodlands. The flowers are greenish with a creamy white ring. The popular cultivar 'Annabelle', has huge, globular, creamy white flowers that will bloom magnificently for up to two months if you cut the bush back to the ground in late winter and fertilize it lightly. You can keep the huge blooms lower to the ground by cutting back the bush each spring.

Hydrangea anomala **subsp.** *petiolaris* (Climbing Hydrangea): This deciduous vine is rarely seen in our area, probably because it abhors our summer heat, but it will grow here, with proper site selection. Plant this climber where it will be in the shade a good part of the day; north and east exposures may be the best bet. Also, allow it to climb on something other than a masonry wall that will heat up during the summer months. Although it starts slowly, this vine will reach 60–80 feet, using its aerial rootlets to attach to structures, trees, rock piles, or walls. It provides a sense of depth and casts seductive shadows in the winter. It has white flowers in the summer and exfoliating, rich cinnamon-brown bark.

Hydrangeas love lots of water. In fact the name comes from the Greek *hydro* (water) and *aggeion* (vessel). Moist, but well-drained soil is best. *H. macrophyllas* do best if not planted in full sun. They require copious amounts of water when first installed; deep mulching helps with this chore by retaining moisture. The most common pruning technique for all hydrangea bushes is to thin out the weak basal growth, leaving the strongest canes. Then cut each cane back by one-third.

AVOIDING INVASIVE PLANTS

WHEN I FIRST WROTE THIS portion of the lesson, it was about some summer-flowering plants that I found fascinating for one reason or another. Included in my list was mimosa tree. I reminisced about one that grew in my childhood yard next to the driveway, perched on a sloping bed of English ivy. Every so often, I see a mimosa tree in someone's yard, but usually I see one sticking out from wooded roadsides or stretching its branches into a field from a bordering thicket. I notice mimosas mostly during the summer months when they bloom with poofs of thin, silky, thread-like pinkish strands, reminding me of the plumage atop a Dr. Seuss character. Smelling their gardenia-type, sweet aroma up close tickles my nose and is heady. I always marvel that mimosa leaves close every night and whenever I take a moment to touch their airy smoothness. It is a magical tree that lends a tropical-like dimension to the landscape.

But mimosa is also an invasive plant, as is the English ivy bedding partner to my childhood tree. And, as I started hearing more about invasive plants, I felt compelled to change the focus of this portion of this week's lesson from summer-flowering plants to invasive plants, although they have nothing to do with hydrangeas. So forgive me for the uncomfortable marriage.

Invasive plants are nonnative; they have been introduced into this area accidentally or, more probably, through the nursery trade as ornamentals. They are robust and do not experience the diseases and insects that keep them in check in their natural environment, so they overtake native plants and dominate areas where, perhaps, they are not wanted. They can change the ecological balance of an area and are, therefore, a problem—one that many experts are attacking by educating both the public and the nursery industry.

Many lists are being produced that suggest alternative plants to particular invasives. I've read the lists with care and question some of the substitutions. For instance, Virginia creeper is a suggested substitute for English ivy. Someone needs to visit my yard! I can't keep up with the "creeper's" growth up, down, and everywhere to be found—but I do love it's fall color. Some invasives make the list because of their propensity to get out of control, but their management doesn't take that much effort, particularly if they're planted in proper places in the landscape. Other listed invasives are more problematic because of their growth rates, kind of growth, or overpowering attributes. Many are deemed invasive due to their ubiquitous reseeding after wildlife has assisted their portage. Does that make my Lenten rose that is coming up from seed all over my yard invasive? To me, that's a private concern and one to which I say, "Invade on!" Or is the real problem the invasion of these ornamentals into uncultivated, unmanaged, common areas where there is no control at all? Now that's a social issue.

When in early 2006, I revisited after several years my writing of this book, I became anxious about this emerging awareness of and effort to eliminate these plants from our landscapes and how I should treat the matter. I had not mentioned the problem or any invasive qualities of plants I discussed. But I was forced to ask myself whether I should exclude mention of all invasives that have made the lists. That would mean eliminating from the book many of the plants that I feel deserve attention to fulfill one of my writing intentions—initiating newcomers to the South to the common elements of our landscape. Should I promote the efforts of those who are adamant about the exclusion of all invasives? I'm not ready for that drastic measure without knowing more. Should I dissect the issues espoused by various groups and color the world gray with questions? I'm not up to such a philosophical debate right now, although I do tend toward that direction below. Should I omit the issue all together? I think perhaps that's not ethical.

I had not yet gotten a handle on the treatment I would give invasives until several months later in the summer when I was sitting in an office in which I had never been, discussing my book and expressing my quandary about invasive species. I noticed out the window the largest mimosa tree I have ever seen, stretching its arms from its large, single-trunked body as if to embrace me through the glass and urge my protection of its beauty. My decision was made in an instant, and you have the results below.

I don't know of any tree quite like mimosa; there isn't a satisfactory alternative in my neck of the woods. The question is: Should I plant one if I want, despite its invasive qualities, and plan to work at managing it, if that's even possible, or should I resist at all costs and plant only noninvasive plants, whatever that really means? Does the question become one entirely of my desires versus the good of society—protecting it from the ravages of an invasion I instigate? Do I need to redefine Thoreau's "weed?"

I sure hate plants going the way of other social issues, which often end up political ones. And I don't mean to make light of this important subject, because if we're going to use our God-given talents to manipulate our landscape, we'd better know what we're doing. But let's be careful that we don't throw the baby out with the bathwater. I need to educate myself more about this matter; perhaps you do too. But for now, I will embrace that mimosa, stroke its leaves, and wiggle its flowers across my face (even as I right now have a branch sitting on my desk, inspiration for protecting our bond—a selfish act); I will refer you to the National Arboretum's Web site for a clear discussion of invasives (see Bibliography); and I will close this subject with a quote from that site:

> An invasive plant has the ability to thrive and spread aggressively outside its natural range. A naturally aggressive plant may be especially invasive when it is introduced to a new habitat. An invasive species that colonizes a new area may gain an ecological edge since the insects, diseases, and foraging animals that naturally keep its growth in check in its native range are not present in its new habitat.
>
> Some invasive plants are worse than others. Many invasive plants continue to be admired by gardeners who may not be aware of their weedy nature. Others are recognized as weeds but property owners fail to do their part in preventing their spread. Some do not even become invasive until they are neglected for a long time. Invasive plants are not all equally invasive. Some only colonize small areas and do not do so aggressively. Others may spread and come to dominate large areas in just a few years.

The site then lists some categories to illustrate degrees of invasiveness:

- Danger! Don't plant it.
  Purple loosestrife is given as an example.
- Warning: If you see it, remove it.
  For example, tree-of-heaven.
- Caution: It's not a problem if you manage it wisely.
  English ivy, for instance.

Needless to say, the degrees are very helpful to me in my moral journey, and I've now, in concluding this essay, made one decision: I won't plant a mimosa, but I'll admire them still.

LESSON 39 ∽ June 11–17
Container Gardening

*If we understand that no artist—no maker—can work except by
reworking the works of Creation, then we see that by our work we reveal
what we think of the works of God. . . . The significance—and ultimately
the quality—of the work we do is determined by our understanding of the
story in which we are taking part.*

—Wendell Berry (b. 1934)
"Christianity and the Survival of Creation" in
Sex, Economy, Freedom and Community

Creative Container Gardening Is Landscape Art

CONTAINER GARDENING HAS BEEN around since the advent of the white-painted tire, overflowing with pink petunias and lying in the front yards of rural America. Right? Actually, no, container gardening dates back to antiquity as shown by the drawings in a 3,500-year-old Egyptian temple depicting people digging up and potting frankincense trees. Then, of course, there were the hanging gardens of Babylon and the Renaissance gardens of Italy with huge pots gracing courtyards and patios.

As a contemporary landscape gardener, you may want to use containers for color, height, texture, filler, aroma, movement, animal attraction, or something simply different. Or you may want to use them to solve a temporary landscaping problem, bring the landscape closer to your doors and windows, or create an easy-to-maintain space. You may want to use containers just because they're another ingredient for beautifying your surroundings, becoming an instrument of landscape integration, not separation (as the word otherwise suggests).

Whatever your motivation for container gardening, your idea will probably work. You just have to decide what it is you are trying to do and why, how much or how little effort you are willing to expend on the project, and what your resources are.

There are numerous elements to consider when landscaping with containers. For example, you must think about the plants themselves: ornamental trees, shrubs, annuals, and perennials, and edible herbs, fruits, and vegetables.

Whether your focus is flowers or foliage, in selecting your ornamental plants first consider their cultural requirements. Your container plants must have the proper sunlight, water, and soil just as they do when placed in the ground. You will not be able to place a hanging basket of geraniums in the shade and expect them to thrive; neither will you be able to combine succulent, sun-loving cacti with water-thirsty, shade-loving impatiens and expect them to prosper.

Next, in choosing the plants, consider their form, shape, texture, and color. Do you want a striking, vertical ornamental grass rising above an understory of brightly colored verbena? Or do you prefer a subtler combination of ferns waving above a covering of moss? Does your landscape demand the colorful accent of a pot of white and purple pansies? Or does it require the subdued effect of variegated ivy? Do you want the interest of four or five plants or the understatement of one?

If you want elegance or formality, you probably should stick with uniform colors or pairs of pastels. If you want a more informal, invigorating look, try combining primary colors. And if you want something in between, there are as many possibilities as there are colors in the rainbow.

Size is also an essential characteristic to gauge when choosing plants since there are aesthetic and practical considerations. Does the plant coordinate with the size of its container? Will it grow to be too high for its spot in the garden, and will you be able to move it to a better location if it does? Will it grow too high for the container, becoming unstable and likely to tip over? Does it fit in your picture; is it attractive in your landscape?

Do you want your plastic container hidden by summer's end with the overflowing foliage and blossoms of a black-eyed-Susan vine? Or do you want your bas-relief terra-cotta pot exposed throughout the seasons, making it functional for bulbs, upright ground covers, and other nontrailing plants?

The questions may seem endless, but so are the plant choices. Whether singly or in combination with others, the possible plant selections and marriages vary across the spectrum from formal to informal, dynamic to understated, simple to complex, whimsical to tasteful. You simply have to try whatever moves you and see if it works. Be bold. Experiment.

There are only two requirements for garden containers: they must be able to hold soil (or planting medium), and they must have adequate drainage. Other than these, there are no other requirements except the use of your imagination and your sense of style.

It's a Matter of Fact

In an unusual use of forsythia, painter Claude Monet trained the otherwise bushy plants into standards with 4- to 5-foot-tall, straight, bare trunks topped with a loose ball of foliage and bright yellow, spring flowers. He placed them like sentinels, in blue-and-white Oriental fishbowl planters, at the bottom of the steps leading from his Giverny garden up to his porch.

From rubber to terra-cotta, the materials for containers are diverse. Plastic containers are light; stone is heavier but will provide a solid and established feel. Medium-weight wood adds a rustic flavor to the garden, while cast-iron and concrete urns make formal statements. Terra-cotta is time honored and provides a sense of simplicity, while a wire basket is utilitarian and nondescript.

You can select plants to go with your container, or you can select a container to go with your plants; either way, be sure to think about compatible heights, colors, shapes, and textures. You don't want your container garden to be the focal point in your garden if it presents an incompatible, unattractive combination of elements.

Although container gardening is replete with creative possibilities, I rarely see the truly imaginative integration of the sculptural element of containers into the garden. This requires flexibility of thought, some daring, and a sense of adventure, so try these ideas on for size, with attention to the container:

- an old bicycle, lying on its side, with petunias cascading from the handlebar basket
- a strawberry jar, dripping with differing plants from each cubby
- an old metal milk can serving as a pedestal to a wooden box with a yucca plant pointing to the sky and phlox draping toward the ground
- a rotting rowboat or canoe filled with a mix of wildflowers
- a wicker basket with daisies standing tall
- glass mason jars stationed along a narrow border with a low-growing sunflower centered in each
- old boots tucked away in the corner of a step with violas and ajuga capping the tops
- driftwood, hollowed out and filled with primrose
- a discarded wagon poised along a pathway, filled with annuals, suggesting movement through the garden
- a wooden whisky barrel, propped up on its side, soil oozing out and filled with running 'Homestead Purple' verbena
- a concrete urn perched on a rock, placed in the midst of a streaming water garden, filled with whatever you choose

Whether you live in an apartment with a tiny deck two stories from Earth, a cluster home with a small yard, or a stately home with roomy grounds, you will benefit from container gardening and find a whole new dimension to the landscape with very few limitations. Containers are an integral part of your purpose and plan. Just consider the basic design elements of symmetry, repetition, contrast, scale, vertical dimension, time and seasonal dimensions, and variety. Then go through your attic, shed, or closet; visit a thrift store. Dream up some container ideas. Experiment and have fun!

CONTAINER CULTIVATION

THERE ARE INFINITE POSSIBILITIES for plant selection and combination in container gardening. However, there's not much choice when it comes to the cultivation of your container garden.

First, decide if you want to move your container garden to varying locations throughout the seasons. Do you want a blue hydrangea next to your favorite bench while it's flowering, but tucked among other shrubs later in the summer? Do you want flowering bulbs on your deck in spring, removed to a less conspicuous spot as the foliage turns yellow? If so, minimize the size and weight of the container.

Second, if your container is large or made of heavy material, go ahead and place it in its landscape spot before filling it with soil. You'll avoid a trip to the chiropractor and will get a feel for its appropriateness to your design intentions.

After you've made these logistical decisions, plant the container. Fill it with a mixture of 80-10-10, a potting mix with 80% organic compost, 10% peat, and 10% pearlite (vermiculite). For an even better soil, mix your 80-10-10 with mushroom compost or other organic compost with manure, in a one-to-one ratio. There'll be more nutrients for the plants, and you won't have to fertilize initially. If you're tempted to use soil from your yard, don't, as it may contain weed and grass seeds, insects, and diseases. Furthermore, it probably won't have the integral and beneficial nutrients available in a bagged mixture.

Once the soil is in place, plant your plants and watch them grow. Remember to water—plants in containers require more watering than those in the ground. Containers with drain holes and no retainer dish dry out faster than others. And plants in terra-cotta pots require more frequent dousing than those in plastic ones since more moisture evaporates through the porous clay. You can help moisture retention in any pot and reduce the need for watering by placing broken bits of terra-cotta in the bottom; the clay will absorb moisture and slowly release it into the soil. This technique also creates some open space, leaving room for excess water, which helps prevent root rot.

I always remember Mom piddlin' around with plants, mostly those indoors or in containers on the patio. Her love for the horticultural pastime was passed on to me. Once we kids were all gone away and home was no longer our daily base, she joined The Rose Garden Club in Atlanta and has maintained her membership and support of its charitable activities ever since. She was mighty proud when she won an award for her hanging basket of Mexican heather in 1989.

Water in the early morning and avoid evening watering since it can encourage fungal pathogens to take hold. Be sure the container has adequate drainage, particularly if it's in the shade. Root rot and fungus may develop in pots that retain too much moisture and never have an opportunity to dry out.

Fertilize your container garden with an all-purpose liquid food. If you use mushroom compost or other organic compost with manure in the soil mix, the first fertilizer application can wait for several months. Otherwise, fertilize just as if the container plants were in the ground.

Prune containerized trees and shrubs as needed or for decorative purposes. Pinch back spent blossoms for more prolonged and prolific flowering. And otherwise maintain the appearance of the container plants as if they were in the ground.

SUMMER

As I PULL YET ANOTHER weed and feel the sweat oozing between my breasts and beneath my hair, I realize that summer has arrived. It has an insidious way of inserting itself upon me. The days grow longer and longer as the sun—straight overhead—bears down on the Earth. I'm never quite sure when the Southern summer starts; it just suddenly seems to have been here for longer than I care. And then it drags on and on.

I feel most like an animal during the sultry season—surviving the entanglement of life. When in the woods, I feel ensnared—thick privet and thorny vines make passage painful. By the creek, I feel vulnerable—water moccasins, cottonmouths, and copperheads make carelessness costly. And in the fields, I feel anxious—fire ants and spiders make standing still risky.

As the heat persists, the earth hardens, and the lushness loses its luster to thirst and dust, I become languid and slow down. I look forward to cooler days and a clearer landscape. I usually pray for rain.

I endure the Southern summer, which defines us to others. Yet the Southern summer, which is a virile interval between birth and death—between renewed life and life eternal—is endearing.

LESSON 40 ✍ June 18–24
Dealing with the Southern Summer

*Man changes the conditions to suit the things. Nature changes the things to
suit the conditions. She adapts the plant or animal to its environment.*

—John Burroughs (1837–1921)
"The Gospel of Nature" in *Time and Change*

Succulents Are Successful in Dry Weather

THERE ARE TIMES WHEN I feel as if I'm in the desert. I know desert
air is dry while ours is humid, but give me the leeway to say it feels
as if I'm in the desert—or oven, if I must—because it's hot, hot,
hot, and the ground is dry, dry, dry. I struggle to get through those
times.

Many plants also struggle through our hot and dry periods,
even when we use the best cultural practices, xeriscaping principles, and maintenance techniques to care for them. We—the plants
and I—have not adapted and evolved sufficiently to withstand
such stress, which is worsening in this area—the heat is becoming
hotter, and the dry periods are becoming more pronounced. Many
experts think it's because of the greenhouse effect and will only get
worse.

Depending upon the rate of change, some plants may adapt
and evolve, developing new mechanisms for coping. On the other
hand, some plants, especially those that are already marginal in
our area, may not be able to adapt quickly enough to the environmental changes and simply won't be able to grow here any more.

Plants have always evolved, responding to environmental
changes and challenges. Succulents, for example, evolved to include
water storage abilities in their structure so they could grow where
fresh water is at a premium. They are mostly seen in areas where

rainfall is low and unevenly spaced throughout the year or where the available water is salty—the desert, rocky seaside cliffs, salt marshes, sandy shorelines, and dry grasslands. Succulents have water-swollen leaves or stems, fewer water-losing pores, chemicals in their cells that retain water, and extensive root systems.

There are succulents in many different plant families growing in different parts of the world. There is one succulent in the daisy family, several in the lily family, and so forth. Cacti are the most well-known succulents with about 2,000 species in the deserts of the Americas. Most cacti don't have water-losing leaves at all, having reduced themselves to water-storing stems.

Many of us have succulents growing as indoor plants. Aloe is a fixture in some kitchen windows—in case of burns. And jade plant is an all-time favorite. Most of these indoor plants are tropical succulents and will not survive our winter climate. However, there are several that will thrive in our landscapes, even if the temperatures reach 0°F, and some will survive short spurts of cold down to about 25°F.

For instance, yucca, with its spear-like leaves and handsome, tall mass of white flowers in the summer, is often seen in our area growing lonesomely in the wild or nicely placed in a landscape. Similarly, various cacti survive our winters and are used to great effect in the landscape, complementing architecture, pool areas, or southwestern motifs. Less hardy cacti varieties are sometimes seen grouped in a suitable microclimate of a large landscape.

I'm particularly partial to the low-growing succulents. They are extremely heat and drought tolerant perennial plants, which can be mounding or spreading in habit. Spreading forms are used as ground covers, and they'll creep or cascade over rocks or walls—areas in the landscape tending to become very hot and dry. The mounding varieties are often used as borders or in mass plantings. These plants come in a great range of sizes (from less than 1 inch to over 2 feet), and they are easy to cultivate and divide.

Sedum spurium 'Dragon's Blood' is a ground cover variety with burgundy foliage and red flowers. *Sedum* × 'Autumn Joy' is a mounding variety with a gray-green leaf color. Its foliage grows 16–24 inches, and bronze-burgundy flowers form 10 inches above the foliage in August, blooming until frost. *Sedum spectabile* 'Brilliant' is similar to 'Autumn Joy' but has a slightly larger leaf. It reaches 12–15 inches in height with bright pink, flat-top blooms up to 5 inches across.

I adore *Sempervivums*, commonly known as hens-and-chicks or houseleeks, and think they're the greatest rock garden plants. Their rosettes tuck within the crevices and pockets of the rocks. Although they don't always flower, they do grow fast. The closely held "babies" start to creep away from the parent, covering the rock as they crawl. These offspring are easily separated and replanted, increasing the family. There are green, gray, and purplish varieties of hens-and-chicks with varying forms. One of the best uses I have made of them is in container gardens. In particular, I like to use a strawberry pot (the tall, round kind with compartments on the sides) and put different varieties in each hole, with a taller succulent at the top.

> ## IT'S A MATTER OF FACT
>
> Cacti do not have leaves, the water-losing components of most plants. Rather, they have spines on which fog and dew collect before trickling down to the roots. The spines also shield the plant from the hot sun, insulating it and lowering the surface temperature by about 20°F. But they are primarily a defense mechanism against animals who would otherwise devour the plant for its store of water in the arid area.

To get the best of all worlds, you can create attractive succulent gardens in decorative pots for your indoor, winter pleasure, using some of the tropical succulents that will not otherwise survive our winters. In the summer, take the containers outside and strategically place them in the garden on pedestals or rocks, or on the ground. Group several of these container gardens together for a more striking effect, using tall tropicals as backdrop and shorter ones in the foreground. (See Lesson 39 on container gardening for more ideas and cultural requirements.)

Most succulents need plenty of sun; all need lots of drainage and prefer to literally dry out between waterings, so they are best placed in the low water use zones of your yard. That's the beauty of them—they can survive on very little rainfall, and little or no supplemental watering, depending upon the severity of the drought conditions. And they don't need to stand alone, since there are many companion plants with similar cultural requirements.

Succulents are a prime example of the adaptive nature of life. The question is: Can plants adapt to habitats that are changing rapidly due to man's alterations, or does the pace of change limit adaptability, leading to death or extinction? The adaptability and evolutionary process reminds me that there's usually a resolution to every problem we perceive—given time. But is there time enough?

BEAT THE HEAT

IT'S SUMMER SOLSTICE TIME, and it's as hot as spicy pork sausage. The sun is as far north as it will go before sliding back to cross the equator in September. It sits overhead and pours its energy on us like there's no tomorrow. The days are the longest of the year, the cooling nights the shortest. The heat is reaching its peak, and will remain for quite some time. We know it, and our plants know it. By August, many of them will look strained—drained of vitality by the parching heat—as well as by weeds, insects, and lack of grooming. Fight back! There are many ways to help your plants to renewed vigor through the withering weather. They'll be happier and prettier.

Watering: There is something of an art here, but anyone can learn it. The basic premise when watering trees and shrubs is to be sure that the deep roots are receiving enough water. Do not water lightly often. Rather, water every 4–6 days *thoroughly*; about one inch of water per week should be sufficient if there has been no significant rainfall. New plantings usually require more frequent watering than established plants, but avoid over-watering.

Weeding: Weeds take their food and water from the same soil that your valued trees, shrubs, perennials, and annuals do. If you keep your beds weed free, other plants will get more nutrients and have a better chance for survival, and they'll grow faster.

Mulching: I never tire of reminding folks of the importance of mulching. Mulch helps the soil retain moisture and also helps with weed control. So if you mulch your beds and around any singly planted specimens, you'll reduce the amount of watering needed *and* the number of backbreaking weed pulls.

Fertilizing: If you're experiencing an extended dry period or drought, don't give plants high-nitrogen fertilizer, which encourages new, water-hungry growth.

Pruning: If you're experiencing an extended dry period or drought, don't prune plants heavily or shear them. If necessary, selectively prune them only. Pruning, like fertilizing, encourages new, water-hungry growth.

Lawn Care: Don't mow turfgrass more than one-third its height. If you're experiencing an extended dry period or drought, raise the blades of the mower even higher for a healthier survival until the rains come.

Care of Older, Large Trees: If you have to make a choice of what to water, take care of the older plants first. It may be costly to replace new plantings that die from lack of water, but older, mature trees are irreplaceable. During drought, water older, large trees under the entire canopy every ten days with two inches of water (or 15–20 gallons per inch of trunk diameter). When watering new plantings that are under old, established trees, water deeply. Otherwise, the more established plants will send their roots up in search of the shallow water you added, and they will overcome the young, tender roots of the new plants. Always give the younger understory plants more water and fertilizer than you would otherwise, since the older plants towering over them will use the nourishment also.

LESSON 41 ∾ June 25–July 1
Daylilies

The green thumb is the gardener who can nimbly walk the line between
the dangers of over- and undercultivation, between pushing nature too far
and giving her too much ground. His garden is a place where her ways and
his designs are brought gracefully into alignment. To occupy such a middle
ground is not easy—the temptation is always to either take complete
control or relinquish it altogether, to invoke your own considerable (but in
the end overrated) power or to bend to nature's. The first way is that of the
developer, the second that of the "nature lover." The green thumb, who will
be neither heroic nor romantic, avoids both extremes. He does not try to
make water run uphill, but neither does he let it flow wherever it will.

—Michael Pollan (b. 1955)
Second Nature: A Gardener's Education

Dazzle Your Yard with Daylilies

DRIVING DOWN A COUNTRY ROAD on a warmer-than-comfortable day, I'm struck by a flash of orange—a flower blooming in the horrendous heat, thrusting its old-fashioned smile in my direction. Dotting an old farmhouse yard like paint splatter, colorful clusters emerge and greet me with memories of trips to Granny's, hot summers, and country calm. That flower—stately, yet homely, with grassy foliage and showy bloom—spent in just a day.

It's the daylily—*Hemerocallis fulva*, or tawny daylily. Naturalized along roadsides and around old Southern homesteads, tawny daylily blooms in early- to midsummer for two to three weeks and reaches about 4 feet in height. Although ideal in a cottage garden or wildflower setting, these tough bloomers can add elegant charm to a formal planting as well.

The tawny daylily of my past is an *old-fashioned* daylily. But there are many new varieties—bred for color, size, bloom time, and other desirable characteristics. One way to group them is to define them as either *reblooming* or *fancy*, their characters baring witness to the group names. The reblooming varieties bloom throughout the warm months and include rugged landscape daylilies that have high durability and ability to multiply. 'Stella de Oro' is the most popular one of these. Its golden yellow-orange flowers display from late spring through fall, and its compact, 12- to 14-inch-tall habit makes it a favorite for smaller beds needing lower-growing color. The fancy daylily hybrids do not bloom all summer, but come in a massive array of colors. They are commonly used as perennial borders and for showy displays; their color and form should dictate their use in the landscape.

IT'S A MATTER OF FACT

Most plants have two sets of chromosomes, one from each parent, and are called diploid. But sometimes during reproduction, a cell fails to separate as usual, and fertilization then produces offspring with three or four sets of chromosomes, resulting in abnormally large flowers and fruits. Scientists have discovered that the use of the chemical colchicine on flower buds can yield the same polyploidal giants, such as tetraploid daylilies (Tets) that have four sets of 11 chromosomes each, for a total of 44 chromosomes. The tetraploid factor enhances the intensity of certain characteristics—larger flowers, thicker petals, robust scapes, greater intensity of color, and bigger price tags. But tets are regal and worth the extra expense.

Each year, in late May and early June, I see signs popping up at country corners and in front yards stating the presence of daylilies. Someone has a bunch and wants to divide and sell them. These "backyard nurseries" are a testament that this perennial is easy to grow, looks great in the landscape, requires little or no care, and is essentially free of diseases and pests.

Although daylilies are tough and durable, if you know certain of their characteristics and cultural requirements, you'll probably have even better success with them. Here's a list of things to know and consider about daylilies:

- The scape is the leafless, flowering stalk of the daylily. It is naked in the lower portion and branched in the upper end where bracts occur at each node.
- Daylily flowers can be eyed or banded, with distinct, darker-color markings surrounding the throat, or may have less distinct eyes, referred to as a halo.
- Daylilies like full sun to partial shade, with at least six hours of sun.
- Many light yellow, pink, and pastel blends have better color value in very sunny situations.
- Some red and purple varieties keep their color better if they are protected from direct sun for at least part of the day, particularly the late afternoon.
- It's best to keep daylilies away from heavy-feeding broad-leaf trees and shrubs that will compete at the surface for nutrition.
- Well-drained, moisture-retentive soil is required for good growth. Soggy, saturated areas should be avoided, and sandy or clay soils should be amended with compost or other organic amendment.
- Daylilies can tolerate very dry conditions, but they perform best with adequate water, and extra watering even helps, especially during the bloom period.
- For best production, fertilizer (13-6-6 or thereabouts) should be applied each year in late winter before flower scapes start rising inside the crown of the plant. Two more applications during the year, but not in mid- or late summer, are helpful.
- Most cultivars should be planted 18 inches apart, with the crown no deeper than, or slightly above, the soil line.
- Daylilies are generally pest free but sometimes have aphids, thrips, and mites. Kelthane is toxic to daylilies and should never be used to control these critters.

Whether you choose old-fashioned, reblooming, or fancy daylilies, they will dazzle your yard with color and height variation. If you really get into them, or find that they've proliferated more than you had dreamed for, you might want to know that almost every part of the daylily is edible—roots, buds, and flowers. Eat the crisp tubers raw or boil the green buds and serve with herb butter. Pork and soy sauce are good accompaniments—so I'm told, but I haven't gotten beyond the visual and olfactory pleasures yet.

DAYLILY DELIGHTS

I FAVOR CERTAIN DAYLILIES, just like I favor certain trees and shrubs. Your preference or landscape needs may differ from my picks, but I'm sure there's a suitable variety for you since there are thousands to choose from, with more every day, it seems. As you read about some of my favorites, know that virtually any daylily variety description will read just as lusciously. Some of my favorites are as follows:

'**Colonel Scarborough**': This finely fragranced daylily has a cool, soft-pastel-yellow flower with very dark, rich foliage. The large, 6-inch waxy flowers have diamond dusting and ribs, an icy-green throat, and pie-crust ruffled edges. The plant grows 16–18 inches high, and the scapes are just tall enough to provide a full view of the bloom.

'**Marcia Fay**': With a textured flower sporting a yellow-green throat and cream midribs on a rose-and-pink blend, this daylily is vigorous growing and has medium green foliage.

'**Dallas Lass**': Flowers of this daylily are 2½ inches, with near-circular form, broad overlapping petals with crisp ruffling, and a rich apricot color; foliage is 18 inches long. Elegant simplicity is at its best in this jewel.

'**Winsome Lady**': Like the name implies, this daylily has a very light-blush-pink, symmetrical flower. The blooms are 5½ inches and repeat well, with lots of fragrance.

'**Pandora's Box**': The 4-inch ivory-cream with purple eyezones flowers on this daylily are crisp and lively, yet cool and inviting. The scapes are 20–22 inches tall.

'**Enchanted Elf**': The earliest to bloom, this daylily has well-branched and profusely budded scapes. The flowers are an orange-tangerine blend with a small, lime-green button throat. Petals are creped, ruffled, and reflexed into a funnel-form shape.

'**Dancing Shiva**': Five-inch flowers on the 22-inch scapes of this daylily have broad ruffled petals that overlap wide sepals to form a round, full shape. This heavy substance and a yellow throat accentuate the rich blend of pink, peach, and apricot colors. This tetraploid has deep-green foliage.

'**Smoke Rings**': This one is exotic looking with distinctly separate petals and sepals that are clearly accentuated by a band of purple in an inverted shape, giving a six-pointed star pattern. The flowers are peach-pink with a purple eyezone and chartreuse button. This tetraploid is slightly ruffled.

'**Stella de Oro**' and '**Stella Supreme**': These two daylilies are short (only 14- to 18-inches tall) and bloom repeatedly throughout the summer and until frost, unlike other daylilies. Stella is golden-yellow-orange; Supreme is yellow.

Lilies, like the one pictured, are not daylilies. They are of the genus *Lilium* and the family Liliaceae. Daylilies were once thought to be a part of that family, but were separated out and given their own family, Hemerocallidaceae.

LESSON 42 ⚮ July 2–8
Edible Fruits

*Nothing great is created suddenly, any more than a bunch of grapes or a fig.
If you tell me that you desire a fig, I answer you that there must be time. Let
it first blossom, then bear fruit, then ripen.*

—Epictetus (ca. 55–135)
Greek philosopher

Red, White, and Blueberries

SOMETIMES I THINK the only real exciting thing about summer is the Fourth of July. Otherwise it's just too hot, too dry, and, to me, downright depressing. But the celebration of independence and our personal freedoms ignites the soul, enlivens the spirit, renews the faith, and is just plain fun. I always look forward to the bursting fireworks, the foot-stomping music, and the food—especially the red watermelon and blueberries. Mix them in a bowl, and feast 'til your belly bursts or floats away.

When I was a child, my grandfather was my watermelon supplier. He would select the plumpest, largest, longest striped version he could find and have it waiting for me when I visited him—or he would send it on the back floor of my grandmother's car when she came to visit. He was proud when he thumped the moisture-filled rind and declared it a fine pick. To this day, I firmly tap a melon, listening for the right tone and vibration before deciding it fit to cut. And I still opt for the long striped melons filled with seeds—just waiting for the spitting contest with my children. I do enjoy the seedless varieties also, but they're not nearly as much fun. Either way, I always eat my watermelon with a touch of salt to enhance the sweetness.

My watermelon supplier, Grandpa (Hubert Olie Godwin), loved to catch a
fresh fish for lunch to accompany his sharp cheddar cheese, saltines, and
hot sauce. When he couldn't make a catch, he ate sardines from the can.

My love affair with blueberries began in the mid-1980s, the
year before our son James was born, when my husband and I took
a trip to the Alma, Georgia, blueberry festival in June. We returned
with a pickup truck filled to capacity with one-gallon blueberry
bushes. There were so many berries that had fallen to the bed of the
truck, we had to sweep them out (after we couldn't eat any more).
We planted those bushes, and many more subsequently, creating a
pick-your-own field. Our freezers are always filled with the huge,
sweet morsels that we eat frozen as snacks, cook into pancakes and
muffins, and put on top of all kinds of confections. But my favorite
way to eat blueberries is to punch fresh ones into vanilla ice cream

and let the concoction sit for about five minutes before eating. In that short time, the berries become slightly frozen and provide a crunch within each bite of the creamy ice cream. You really should try it.

My true passion for blueberry bushes began when I witnessed them blooming in spring with their profuse covering of tiny flowers that yield a heavenly pinkish glow created from the combination of off-white, almost translucent petals cupped on the bottom with a blue "shell," the precursor to the fruit. Then, when I witnessed the blueberry's fall glory—bright red and orange leaves, tenaciously hanging on until the end of the season—I knew for sure that the bush of divine fruit is also a bush of beauty.

Blueberries are the easiest fruit to grow; rabbiteye blueberries (*Vaccinium ashei*) are the best growers in this area. Although northern highbush varieties will grow in some sites in the Piedmont and North Georgia Mountains, rabbiteyes are the choice for the non-mountainous areas of Georgia.

With the introduction of improved rabbiteye varieties, Georgia has become one of the top five blueberry producing states in the nation. You can join the ranks and grow them right in your backyard. By planting early-, mid-, and late-season varieties, you'll have fresh blueberries from mid-June through mid-August. 'Brightwell', 'Climax', 'Premier', and 'Woodward' are good early-season producers. 'Bluebelle' and 'Tifblue' have huge mid-season berries. And 'Delite' is a delightful late variety.

The single most important thing to know about growing blueberries is that there must be at least two, and preferably more, varieties that bloom at the same time in your yard. If there's not, the plants won't cross-pollinate adequately, and acceptable fruit-set will not occur.

There's not much else to blueberries since they're so easy to grow. Plant rabbiteyes in full sun about 6 feet apart in a row, with 12 feet between rows. Single, specimen plantings can be spotted however you like. Prepare the soil as you would for any other plantings, keeping in mind that blueberries like acidic soil (pH of 4.0–5.2) and therefore don't need added lime. Cut back the bushes about one-third at planting time and remove low branches. Do not fertilize when planting, but apply a 10-10-10 or equivalent fertilizer after new growth in March/April and again in June. Do not overfertilize and do not apply mulch within 6 inches of the trunk. After the third season, use a fertilizer with micronutrients.

The first year, remove any flowers to promote faster growth. Water blueberries throughout the growing season if there isn't enough rainfall. Don't worry about spraying for pests since you probably won't have any worth fooling with. But if you do have a problem, seek advice from your Cooperative Extension Service.

Be prepared to pick to your heart's delight and your family's contentment and your neighbors' joy. See how much you can take to the house . . . and how much you consume en route. Eat all you can while they're fresh—they keep well in the refrigerator for 7–10 days, or more, and freeze the rest by simply putting them in a plastic container, without washing. Then take out just the amount of the frozen ones you want, wash them, and have fun preparing dishes and eating them.

It's a Matter of Fact

Fuzzy, drippy peaches—Georgia's prize fruit and the makings of delectable ice cream and cobblers—originated in ancient China. They were carried westward through Persia (hence their botanical name *Prunus persica*), and on to Greece and Rome where they were called Persian apples. Spanish conquistadors took peaches to Mexico in the 1600s, then to the southwestern part of the United States. It was only a matter of time before they reached the Southeast and became one of its beloved fruits.

Melons and berries. It just doesn't get much better—until fall when the blueberry bushes turn their gorgeous bright red and linger until autumn frosts finally force the leaves to fall, and the chill hours start ticking away, determining the production ability for the following year.

FRUITING FACTS

MOST OF THE PLANTS in the world have flowers; we call them angiosperms. After pollination, their flowers change and fruits develop to protect the fertilized seeds until they find a suitable place to germinate. The fruits are the ripened ovaries of a flower; the seeds of the fruit are the beginnings of new life. Those that we eat we call fruits, nuts, grains, or vegetables, although botanically they are fruits.

The fruits that we eat, and call fruits, are primarily fleshy simple fruits such as apples, melons, bananas, peaches, and pears, and complex fruits such as strawberries and pineapples.

Some fruits that we eat we call vegetables. Tomato—considered a vegetable by most folks—is actually a fruit, the ripened ovary of a single flower. Peas are dry fruits. And each kernel of corn and each grain of rice or wheat is a ripened ovary of a flower—a fruit.

When Grandpa wasn't fishing, napping during a baseball game on TV, or picking out watermelons for me, he was lawyering. He did not attend school to become an attorney. Rather, he "read the law" while serving as a telegrapher for the railroad, and passed the bar exam on his third attempt. He later became mayor of Social Circle, Georgia, and was a Justice of the Peace. In deference to his standing, many folks called him Colonel Godwin, a customary courtesy title dating back to the War Between the States. Granny called him Mr. Godwin, and many others called him Mr. Olie. (Photo: 1927 when admitted to practice.) Although advised by Grandpa otherwise, I too became a lawyer. But my love of Nature and the pull of the nursery, as some like to say, "reformed" me—sort of.

LESSON 43 ❧ July 9–15
The Forest Shade

This is the forest primeval.
The murmuring pines and the hemlocks,
Bearded with moss, and in garments green, indistinct in the twilight,
Stand like Druids of eld . . .

—Henry Wadsworth Longfellow (1807–1882)
Evangeline: A Tale of Acadie

Mountain and Shade Plants Create a Primeval Forest

EVERY YEAR AS THE MOUNTAIN laurel and rhododendrons bloom, customers come to the nursery seeking them and information. These plants, along with pieris, sourwood, leucothoe, deciduous azaleas, and many others, are members of the Ericaceae family. They are native to the hills and mountains of the Southeast, growing in our acid soils. Some grow in swamps, but most prefer moist, well-drained soils.

When I was a child growing up in Atlanta, a common means of obtaining a large-leafed, evergreen rhododendron for one's yard was to take a trip to the North Georgia Mountains. With shovel in hand, a wild one was easily snatched. For those blessed with mature, shade-providing hardwoods and a moist, protected habitat, rhododendrons brought those mountains to the city with their late-spring splendor.

I think we all know now that taking plants from the wild is unsavory behavior, usually illegal, and not necessary. There are hundreds of hybridized varieties of our native Catawba rhododendron (*Rhododendron catawbiense*) being grown and sold in nurseries. Cultivated to improve certain qualities of the plant, rhododendron cultivars have been developed with better foliage, better flower color and quality, cold hardiness, and better growth rate and habit.

The huge rhododendrons covering our Southern Appalachian slopes usually bear light pinkish to purplish rose flowers, marked with yellow-brown or green on the inside. The dark green foliage rises on somewhat contorted, brown branches to 6–10 feet or more and spreads 5–8 feet or more. Their mid-May through June flowering season is slightly later than ours in the warmer foot- and toehills (late April through late May).

Flower colors vary among the cultivated varieties—white, pink, coral-red, purple, light yellow, peach-pink, lavender, light salmon, chartreuse, bright red, and more—while other attributes distinguish some cultivars. For example, 'Chionoides' has narrow foliage that grows densely on the broad, compact shrub, which reaches only about 4 feet and has white flowers with yellow centers that make numerous domed-shaped trusses.

In contrast to the usual slow growth of Catawba rhododendrons, 'English Roseum' grows rapidly and vigorously to about 6 feet. Its leaves are a smooth, glossy, dark green, underscoring the soft rosy pink flowers. 'Roseum Elegans', an old favorite in gardens because of its flowering reliability, has excellent heat and cold tolerance, as does 'English Roseum'.

In our neck of the woods, rhododendrons usually suffer from the searing sun and the compact clay soils. Don't expect to be able to grow them below the Fall Line (or perhaps I-20) in Georgia. But, with a little bit of extra care, in North Georgia you can alleviate the growing difficulties. Like most other ericaceous plants with shallow roots, rhododendrons like acidic soil that is porous, moist, highly organic, and well-drained. Plant them in a protected area—preferably on the shaded north or east side of your house or tucked into a wooded area with dappled light. Too much shade will retard flower production.

Dig a hole and then fill it completely with a mixture of 50 percent organic material such as compost, bark, or leaf mold and 50 percent finely chopped native soil. Finger through the roots of your plant and place them over the surface of the filled hole. Cover the rootball with a thick layer of organic material such as soil conditioner (composted, pulverized pine bark). Continue adding conditioner, building a raised mound with a flat top around the root-ball until the top surface is 100 percent bark. Water thoroughly.

In our area and because of the planting method, rhododendrons, and other ericaceous plants, need supplemental water, so plan to water periodically as needed. Rhododendron leaves droop dramatically when the plant is thirsty, but try not to wait for this distress sign. Rather, feel the soil beneath the mulch, sticking your fingers several inches down to determine if it is dry. Fertilize in spring after bloom and in early- to midsummer using a general-purpose fertilizer with micronutrients, and without acidic additions since our soils are acidic enough. Prune after flowering to remove diseased or damaged stems but not to tame or shape.

Other ericaceous plants need similar cultural care, and the key to successfully growing them starts with replicating, as much as possible, the growing conditions of the plant's native environment. For most of these plants, including rhododendron, azalea, mountain laurel, and pieris, this dictate means having or creating part-shade or full-shade beds. Planting under large, mature hardwood trees is ideal. Short of that, planting on the north or east side of the house usually will suffice. Although these plants need moisture, they should not be planted in constantly wet soil.

Fertilize these "mountain" plants in spring after bloom or in early summer. Water them thoroughly after planting and then periodically as needed. The "as needed" can be the tricky part. Soil moisture depends on three things: transpiration, evaporation, and gravity. You can reduce evaporation of moisture from the soil by using mulch, but you can't control transpiration—the movement of moisture from the soil, through the roots, and out through the leaves. Nor can you control the force of gravity, which pulls water away from your above-ground-level planting. Therefore, watering your ericaceous plants is a must in the summer.

Think about adding some companion plants to create a forest floor with a mixture of native and introduced varieties that will transform your yard from a cookie-cutter landscape into a private, natural oasis. To do this, three groups of plants are a must: ferns, hostas, and Lenten roses.

Hardy ferns, both deciduous and evergreen, carve character in the landscape, whether in masses, as ground covers, or in small clumps as specimens. Ferns are tough and often grow in areas uninhabitable by other plants. The fronds are usually green, but the range of shades and textures make them extremely versatile. Evergreen fern varieties add winter interest with their unique texture, while deciduous varieties display differing traits throughout the four seasons: their naked winter dormancy opens up the garden and brings focus to other plants, their coiled spring fiddleheads offer daily change in their unfurling, their lush summer-green fronds cool the garden, and their fall color mixes with the falling leaves.

Fern fiddleheads that emerge in spring become luxuriant
forest floor plants by early summer.

Hostas are another group of perennial plants that will do well on your forest floor. Also known as plantain lilies or funkias, hostas have been around for years, but renewed interest has breeders introducing new varieties every year. Although hostas are grown primarily for their foliage, they do send up stalks of flowers that can be very fragrant. Leaf shape varies from long and slender to rounded, leaf size varies from 1–2 inches to 2 feet, and color varies from green to golden yellow on one end of the spectrum to blue-green on the other. Hostas are good for mass-planted ground cover or borders. Varying colors and leaf shapes make a truly dynamic forest floor.

IT'S A MATTER OF FACT

Mosses and ferns predate the seed-bearing gymnosperms (no flowers and naked seed) and angiosperms (flowers and covered seed) in the evolution of plants. Mosses are more primitive, lacking true roots or a vascular system that easily transports water and having often undifferentiated roots, stems, and leaves.

Helleborus is a third group of plants sure to add interest to your primeval paradise. These winter/early-spring-flowering perennials are most appealing between the time of the colorful fall supplied by the ferns and the emergence of the fiddleheads in spring. They flower for a long period in North Georgia, sometimes as early as December and continuing into May, but primarily from January to April. Nodding flowers range in color from white to green and pink to deep purple. (See Lesson 19 on Lenten roses, *H. orientalis*. Other species that are equally valuable in the landscape are *H. argutifolius*, *H. foetidus*, and *H. niger*.)

Many other native plants and wildflowers and their newer cultivars make excellent forest floor additions. Look at books, visit the Web, and go to nurseries for shade-loving perennials and pick those that you like, maybe adding a few each year as your budget allows. If blessed with relatively heavy shade, you'll be amazed at your ability to create a microclimate in your landscape like the forested mountains we all seem to love to visit. And while you're at it, don't forget about mosses, which will complete the setting.

MUSHROOMS MATTER

MOST PEOPLE DON'T THINK much of mushrooms—except when deliciously prepared and served with a meal or made the source of extrasensory experiences. But they play an extremely important part in the life of a forest and other ecosystems.

Mushrooms are the most advanced of the fungi, some of the most simple and primitive members of the plant kingdom. The part we see above ground is merely the flowering part of an underground growth of fungus and its long, thin filaments called hyphae. The mushrooms are temporary structures sent up to make and release millions of reproductive spores (as much as ten million per hour for several days). The hyphae grow underground in all directions, sometimes stretching for acres. A group or "fairy ring" of mushrooms is likely evidence of one large organism.

Most mushroom-forming fungi feed off of dead and decaying organic matter. In a forest where the floor is covered with decaying leaves and fallen trees, fungi consume the death and recycle it back into the ecosystem in the form of rich humus, releasing the nutrients the dead organisms had accumulated during their lives, making food for new life to grow.

Mushroom-producing fungi also form a symbiotic relationship with living organisms in the forest. Trees use the mycorrhizae (fungus filaments) that surround and penetrate their roots, increasing their absorption surface. Some trees, like pines, do not have any root hairs and rely upon the additional mycorrhizae surfaces; others simply increase what they already have. As a result, a tree growing among fungi extracts hundreds of times more nutrients, as well as some minerals and water from the soil, which would not otherwise be available to it. In return, the fungi get their energy from the tree's roots, the above-ground tree acting as the photosynthetic mechanism for the light-deprived underground organism. Some biologists think this mutual relationship may have been the determining factor that supported the evolution of large trees with their vascular systems.

Truffles—those delicacies of many a gourmand—are prime examples of the fungus root, but truffles, like those who eat them, are picky. Each variety selects a particular species of tree as its host. Reports indicate that the truffles associated with our Southern pecan trees are a delicacy of the highest repute—prized and priced in extreme.

LESSON 44 ⤳ July 16–22
Water Gardens

*Waterfalls are musical landscapes, not only beautiful to observe
but also pleasant to hear.*

—Eugene P. Odum (1913–2002)
Essence of Place

Make a Splash in Your Landscape with a Water Garden

WHEN I WAS A CHILD, our next-door neighbors had a tiny pond in their backyard. The rough-concrete, kidney-shaped affair, as well as the surrounding plants, were somewhat ramshackled and wanting for attention. As a child, all I saw was a stone-encircled pool filled with tadpoles—a place to float a leaf or acorn shell. But as an adult, I realize the untapped possibilities that pond held, and I'd give anything to be able to revisit it and work its wonders.

A landscape—one that truly incorporates nature's elements—includes a water feature. It can be as understated as a large pot filled with water, a small pump, and some water plants. It can be a waterfall cascading over rocks through various ponds, ending in a fish-filled pool surrounded with lush plants. Or it can be a small, simply designed pool like the one of my memories. Either way, the water—its sound and ceaseless movement—will add a component to the landscape incomparable to any other device.

It's Easy—When we first decided to build water gardens at our nursery, we found that, like vegetable gardening, most people with water gardens have their own way of doing things. We worried about pumps and filters, plants and fish, in-ground or above-ground, and many other issues that had to be resolved. But after talking to some truly experienced water gardeners, we decided to stop our worry and simply proceed. Amazingly, most of the "problems" disappeared, and we were rewarded with a very pleasant, low-maintenance, tranquil water garden area in the nursery. The task was so easy, in fact, that our first two ponds soon became six.

Need Sun—The first step in building a water garden is to decide where to put it. Most water plants need at least six full hours of sun per day. If this is impossible, all is not lost since it's possible to have a water feature in a shade garden, just one without water plants or with plants that require less sunlight.

Sitting Area Close By—Place your water garden area where you can enjoy it while relaxing. Put it near or on a patio or near your favorite garden bench. Or add a water garden and bench in a serene spot in the yard.

Think Long Term—When deciding upon your water garden placement, think long term. It's very likely you'll want to add features to the garden, so plan for enough room to do so, as water gardens tend to evolve over the years. You may install a pond this year, add a waterfall next year, and add plantings or hardscaping around the pond in future years. Or you may become addicted and build more ponds. Plan for this!

Must Be Level—One of the most important things to remember when building a pond is that the edges must be level, and groundwater must flow away from the pond. This does not mean that you must have a level place to put a pond since you can build a pond into the side of a hill by building up the front edge, leveling the pond, and allowing for a very natural waterfall out of it.

Preformed, Rigid Ponds—There are two basic kinds of ponds, the first kind being rigid. Preformed ponds are manufactured specifically as ponds, come in a variety of shapes, and usually have shelves for bog plants. Then there's other types of containers such as animal stock tanks, large nursery pots, or flower pots that can be used. When considering the container that suits, be sure it has enough depth, which means at least 20–24 inches for lilies and 8–10 inches for bog plants. The actual depth needed is determined by the pot the water plant is in.

Free-Form, Flexible Liner Ponds—The other kind of pond is free-form. Small or large, most ponds of this type use a liner to hold the water. You can combine free-form and preformed ponds. So, for instance, you might use small preformed ponds to form a creek or waterfall flowing into a large free-formed pond.

Pump Choices—Simplify your decision-making about your pump choice by considering their two uses: water circulation and water feature creation. Regarding water circulation: as a general rule, use a pump that will circulate one-half the volume of the water in the pond every hour. If you have a filter, or do not intend to clean the strainer on a daily basis, size the pump slightly larger.

The second pump use is to create a water feature. When building a waterfall or creekbed, the flow of the water is critical to making a natural look. One way to measure the volume needed is to pour water from a container through the water feature, noting the volume poured and the time it takes to reach its destination. Another way is to purchase a pump that has more than enough capacity to provide the flow and use a valve to control the amount that goes to the feature. We prefer the second approach since, as our pump supplier said: "Too big is wonderful; too small can be a disaster."

The Final Touch—One of the most difficult choices to make when constructing a water garden is how to finish the edges of the pond, which can be done with bricks, wood, tile, rock, stone, or any number of other products. You are limited only by your personal tastes and imagination.

Be Prepared for Green Water—Once the water garden hardscape is complete, you can install the water plants—and fish. That's right. You'll want to have both, not only for your enjoyment, but also for the promotion of clean water. A well-balanced pond that is free of green, pea-soup algae gunk generally includes a variety of water plants and fish. The trick is to reach and maintain a balance of oxygen and nutrients in order to promote plant growth while reducing algal growth. You'll need plants that are oxygenators to produce oxygen. You'll need fish to consume the oxygen and produce waste nutrients for plant growth. And you'll need floating plants that reduce the amount of sunlight reaching below the water's surface since high levels of sunlight and excess nutrients like nitrates and phosphates promote algae growth. While the pond is striking a balance, you can help reduce or prevent algae growth by using flocculents (clumping agents), filters, and ultraviolet clarifiers that kill algae cells and bacteria.

Enjoy—Having a water garden can be a relaxing hobby. The tranquil sound of moving water is a great addition to any yard or garden. You'll love water gardening. And yes, it is addictive.

The neighbors with the fabulous pond also had a wonderful vegetable garden. My sister, Elizabeth (right), holds a turnip just given to her in 1961. Mom and I enjoy the gift with her.

THE WHAT'S OF WATER PLANTS

THERE ARE SEVERAL CATEGORIES of plants for water gardens:

Hardy water lilies are the perennials of a water garden. They are frost tolerant and survive the Georgia winters. They bloom all summer, and each flower lasts 2–4 days, staying open only during the daylight hours. The flowers float on the surface of the water, as do the leaves. Hardy water lilies need lots of fresh soil, sun, and nutrition. Use large containers for planting them. Fertilize every 4–6 weeks; divide every 2–4 years.

Tropical water lilies are the annuals of the water garden. Though they can be overwintered in a greenhouse, most gardeners treat them as annuals. Tropical lilies have very fragrant flowers, which typically bloom on stems 8–12 inches above the water surface. Some varieties bloom at night, making it especially nice for day workers, who can return home to relax by their water garden in the evening.

IT'S A MATTER OF FACT

The Okefenokee Swamp in southeast Georgia is a huge water garden of sorts, housing all kinds of water and bog plants, several of which are carnivorous (flesh-eating). The pitcher plant (flycatcher) attracts insects with its sweet fluid and enticing flower. The inner surface is covered with hairs that allow a visitor entry but not exit. Moving in the only direction possible, the victim ends in the fluid-filled bottom where it drowns. The plant absorbs the soft parts of the body while the skeleton remains in the bottom of the vat.

Lotuses are similar to water lilies. They have beautiful, large leaves and striking flowers that open during the day until midafternoon. The seed head is like a round watering can head with large holes and makes a delightful dried addition to an indoor flower arrangement. Lotuses are unsuitable for small ponds since they tend to take over.

Floating plants are just that—they float on the surface of the water with their roots only in water, not soil. They can be very effective biological filters for fish waste. In fact, sewage treatment plants use them to filter out excess nitrogen. They multiply quickly and can become a weed in the pond, but those that are easy to pull out make a great addition to a compost pile.

Submerged plants are those whose leaves are at least partially under water. They are oxygenators, helping to maintain clear water, but they also grow quickly and can overrun a pond. Most root at the bottom of the pond in a soil layer and have stems that are not self-supporting out of water.

Bog plants (marginal plants) grow in constantly wet soils. They will grow around the edges of ponds in "artificial" bog areas or on shelves in a pond, and they add contrasting texture to the lilies and a verticle dimension to the pond.

Some quick tips:

- A half whiskey-barrel planter with a waterfall liner insert makes a great biological filter for ponds with too many fish. Just fill the barrel with water hyacinths and let the water circulate through it before falling into a larger pond below.
- If you must walk in your pond to perform maintenance, do it barefoot. If you step on something that cuts the liner, you will know it and will be able to fix it before it creates other problems.
- When placing potted plants around your pond, anchor them so they can't fall in. Most potting mixes float and make a mess in the pond.
- After potting water plants, place washed stones with rounded edges on top of the pots. The stones will help hold the soil in the pots, deter some types of predators, and will not damage the pond liner if they fall out.

LESSON 45 ℣ July 23–29
Ground Covers

The natural environment we treat with such unnecessary ignorance and recklessness was our cradle and nursery, our school, and remains our one and only home. To its special conditions we are intimately adapted in every one of the bodily fibers and biochemical transactions that gives us life. . . . That is the essence of environmentalism. It is the guiding principle of those devoted to the health of the planet. . . . The relative indifference to the environment springs, I believe, from deep within human nature. The human brain evidently evolved to commit itself emotionally only to a small piece of geography, a limited band of kinsmen, and two or three generations into the future.

—Edward O. Wilson (b. 1929)
The Future of Life

Gaining Some Ground Cover Means Losing Some Lawn

WE ALL NEED TO CHANGE the paradigm that dictates our loyalty to lawns (see Lesson 29), so lose your lawn—at least a good part of it—and don't fret. Just replace it with more interesting, hardier, easier to establish and maintain ground covers. It doesn't matter if your yard is shady or sunny, hilly or flat. There are ground covers that will thrive and become virtually maintenance free, demanding no chemicals and far less water, money, and energy from you and our earthly resources. Better still, you'll have green where grasses won't grow.

When I say ground covers, I mean herbaceous and woody perennials that spread rapidly, growing low to the ground and easily covering large areas. Some are evergreen, some not. Some have outstanding flowers, some not. Some take over like weeds, and some not.

The most common—and perhaps overused—ground cover I see is *Liriope*, sometimes known as **lily turf**. Ironically, it's usually seen running alongside walkways, encircling trees, and edging flower beds. But it does work magnificently in its own right filling a bed. The slender leaves bunch in clusters, arching upward and then cascading toward the ground, like a fluffed ponytail atop a young girl's head. Most bear lilac-colored flowers above the foliage during the summer, although some, like 'Munroe White', have white flowers. Most have green foliage that blends into the surrounding landscape, but some, like 'Gold-banded', are variegated. It's lightened leaves provide contrast to perhaps an otherwise dreary sea of green.

Liriope likes full sun or shade, depending upon the variety. Some are spreading in habit; some are clumping. Use the clumping types for edging, the spreading types for ground cover. Plant the sprigs or clumps 8–12 inches apart. Anytime after their black berries have faded in late fall, but before new spring growth emerges, run a lawn mower over the plants. Then, if the clumps have become larger than you like or need, divide the plants and give some away, or create more beds.

Another ground cover that I have enjoyed throughout my life is *Ajuga reptans*, **common bugle weed**. Although this fast-growing plant will tolerate full sun, it performs best in partial shade. Because of its invasive qualities, you should keep it away from lawns. But put it on a bank, and its rough, velvet foliage (which varies from bronze, gray-green, whitish, to pinkish—depending upon the cultivar) will fill the area with year-round beauty. In spring, the flowers stand on spikes, creating a colorful carpet of blue, white, pink, or lavender. (I like the old, common blue myself.) Ajuga is easily divided almost anytime.

Common periwinkle (*Vinca minor*) has also been a part of my landscapes since I can remember. Although it likes partial to full shade, I've had it grow in full sun with some success. Its spring flowers of purplish blue, white, or burgundy add a gentle touch at just the right time. The lustrous green leaves shine (if in shade) during the hot summer months, giving a sense of coolness. Despite its fine qualities, however, periwinkle is truly invasive and should be avoided, unless you have defined barriers to pen it in and no other plants in the area over which it will grow. (See Lesson 38 about invasive plants.)

Pachysandra terminalis (**Japanese spurge**) is a shade-loving ground cover that first caught my attention when my husband was asked to design and install a shade garden during our early years in the nursery business. He recommended this rapid-growth plant for a heavily shaded area under trees where other plants would not be able to compete for nutrients. The plants, with their dark green leaves whorled atop the 4- to 6-inch-tall stems, quickly spread and filled the space. I particularly like this simple green plant (that also comes in variegated varieties) when the breeze blows and makes it dance, providing movement at ground level. Its spiked, white spring flowers are also attractive.

Some ground covers love the sun and excel in color, and one group, **dianthus**, caught the attention of horticulturists and gardeners in the early 1990s. While running the risk of perpetuating a trend toward its overuse, I'd like to mention it since I have found it exceptionally easy to grow and maintain, and a vibrant addition to my yard.

Several varieties of dianthus stand out in my mind. My favorite to date is 'Mountain Mist' (*Dianthus plumarius* 'Mountain Mist') with its blue-green, long and narrow foliage and single pink flowers on 10-inch stems in the spring. The foliage remains a colorful complement to the cold winter landscape and is especially attractive placed around the base of a winter-colorful tree like a red-stemmed Japanese maple. Nike, our now-deceased pure white cat with bright blue eyes, made a picture-perfect sight when she sat among our Mountain Mist dianthus in what must have seemd like a field of flowers to her. Bath's Pink (*Dianthus gratianopolitanus* 'Bath's Pink') is a Georgia Gold Medal Winner with gray-green foliage and soft pink, fringed flowers. Firewitch (*Dianthus gratianopolitanus* 'Firewitch') has a deeper magenta flower that blooms in spring and again, somewhat sparsely, throughout the summer. The most delicious thing about dianthus is the heavenly cinnamon scent that wafts as you pass a blooming bed. The cultivar Vanilla (*Dianthus plumarius* 'Vanilla') thrusts the mouth-watering aroma of the same name into the air.

Low-growing junipers are also good, sun-loving ground covers and are very low maintenance, evergreen, drought tolerant, and quick growing. The gray-green and blue-green hues add contrast to a yard if used creatively with other plants and if not overdone. The lowest growing junipers (*Juniperus horizontalis*) creep in mats with their spreading, horizontal branches. 'Blue Rug' and 'Bar Harbor' are probably the most popular of this species. *J. conferta* is another choice that works better in sandier soils and tolerates some shade, and 'Blue Pacific' is a popular variety in the *J. conferta* group that will also tolerate some shade. *J. procumbens* varieties are often selected for their finely textured, blue-green foliage. 'Sargent' (*J. chinensis*) and 'Parsons' (*J. davurica*) are also good choices for ground cover.

There are three things about junipers that I'd like to leave with you: (1) don't plan a huge area for junipers since they can become quite boring rather easily, although they are quite cost-effective; (2) always wear gloves and long sleeves when fooling with junipers (or do otherwise to find out why); and (3) be sure your juniper bed is well-drained, and do not overwater since junipers do not tolerate wet feet.

There are many more ground covers that I adore, but those mentioned are some of the most traditional, commonly used ones in Southern landscapes. The list of ground covers is extensive, however; offers interesting alternatives to the traditional choices; and includes those that are very low-growing (creeping Jenny, *Lysimachia nummularia*, for example) to those that have some height (such as ferns).

Whether a plant is called a ground cover or not depends upon your use of it. For instance, hostas, ferns, daylilies, black-eyed Susans, and pincushion flowers—all quite tall—are called ground covers by some and simply perennials by others. In fact, many plants that serve as ground covers have been honored by inclusion in the Georgia Gold Medal Award list under the perennial and vine categories: Bath's pink dianthus, Lenten rose, autumn fern, anise hyssop hybrids, Georgia blue veronica, creeping raspberry, and perennial plumbago, for example.

When selecting ground covers, decide how much of one plant will provide interest, not boredom, in a particular area and go with your personal preference for flower and leaf color. Don't confine your thinking to one plant, and break a large area into smaller plots using different ground covers, with turf grass being just one of them. By so doing, you may be able to change your paradigm—thinking of your lawn as just another ground cover that should be limited in scope and incorporated into the grand scheme of the landscape, rather than dominating it.

IT'S A MATTER OF FACT

There is some good news about kudzu: (1) You can eradicate it with goats, a fact to which I can attest since we had great success with the living exterminators at our Loganville farm, and (2) it ostensibly represses alcohol consumption; medical research is getting closer to validating the 2,000-year-old Chinese tradition of using the vine for treating the disease.

KUDZU CAN'T COMPETE WITH IVY

WHEN I WAS A TEENAGER we moved to a neighborhood newly constructed in the hills in north Atlanta, inside I-285. Our yard was vertical—front and back—with a narrow, flat spot in the middle for our house, turnaround, and side yard. After a few rains and mud-soaked basement floors, my father threatened to plant kudzu (*Pueraria lobata*) on the banks to hold the red clay in place. We thought he was joking. He wasn't.

But it didn't happen, thank goodness. His temporary lapse of patience and prudence was beaten by my mother's quick retort and resolve to plant seedling trees (which we bought from the Georgia Forestry Commission and planted with a dibble—an interesting task on the steep slope) and English ivy (*Hedera helix*)—lots of it. That ivy still climbs those trees and flows off the brick retaining walls. I think of what might have been. And now I'd like to compare the two contenders for our hillside stabilizer.

Kudzu, a native-Asian vine, was introduced to this country in 1876 at the Centennial International Exposition in Philadelphia.

We moved from Druid Hills to the Buckhead area of Atlanta in the late 1960s. In this 2002 photo, at age 84, Dad (John T. "Jack" Godwin) sits on the patio in front of Mom's Coral Bells azaleas and the steep bank of English ivy that we planted to prevent erosion (rather than the kudzu he had threatened to plant). Dad was a pathologist and investigated life, and death, at the microscopic level. He was truly a very wise man.

After a showing in the Japanese pavilion at the New Orleans Exposition (1884–86), Southerners adopted and used the "foot-a-day" plant for shade on porches and arbors. Encouraged with payments by the federal government, farmers planted and used kudzu for erosion control and, in times of drought, as fodder for cattle. Now covering millions of acres of Southern forestland, the vine is categorized as a weed—an *invasive* weed. It has enveloped trees, shrubs, automobiles, buildings, telephone poles, and anything else worth climbing—fast—covering it all, y'all. It also has encouraged research, leading to its possible use as fuel and yeast.

Although also invasive, English ivy isn't as threatening as kudzu. Contrary to popular belief, it is not parasitic and doesn't choke and strangle healthy trees and shrubs. Like kudzu, however, it will rob a host plant of light if it becomes too thick. And it can become too weighty for weak trees, particularly when the winds pick up.

I was always told that climbing ivy damages walls. This assertion is also false—sort of. Ivy will aggravate loosened mortar and will climb through, widen, and weaken existing cracks. It will leave spots on wooden siding, invite insects into its nest, and pull at damaged structures when you tug at it. But you can prevent damage from ivy with remedial repair prior to planting and vigilance during growth.

English ivy reached its height of popularity as an ornamental plant in the late nineteenth century—the same time kudzu was introduced in this country. It has been used since time immemorial and for good reason. Its shiny, evergreen leaves lushly blanket all it intercepts. It clings gracefully and flows over obstacles like oozing mud. It enjoys deep shade as well as sunshine, and tolerates drought and pollution. Ivy grows rapidly and is extremely hardy. Although a good choice for ground cover in large, shady areas where you can control its growth, be aware that you *must* continue to keep control of its invasive nature and tree-climbing habit. Other ground covers may prove as effective with less maintenance and potentially harmful effect, so consider them first.

If you park for too long in these parts, kudzu is liable to take over, as it did in 2007 to a neighbor's bulldozer.

LESSON 46 ꩜ July 30–August 5
Crapemyrtles

Gardening, in whatever form practiced, provides positive emotional and spiritual experiences that are available nowhere else. For most of us, lack of time is the greatest frustration. We go to work in the dark, and return in same. Perhaps the garden offers the mini-sanctuary where we can reflect on the craziness that, at times, appears to control our lives. A garden is indeed the forum for creativity, reflection, repose, and spirituality.

—Michael A. Dirr
Manual of Woody Landscape Plants: Their Identification, Ornamental Characteristics, Culture, Propagation and Uses

Crapemyrtles Strut Their Stuff Year-round

THERE ARE A FEW THINGS TRULY SOUTHERN—iced tea, magnolia trees, fatback cooking, and crapemyrtles (*Lagerstroemia indica*). In the Old South towns, towering specimens of the watermelon-red flowering crapemyrtle tree speak of the Victorian era of the houses they grace. In newly constructed city corridors and suburban neighborhoods, a variety of colors and sizes of this flowering showpiece shocks the summer-green landscape.

The old farmhouse seedling varieties of crapemyrtle are of tree proportions, sporting spots of flowers high above comfortable eyesight. But today there are many cultivars of smaller proportions, some looking like large bushes and some only reaching 18 inches in height, making excellent patio container plants. Some crapemyrtles have single trunks, others are multistemmed. Some have huge panicles of flowers, while others have a more demure design. Some varieties have so many flowers that they gracefully weep over with the weight, creating wide masses of color, while others maintain their vase shape throughout the flowering season.

Common traits among the newer cultivars are improved mildew and disease resistance, as well as cold hardiness. Flower sizes are larger and colors are often more intense than in the older varieties, with a broadened palette of color and hue selection. Spring and summer leaf color is more varied with the new cultivars, and the fall colors have evolved into a spectacle. Cultivar improvements also include enhanced and varied bark colors as well as mottled and exfoliating bark variations. Most exfoliation occurs on older plants, and some leaf and bark coloration settles in with age. But regardless of age, crapemyrtles shine from spring leaf-out through summer flowering, fall coloring, and into their winter bark displays.

There's not much to the cultivation of crapemyrtles. They like to be planted in full sun for the best growth and flower production, and they prefer moist, well-drained soil. You should fertilize established crapemyrtles in the spring (and again in summer if needed) with a general-purpose fertilizer (8-8-8, 10-10-10, 12-4-8, or 16-4-8). Fertilize newly planted crapes once a month or so from March to August, unless you use a slow-release fertilizer that lasts longer than quick-release varieties.

Although they are drought tolerant, crapemyrtles fare better if you water them when they are wilting or the flowers are declining. By cutting spent blossoms, you can prolong their flowering (a September pick will yield more flowers as fall progresses). You can remove the winter seed capsules, or not—it's a matter of taste.

On the subject of cutting: the proper pruning of a crapemyrtle is one of the most perplexing problems and controversial issues in plant maintenance. There are many schools of thought, but there are some certainties to help guide the process. The first is when to prune. If you do so in late summer through early winter you run the risk of reducing the cold hardiness of the plant, leaving it susceptible to winter damage. Pruning is best done in late January through early March—when the plant is dormant and before new spring wood grows, on which the flowers are produced. Another certainty involves the how to prune. If you prune crapemyrtles to the same point each year or trim stems and trunks that are much larger in diameter than a pencil to tame their height, you will produce trunks with calloused tips that look like mini-Sputniks—for sure—and the heavy summer flowers will nod and bob about on floppy stems shooting from the stumpy knobs. You will, in fact, be guilty of crape murder. And here the certainties end.

A properly pruned crapemyrtle does not have knobs on the trunks. Interior, crossing branches and suckers are removed each year. And in the case of this one, the seed capsules and a very short amount of the end growth was cut back. Although pruning the branch ends is not necessary, it does promote more abundant flowering.

Some people think crapemyrtles should not be pruned at all, but this approach results in unhealthy, unsightly, and far less vigorous plants. Others like to whack back their crapemyrtles to within 2–3 feet of the ground each year, but this approach prevents the plants from ever reaching their mature heights and beauty and results in ugly trunks—crape murder once again. Many like to do minor pruning, removing the dried fruits they find offensive. (Again, it's a matter of taste; I like to cut just a few for dried arrangements in the house.) And some people choose to hack at the smaller, brittle branches on occasion, considering them a maintenance problem, although it's a slight problem, at best.

But actually, crapemyrtles should be treated like other trees and shrubs and be given an annual maintenance pruning in January through early March, only if needed. First, remove all the suckers, crossing branches, and branches pointing toward the center of the tree, keeping in mind that you want to allow light into the center of the plant for maximum flower production. Then, selectively prune the top—or not—to the desired shape, trying to leave a minimum of 6–8 inches of the most recent growth and trying not to cut any stems that are more than about the diameter of a pencil. Note that the pruning point then changes each year as the plant grows to maturity. Be sure that you're not trying to keep your crapemyrtle at a height unnatural to its habit. For example, don't try to keep a tree-type variety that normally grows to 20–30 feet at 6–8 feet. If you do—or must—then you have selected a variety that's inappropriate to its spot in your landscape or to your tastes.

By carefully pruning your crapemyrtle each year in this manner, you will enjoy massive flower bloom in the summer and gorgeous trunk exposure in the winter. You will enhance the natural beauty of this Southern fixture that struts its stuff year-round.

CRAPEMYRTLE CULTIVAR CHOICES

THE LIST OF CRAPEMYRTLE CULTIVARS is quite extensive and is growing each year as horticulturists experiment with new crosses to produce better plants in terms of disease resistance, cold hardiness, variation of bloom color and time, and leaf and bark attributes. I've selected a few that are popular.

'Acoma': Low spreading, semi-dwarf (10–15 feet), multistemmed with pure white panicles with golden anthers. Blooms late June to September. Light gray bark, red-purple fall color.

'Basham's Party Pink': Large (up to 20 feet), rapid growing with soft lavender-pink blooms first appearing in late June. Orange-red fall color, good exfoliating bark.

'Biloxi': Tall (23–33 feet) upright, multistemmed tree-type. Pale pink panicles blooming from July to late September. Orange-red to dark red in fall. Dark brown bark, exfoliating on older branches.

'Carolina Beauty': Dark red, intense flowerer blooming in mid-July and later. Upright to 20 feet or more. Handsome gray-brown bark, poor mildew resistance.

'Catawba': Compact inflorescences of dark purple florets late July to September. Relatively short (10–11 feet). Excellent reddish fall color, somewhat slow growing.

'**Choctaw**': Large, multistemmed, vase-shaped form. Clear, bright pink flowers, maroon fall color, and fabulous, dark brown trunk. Highly mildew resistant.

'**Dallas Red**': Nice deep-red flowerer. Fast grower (up to 20 feet).

'**Hardy Lavender**': Upright that reaches 20 feet with medium lavender flowers starting in late July and lasting until frost. Red fall color.

'**Lipan**': Broad upright to about 13 feet. Medium lavender blooms from mid-July to mid-September. Light orange to dull red fall color. Mottled near-white to beige bark.

'**Miami**': Upright, multistemmed to 16 feet tall and 8 feet wide. Dark pink flowers early July to September. Orange in fall. Handsome mottled, dark chestnut-brown bark, exfoliating as it matures.

'**Muskogee**': Fast growing, 21-foot high by 15-foot wide. Light lavender-pink flowers, in 4- to 10-inch-long panicles. July to September bloom time. Light gray to tan bark. Good red color in fall.

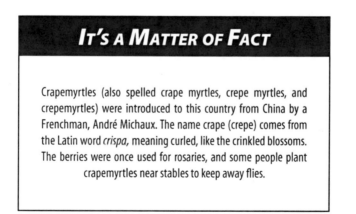

IT'S A MATTER OF FACT

Crapemyrtles (also spelled crape myrtles, crepe myrtles, and crepemyrtles) were introduced to this country from China by a Frenchman, André Michaux. The name crape (crepe) comes from the Latin word *crispa*, meaning curled, like the crinkled blossoms. The berries were once used for rosaries, and some people plant crapemyrtles near stables to keep away flies.

'**Natchez**': Large tree up to 21 feet high and wide. Gorgeous dark cinnamon-brown mottled, exfoliating bark throughout the year. Pure-white flowers late June/July into September. Orange and red fall color.

'**Potomac**': Upright, medium height (10 feet) with clear medium pink flowers mid-July to October. Not particularly mildew resistant or cold hardy.

'Sarah's Favorite': Large shrub (up to 20 feet) that's good for tight spaces since it's narrower than other crapes. White flowers, cinnamon-brown bark, and spectacular fall color. Cold-hardy variety.

'Sioux': Upright, multistemmed up to 14 feet tall by 12 feet wide. Intense dark pink flowers from late July to mid-September. Light, medium gray-brown exfoliating bark. Super dark green summer foliage turning to bright red in fall.

'Tonto': Semi-dwarf, multistemmed shrub (10 feet by 8 feet). Fuchsia-red flowers July through September. Bright maroon in fall.

'Tuscarora': Large, 15-foot-high and -wide tree. Superior dark coral-pink flowers in panicles up to 12 inches long and 8 inches wide. Blooms early July through late September. Fabulous mottled, light brown bark. Late frost damage possible.

'Victor': Dwarf compact that reaches 3–5 feet. Dark red flowers July through August. Reddish yellow fall color. Good mildew resistance.

'William Toovey': Often called watermelon red. Vase-shaped up to 15 feet with pink-red flowers, blooming July through August. Red-orange fall color. Good mildew resistance.

'World's Fair': Dwarf variety with watermelon red flowers.

'Yuma': Upright, multistemmed 13-foot-high by 12-foot-wide form. Long, tapered panicles with finely clustered flower heads of bicolored medium lavender. Blooms late July to late September. Light fall colors, light gray exfoliating bark.

Dixie Series: 2- to 3-foot high "ground cover" miniature, weeping forms that flower mid-May to October. **'BatonRouge'**: deep red; **'Bourbon Street'**: watermelon red; **'Delta Blush'**: pink; **'New Orleans'**: purple. May die back to the ground in the winter but will come back from the roots.

The Razzle Dazzle® Crapemyrtle Series: Dwarf (2- to 5-foot high) varieties that bloom from summer into fall. **Cherry Dazzle®**: brilliant red with red fall foliage; **Dazzle® Me Pink**: profuse pink blooms; **Raspberry Dazzle®**: upright with wavy dark green foliage that has brilliant fall color; **Ruby Dazzle®**: bronze red foliage and pink flowers; **Snow Dazzle®**: white flowers, mounding habit.

LESSON 47 ∽ August 6–12
Vines

As one moves about the flower beds, weeding, propagating, pruning the
apple tree, shifting the rock in the rock garden an inch or two to make room
for the roots of a healthy erica, one becomes a subtle and powerful
force of natural selection in that place, placing one's stamp on the future of
the biosphere . . . .

—Frederick Turner (b. 1943)
"Cultivating the American Garden" from *Rebirth of Value:*
Meditations on Beauty, Ecology, Religion, and Education

Vines Define a Garden

IF I HAD TO PICK ONE KIND OF PLANT that firmly justifies to me the use of the term *garden*—as opposed to *yard*—to describe a cultivated area, it would be vines, growing vertically in some fashion. They frame, embrace, invite, and soften. They shade, conceal, and camouflage. They create entrances, pathways, canopies, and defined spaces. They direct attention upward while anchored downward, connecting heaven and Earth. They pull it all together.

There are all kinds of vines: annual and perennial, woody and herbaceous, evergreen and deciduous, fancied for flowers and fancied for foliage. Many make great ground covers, and others create cascades in hanging baskets, over walls, and in containers. But all climb, if given the support they need, and the possibilities for support are endless.

There's one basic precept for vines: they like shady feet and sunny heads. Generally, this requirement is not a problem since their very structure allows for this cultivation, especially when they grow vertically rather than horizontally or draped. Vines require relatively little room for their base, about 1–2 square feet.

In contrast, their rapid growth extends the plant to great heights and breadths. In fact, the very nature of vines is to grow in order to reach the light, so the foliage from the growth fills out to reach the sun while shading the ground beneath. In some instances, the stems themselves remain bare near the bottom of the viny structure where sunlight fails to penetrate.

Select one of the many vines just as you do any other landscape plant. Do you like it? Does its color at various times of the year blend with the rest of your plants and architecture? Does it carry a scent that pleases you? Can it be combined with other climbers to nice effect? How easy or difficult is it to maintain? Is it hardy at your site? Is it a perennial or an annual? Is it evergreen or will it lose its leaves in winter? Will it work for the purpose you intend—providing shade, creating an entranceway, adding vertical dimension, etc.? Does it attract birds and butterflies? Will it be appropriately supported by your choice of walls, frames, arbors, rocks, fences, sculpture, or other garden structures?

The two most *basic* questions you need to ask are whether the vine you think you want is perennial or annual—will it keep coming back year after year or not—and is it evergreen or deciduous—will it have leaves year-round or not? As a general rule, evergreen perennial vines are going to give you good, solid green foliage without much in the way of striking flowers. But you'll delight in the visual effect all year. On the other hand, the more floriferous vines tend to be deciduous perennials or annuals that lend little visual appeal to the landscape in the winter, although they do act as protective havens for many birds.

Climbing roses are good examples of the floriferous, deciduous vines. I planted a *Rosa banksiae*

IT'S A MATTER OF FACT

Vines attach themselves to things in one of four ways: they grab with tendrils that remain straight until finding something to wrap around; they cling with discs, hook-like claws, or small roots; they lean and anchor themselves by resting on adjacent supports or by using thorns for stabilization; or they twine, twisting new growth around a support. Some vines twine only in a clockwise manner, others only in a counterclockwise direction.

'Lutea' (yellow Lady Banks' rose) next to a chain-link fence in our backyard many years ago. It grew extremely rapidly, climbing up the 6-foot fence and then some, and spreading out on either side. Its long stems continued reaching upward, so a string support running to the top of the second floor roof gave the plant new heights, framing the end of an open-air porch. Back down at the ground, the vine grew more than enough so we could shape it on one side of the fence to create a natural arch under which we placed a bench in its shade. The chain-link fence became so inundated with the vine that it was hidden from view, even in the winter. The profuse dainty flowers in early spring brightened everyone's spirits. And the birds nested in the tangled web, giving us constant delight from our breakfast room window. Now that's a multipurpose vine!

My Lady Banks' grew on a fence for good reason: we didn't want to let it grow on the side of our house because moisture buildup behind vines may eventually cause damage to structures and will stain them. You should place a trellis next to your house, garage, or building and train the vines to grab hold of it rather than the walls.

Not all vines can do what my Lady Banks' did. But you can use them for any number of purposes and designs, including espaliers, topiaries, or standards (a single trunk limbed up). Add them to your plant list and try some. Give your yard the mark of a garden.

Picking Perennial Vines

IF YOU WOULD LIKE TO DEFINE your garden with vines, start with perennial ones—deciduous or evergreen—that will come back year after year. There are many choices:

Clematis: There are lots of varieties, ranging from 8 to 30 feet, with flowering times ranging from late winter to autumn. Flowers vary from large and showy to small and dainty in pink, blue, purple, white, red, or multicolor; fragrance rises from the smaller flowered varieties. Clematis climbs on supports using leaf stems. Because there are four possible scenarios for how and when to prune clematis, you will need to find out what is right for the variety you have.

Wisteria: The most popular are the Japanese varieties (*Wisteria floribunda*), blooming purple, pink, or white in spring and early summer with huge racemes (groups of flowers) and marvelous fragrance. For more blooms, pinch back side shoots and prune after flowering and again in winter. Do not fertilize if there are no blooms since there may be too much nitrogen encouraging leaf growth rather than flowering. Root pruning may renew older vines. Wisteria needs strong support and protection from heavy winds, and it's best grown away from houses and any other plants or structures since it is invasive and becomes impossible to control. But, as has become the norm in horticulture it seems, there is an improved cultivar that solves the problem: *W. frutescens* 'Amethyst Falls', which is less aggressive and easier to manage. This 2006 Georgia Gold Medal winner blooms at an early age, blooms a bit later in the spring (avoiding a late bloom-killing frost), and will rebloom in the summer if you trim the spring flowers after they are spent.

Climbing Roses: There are hundreds and hundreds of varieties, of which old-fashioned, own-root roses are the easiest to grow and maintain and carry wonderful scents. Climbing roses are useful in all sunny locations.

Fiveleaf Akebia: With its interesting, small rounded leaves, this foliage vine is semievergreen in our area. It twines in counterclockwise fashion and has small fragrant flowers in early spring. Growing in sun or shade, akebia is extremely vigorous with a lush feel.

Other Perennials: To just name a few, there's Dutchman's pipe; wintercreeper; Virginia creeper; climbing hydrangea; Carolina jessamine; Confederate jasmine; trumpet vine; and bittersweet, which needs male and female plants to produce yellow and orange berries in fall for brilliant dried arrangements and is noted for overrunning an area easily.

LESSON 48 ⌇ August 13–19
Trees

He that plants trees loves others besides himself.

—Thomas Fuller (1654–1734)
Gnomologia: Adagies and Proverbs

A Future with Trees Requires Plan(t)ing

I GREW UP UNDER OAK TREES—tall, straight pillars wrapped in thick bark, shrouded in luxuriant leaves, and exuding a sense of stability and endurance. My oaks were too big to climb, the branches reaching upward from high above the ground. But the trunks, where they flared into feet to meet the ground, provided surprising pockets for play toys and imaginary games.

I loved those oaks in the summer when they shaded our yard and house; I anxiously anticipated arriving home where it was dramatically cooler than much of the surrounding urban scape. I also loved the oaks in the fall when they dropped their legion of leaves and acorns; there were so many leaves to mound and so many acorns that fell through to the ground that we always had the makings of forts and battles, and places to hide. The oaks were supremely sublime in the winter, casting their nakedness against the sky, reminding me of the rhyme and rhythm of nature as the warm sun allowed passage to the cool earth. And the spring oaks were equally evocative—a canopy of new green progressively brightening the landscape while masking the oncoming heat . . . that the summer oaks cooled.

I was privileged to grow up in an Atlanta neighborhood called Druid Hills, which Frederick Law Olmsted, the father of American landscape architecture, had a hand in designing. For an urban community with sidewalks, stop signs, a few stoplights, and electric trolleybuses (replaced during my tenure there with noisy, stinking, diesel buses), it was quite pristine with all of its tall hardwood trees and lushly landscaped yards. Druid Hills was possible because of the vision of Olmsted and his progeny—the incorporation of the natural landscape with the man-made. It was the result of a reverence for trees and an absolute understanding of their importance to man and his psyche.

The oaks of my childhood were white oaks. This most august of species is still a part of my life, creating much of the woods on our farm. But the fields in our nursery are filled with many other kinds of oaks. Their characteristics differ, as do their most desirable uses, but all are enduring trees—trees that tie generations to generations, the past to the present, to the future—their hardwood supreme evidence of their patient, solid growth.

There are many choices of oaks for use as shade trees or ornamental specimens in your landscape, and I mention here just a few.

White Oak (*Quercus alba*): This is, without a doubt, the stateliest, grandest of the oaks. It slowly grows to 50–80 feet or more in height (over 100 feet in the wild) with an upright-rounded to broad-rounded head and wide-spreading branches out to 50–80 feet. Bark on the old trunks is scaly, light ashy-gray. The leaves are large with rounded lobes, and the acorns are large. This is a regal specimen for a large area.

Nuttall Oak (*Quercus nuttallii*): Nuttall is another medium-large oak, growing relatively rapidly to 60 feet. It's very similar to pin oak and shumard oak in that it tolerates wet soils, but it's more adaptable to adverse conditions. The leaves are deeply lobed with pointed tips; new foliage has a rich reddish purple color that continues to tint the summer tree, and the fall leaves are reddish. The canopy develops more fully at an earlier age than many of the other oaks.

Chestnut Oak (*Quercus prinus*): This is a medium/large-sized oak that grows up to 60–70 feet with a comparable, irregular spread, which is rounded and relatively dense. The leaves are broad with 10–14 pairs of smooth teeth, and they all fall in the autumn. The bark is brown to almost black on older trees. Chestnut oak does well in dry, rocky soil but it will maximize growth in moist, well-drained soils. As an added attraction, its large, sweet acorns entice wildlife.

Water Oak (*Quercus nigra*): Also called possum oak, this conical to round-topped tree reaches 50–80 feet. It has long, narrow leaves that are three-lobed at the top, although multilobed in youth. The leaves vary in size and shape and persist into late fall and winter. As the name suggests, water oak tolerates wet soils, and it makes a good shade or street tree.

IT'S A MATTER OF FACT

In the past, the Japanese adored the fall foliage so they built paths on stilts among the trees; they got up close and personal with the changing leaves. The Italians carefully pruned their trees and interwove the branches, creating a sphere of space within the boughs where they could put a chair and sit. What inventive, and respectful, alternatives to nailed-into-place tree houses these creations were.

Willow Oak (*Quercus phellos*): A relatively small oak, this 40- to 60-foot-tall, 30- to 40-foot-wide tree (which can grow larger in ideal conditions) is pyramidal in youth, growing to dense oblong-oval to rounded in maturity. The leaves are long, narrow, and wavy, but not lobed. The tree has a medium growth rate and prefers moist, well-drained soils but can adapt to most conditions. It provides texture in the landscape, especially along avenues and in large-area uses. In contrast to other oaks, its small leaves, which all fall in the autumn, and small acorns make this oak the cleanest and most desirable for low-maintenance landscape requirements.

Pin Oak (*Quercus palustris*): Also called swamp oak, this is a fast-growing tree that tolerates wet soils. It has very horizontal branching, lending interest to the winter landscape. Some of its leaves hold through the winter, requiring more cleanup time. Pin oak usually has decent red fall color.

Scarlet Oak (*Quercus coccinea*): This oak is similar to pin oak, but the leaves do not develop the chlorotic, off-colored look so often found on the pins. The pointed-tipped, lobed leaves turn from a glossy dark summer green to a fall scarlet late in the season.

Chinese Evergreen Oak (*Quercus myrsinifolia*): This oak does not lose its leaves in the fall but remains green year-round. It's cold hardy in zones 7–9 and is the most cold hardy of the evergreen oaks. (The live oak of coastal plantation, draped-in-moss fame is usually, though marginally cold hardy in Zone 7 but has a much slower growth than those found further south.) Chinese evergreen oak grows 20–30 feet with a slightly smaller or similar-sized spread. The leaves have serrated edges while the bark is smooth and gray. It is extremely tolerant of virtually all soils and heat and will grow in full sun or partial shade.

Hightower Willow Oak (*Quercus phellos* 'QPSTA' P.P. #13677 Hightower® Willow Oak): Despite the nightmarish nomenclature (which I have included in full here just for demonstration purposes—see Lesson 11), this new, patented willow oak is touted as a "grower's dream tree and landscape architect's easiest specification" by Michael Dirr, who selected the cultivar from a field of seedlings. It is the first clonally produced willow oak, being vegetatively propagated by Tree Introductions, Inc. The leaves are lustrous green and all drop in the fall. It is predicted to grow 55 feet high and 35 feet wide with a central leader (trunk), uniform distribution of branches, and upswept branching habit. Because of the propagation method, the trees will be consistent, uniform, and predictable.

Highbeam Overcup Oak (*Quercus lyrata* 'QLFTB' P.P. #13470 Highbeam® Overcup Oak): Another clonal oak, this one is unique for its lustrous leathery dark green leaves that change to yellow and bronze-red in the fall. The bark exfoliates similar to that of a white oak. It is fast growing (up to 50 feet with a 40-foot spread) and has upswept branches.

I'm eternally grateful to Olmsted and others who had the foresight and willingness to leave trees in the face of "progress" and to plant them for the future. Those old trees had an immense influence on my life. As a child, I played among them constantly and basked in their greenery. Through my open window in our air-conditionless house, I breathed in their moisture while napping in my room. I listened to their leaves, tickled by the wind, and anticipated and savored their shade and coolness in the hot summer months. I fell in love with them, and still am.

I cannot live without trees—and neither can you. So plan(t) for the future. Plant trees, especially hardwoods, which will last for lifetimes to come. You will be creating a bridge to the future, and, with your patience, you'll breed solidity, longevity, and endurance—especially with oaks.

A postscript: Several years ago I read a book about sudden oak death found on the West Coast. Learning of the massive mortality caused by the fungus *Phytophthora ramorum,* it deeply disturbed me, although I was a bit relieved to learn that it was not yet found on the East coast. But, as has been the case for all of history, man has a way

Tree of Four Seasons

of transporting diseases, in this case via ornamental plants grown in nurseries in California and Oregon and sold to nurseries in the East. And now, the pathogen has been identified in a few nurseries and retail garden centers in Georgia on host plants, and I have heard of one siting in the wild along a creek bed, near one of the nurseries. Although researchers do not yet know the exact course this problem will take, they do know that the danger is real to our oaks as well as other thin-barked trees like beech, elm, and maple. It is imperative that research continues looking for ways to combat this potentially deadly scourge to our forests and their ecosystems, but those with the funding don't yet seem to feel an immediate need. So, just as the American chestnuts disappeared a century ago, so might our oaks, as well as other susceptible trees. Although John and I have witnessed many of the oaks in our woods die within the past year and feared the worst, we have been told by our Extension agent that it is not sudden oak death but rather decline most likely due to drought stress. But my anxiety remains.

Rings Around a Tree

Everyone seems to know that you can tell the age of a tree by counting its rings. But do you know how those rings were formed?

A tree trunk, from inside to out, has four essential layers: xylem, cambium, phloem, and bark. The cambium layer is extremely thin and is the only part of the tree that actually grows. As the cambium cells divide, the new cells become the interior xylem and the old cells become the exterior phloem. The diameter of the tree enlarges.

Cambium that grows in spring produces larger cells than those produced in summer, which also look darker because they are more compact. The alternation of the lighter spring growth with the darker summer growth creates the rings on the tree. So counting all of the dark rings or all of the light rings will reveal how many years a tree has been alive.

If a tree is stressed, the width of the growth rings is affected, and more wood develops where needed to remedy the stress. So, for instance, a young tree that is bent over will grow thicker on the underside, which provides protection from further bending and eventually, with more expansion, pushes the tree back in the other direction toward righting itself. Asymmetrical growth rings tell you if a straight tree was ever leaning and in what direction; the thicker rings are on the side to which the tree leaned.

Since it does not actually grow, the interior xylem is sometimes said to be dead. Nevertheless, it pipes water to the leaves and adjacent cells, stores food, and forms support for the tree. The younger xylem is called sapwood. When the older, most interior xylem ages and becomes clogged with gum and other substances, it becomes darkened heartwood and ceases to conduct water and food (perhaps similar to clogged arteries in humans).

Phloem, on the outside of the growing cambium layer, carries food in sieve tubes up and down the tree for the first few years after it is formed. But water and food from the inside of the tree are eventually cut off, and the phloem begins to die, building up the protective outer bark of the tree.

LESSON 49 ⚭ August 20–26
Practical and Inspirational Touches

The trail is the thing, not the end of the trail. Travel too fast and you miss all
you are traveling for.

—Louis L'Amour (1908–1988)
Ride the Dark Trail

Walkways Work Where You Have Gone

WHEN IN LAW SCHOOL, I wrote a paper about the development of roads and bridges in the Massachusetts Bay Colony in the 1600s. One of my most poignant statements was the fact that the shortest distance between two points is a straight line; I got an A anyway. One of my conclusions was that the roads and bridges developed where they did for one of two reasons: they followed trails already set down by predecessors (usually Native Americans), or they were new routes designed to get the traveler from one point to another in the least distance—given the natural barriers and lay of the land. I also mentioned a few other factors, like politics and avoidance of enemy territories—but I'll just go with the first two for this discussion.

Like roads and bridges, one usually develops walkways and paths in the yard or garden for the simple, utilitarian purpose of getting from here to there—from the backdoor to the swing set, for instance. You may have additional purposes in mind, however. Perhaps you want to provide a means of movement through your garden, or a detour from one spot in your yard to another. Maybe you want to go a step further and lure the traveler to special features or vistas in the garden, drawing the eye and the traveler to points around the bend. Or maybe you're more interested in defining separate areas or themes of the garden or in ornamenting and complementing the garden design and structures.

Hopefully your paths and walkways will serve all of these purposes, as well as provide additional benefits such as preventing soil compaction around plants by keeping people, wheelbarrows, and other heavy objects off the surrounding dirt; creating an area for foot traffic that's easy to maintain; and creating a cleaner avenue for your outdoor rompings.

Some of the best paths are not planned but are developed through use—dogs, kids, and adults alike keep on taking the most direct route, wearing a road into existence. Designing your garden around these highways is often the best plan. But you may have to change routes and create natural barriers to the old ones if they're bothersome to your design ideas.

If you're starting from scratch and designing your entire landscape, you can incorporate paths, getting the best of their utility and design qualities all at once. But do you really know yet where those dogs and kids are going to go? On the other hand, if you let your garden evolve as you have the time, money, and inclination to develop it, your paths will probably evolve with it, and you will achieve the most natural incorporation of paths and plants.

Either way, the design elements of walkways should complement plantings and coordinate with the architecture they seek to connect. When deciding which type of material to use, consider the house and shed, old stone walls, new blacktop driveway, old brick barbeque pit, themes in the garden, existing plants, and plants dreamed of. For instance, a woodland setting may call for a path covered in pine bark mulch, whereas a formal entry by an Italianate home from the driveway to the back patio may require cut sandstone blocks placed closely together. You may need a simple grass path through the back corner of your yard where large flowering bushes grow, or you may need granite stepping stones through a large perennial bed. With so many possibilities, you can really get your creative juices going on this one.

When deciding on style and materials, think about the following pointers:

- Try to create a balance between unity and variety, both with the walkway itself and between the walkway and the surrounding landscape.

- Use designs and materials that complement the theme(s) of the garden as well as its colors and textures, year-round. Choices include grass, wood, sand, gravel, tile, glass, pebbles, stones, rocks, bricks, and so forth.
- Make the length of the path suit its purpose—nothing more, nothing less.
- Use straight walkways to evoke formality, and curving, meandering ones for informality.
- Use paths that have breaks in the hard material, like those made with stepping stones, for a slower pace, encouraging more time in the garden, more pleasures to behold.
- Broaden a path at some point, opening it up, inviting a pause in one's travels—a time to stop, turn in another direction, take in another vista.
- Make the walkway wide enough to accommodate travelers and growing plants that will eventually invade its path. The more informal the path, the more tolerance allowed for brushing against plants. The more functional, as in getting from the driveway to the house without getting ones clothes and feet wet or dirty, the less tolerant.
- Consider all the seasons in the yard when designing.
- Consider the presence of sun and shade on the pathway. Algae grows on some surfaces in shaded areas, making

IT'S A MATTER OF FACT

Different stones have different working qualities. Igneous rock, like granite, is very strong, hard, and difficult to cut, leading to a natural look. Sandstone and limestone, sedimentary rocks, are very workable and often used for uniform cutting and design. Other sedimentary rocks that are formed in flat planes like bluestone split easily horizontally but not vertically, making them stacking candidates. And metamorphic rocks like slate and gneiss have major cleavages where they will naturally break, making them easy yet delicate to work with. Granite from Stone Mountain and Elberton, Georgia, was often used for walkways in the early to mid-1900s.

safety and cleanliness a concern. And sun heats up some surfaces so much that they are undesirable.

- Consider using neutral colors, such as tans (not whites) and grays (not glossy blacks), in most instances in order to reduce glare problems.
- Make steps as necessary, keeping those in high traffic areas a height and depth that's an easy and natural climb for most people.
- If compatible with the design, use curved corners rather than right angles, to discourage cutting corners and to help in sweeping and other maintenance.
- Use container plantings, benches, or other garden ornamentation on sharp corners to discourage cutting them and to soften the angle.
- Use lighter colored surfaces and walkway lighting where necessary for evening journeys.
- Use nonslip surfaces where warranted, especially in high traffic areas.
- Try to mimic nature for additional charm. For instance, make the path through an alpine garden look like a mountain streambed by using crushed slate or gravel.
- Use a stepping-stone-like walkway to pocket small plants that might otherwise become lost in larger beds.
- Use paths and spots of repose as places for brushing against fragrant flowers, releasing their aromas.
- Use old, weathered materials that have patina to best achieve the look that the walkway has always been there, is part of the landscape, and is not a separate element in it.
- Have a beginning and ending point. Use gateways, arbors, benches, sculptures, water features, and openings to a landscape below. Give the traveler a destination, a reason for walking the entire path.

Years ago, I laid a brick, basket weave entryway at our Cape Cod–style house in Massachusetts. It was a lot of hard, tiring work, and the result was less than perfect, but it added so much to that landscape, while giving us the enlarged surface we needed for greeting guests, walking to and from the gate to our driveway and mailbox, and shoveling snow in the winter. I used old bricks, so it didn't take long for some moss to grow in some of the cracks, adding to the charm. It was a natural addition to our landscape just as all walkways should be, with a practical purpose and an ornamental aim. It worked.

COMPLETING THE PICTURE WITH GARDEN ART

Gazing ball in nursery.

GARDEN ART IS THE FINAL touch in a landscape—the element that expands the spirit of the garden and enhances the mood you have created. The components of garden art are limitless. They can be bronze, marble, concrete, or terra-cotta statues; bird baths and houses; benches and stoops; gates and fences; tables and chairs; pavilions and gazebos; gazing balls and pottery; tree stumps and boulders; wire figurines and metal chimes; sundials and tiles. Garden art may double as hardscaping, plant containers, walkways, or wildlife habitat. It doesn't matter what you call it, just how you use it.

Some of your garden art may have no deep significance to you. Most of the mass-produced knickknacks found in garden centers and gift shops fall into this profane realm. If, on the other hand, the art you have chosen has special significance or importance to you because it was a gift from a special friend, a souvenir from a special place, or a memento from a special time—it is sacred. Whether sacred or profane, if you find, buy, are given, or create something that you know in your heart belongs in your garden to ornament and enlarge its statement and purpose, whether serious or whimsical, then it's garden art.

Just as your garden design and choice of plants will change as you and your garden mature, your garden art will change. It will reveal your evolution, keeping your soul alive and vocal. So ornament your sanctuary with whatever floats your boat that you keep rowing, hopefully, gently down the stream.

LESSON 50 ᦟ August 27–September 2
Japanese Maples and Gardens

Actually, the garden's intricate and deep structure is really just a shell. For in the end, the garden speaks for itself. The length of shadows in winter, the seed pods that carpet the ground in spring, and the direction and sound of the wind are some of the many things the gardener can't control. He doesn't try to. They are as much a part of the design of his garden as the rock or lantern. By giving nature its freedom, the gardener opens himself to the new relationships that nature will suggest.

—Kiyoshi Seike and Masanobu Kudo
A Japanese Touch for Your Garden

Japanese Maples Are Elegance at Its Best

THERE WAS ONE JAPANESE MAPLE in my childhood yard. It wept over a slight embankment next to the driveway. The leaves were red and floated on the shaded breeze. It was elegant, like all of the other Japanese maples I have seen.

Japanese maple (here meaning the *Acer palmatum* group and the *Acer palmatum dissectum* group) is a general term for an enrapturing variety of trees used to ornament landscapes. There are tall ones and short ones; green, red, and variegated ones; shrub-like, weeping, spreading, and upright ones. Large, upright Japanese maples (15–30 feet tall at maturity) can be used as stand-alone specimens, shade trees, accent plants, outline plantings along walkways and driveways, or companions to other similarly sized trees. Medium-sized ones have similar uses and make exceptional additions to plantings of similarly cultivated rhododendrons and other flowering shrubs. Small Japanese maples can fit in tight spaces or accent a bed of shrubs. And dwarf ones add texture to low-growing plantings of shrubs and perennials or to rock gardens.

Some of the loveliest Japanese maples, known as *dissectum*, have thread-like leaves. Also known as cutleaf or laceleaf Japanese maples, virtually all of these trees are of the weeping or spreading habit, many with lovely contorted and twisted branching patterns. Members of the *dissectum* group do not become large as do many of the upright varieties—15 feet being about the tallest. They are more delicate in appearance and growth, are slower growing, and have a refined, graceful beauty that surpasses the nondissected varieties.

In addition to the form and size of the tree, when choosing a Japanese maple for the landscape, the leaf, bark, and stem colorations, which depend upon the cultivar characteristics, temperature, and the sun and shade available, are important considerations. Leaf color can be more reliable, and less dependent upon the environment, in some cultivars than others.

In general, green-leafed varieties like to be in full sun, with afternoon shade to prevent leaf scorch from the extreme heat. Red varieties prefer some shade, but maintain deeper red color if in sun for part of the day, but not during the searing afternoon. If they are planted in heavy shade, the otherwise red leaves will turn dark green in the summer months. Upright trees with variegated leaf forms need semi-shade and protection from the afternoon sun; the golden variegations need more protection than the pinks and whites. *Dissectums* with variegated leaf forms need ample shade.

Although Japanese maples readily adapt to many cultural situations, they do require slightly different care than most of the other trees we have ornamenting our landscapes. They have a fibrous root system rather than a deep taproot system, so they like conditions similar to ericaceous plants such as rhododendrons. And because of their shallowness, they are ideal container and rock garden plants.

Japanese maples like well-drained, mid-range pH soil (slightly acidic to neutral) that is somewhat sandy with some organic matter. In contrast to taproot trees, they require uniformity of watering, preferring constant amounts, rather than spurts of large amounts. They don't need large amounts of fertilizer, and they like to be pruned of dead material.

In our clay soils, it's best to plant Japanese maples in a somewhat shallow hole with the plant left slightly above ground level. Cover the roots with a mound of soil and the soil with a thick layer of mulch.

Japanese maples are naturally slow-growing, particularly in the South. In fact, the red varieties typically stop growing during the summer months here, so you can rely only upon a short spring growing season and some fall growth. If the soil is too rich or the fertilizer too much or frequent, the tree will grow too rapidly, becoming leggy. On the other hand, the less water a Japanese maple gets, the shrubbier it grows. Again, however, uniform watering is best, for if you allow your maple to dry out, it will die, and if you water it a lot at irregular intervals, its leaves will become scorched or will drop. (If that happens, a deep, thorough watering may save the tree, and new leaves may appear in the summer or early fall.) By reducing watering somewhat in late summer, you can encourage more intense fall color because of the slight stress to the tree.

The shape and health of a Japanese maple depends upon thoughtful pruning. You can, and should, remove dead twigs any time of the year since they invite insects and disease to this otherwise relatively disease- and insect-free plant. You can also do corrective and training pruning anytime, but you should do any major pruning while the tree is dormant, prior to the spring leaf-out. Cut large limbs near the base, leaving a ¼- to 1-inch stub to promote faster healing. Cuts just beyond a pair of buds on a twig or branch will produce two side shoots. At times you may see your maple go through some dieback, which may be its way of naturally pruning itself due to disease, soil chemistry, climatic conditions, or cultural practices.

There are hundreds of Japanese maple varieties, but I'll mention just a few that are typically seen and commonly available:

var. *atropurpureum* **'Bloodgood'**: This nondissected variety is the most popular cultivar, growing in an upright habit to 20 feet. It has large red leaves with dark green undersides and excellent, dependable red fall color. It also holds its summer red color well, and in spring displays bright red seeds.

'**Vandermoss Red**' (formerly 'Christy Ann'): Similar in color to 'Bloodgood', this variety has narrower leaf lobes that are more serrated, feathery, and deeply divided. Fall color is deep orange and vivid red. The upright, rounded tree spreads wider than 'Bloodgood' but does not grow quite as tall.

IT'S A MATTER OF FACT

Cultivation of Japanese maples reached its peak in Japan during the peaceful Edo era (1603–1867), when there were more than 250 cultivars. People brought the trees into their gardens, created bonsai, and held maple-viewing parties in the wild. During the 1940s war years, many Japanese maples were lost when cultivated areas were destroyed or transformed for food production. Large collections were cut for firewood.

var. *atropurpureum* 'Oshio Beni': This variety is slightly faster growing than 'Bloodgood'. It grows upright, 15–20 feet with arching branches, making it somewhat spreading in habit as is matures. The spring leaves are vibrant orange-red to red; in summer the leaves are bronze to greenish red, turning to rich scarlet in fall.

var. *atropurpureum* 'Sango Kaku': A green-leafed variety growing 20–25 feet high by 18–22 feet wide, it is also called coral bark maple because of the brilliant fall and winter stem color. The leaves emerge in spring red-tinged, becoming medium green in summer. The fall leaves are spectacular—yellow-gold with light red overtones.

var. *dissectum atropurpureum* 'Crimson Queen': A red-leafed *dissectum*, this tree reaches a mature size of 8–10 feet with a 12-foot spread of cascading branches. It holds its summer color well with little sunburn, although the leaves do become more bronze-green in the summer.

var. *dissectum atropurpureum* 'Garnet': This tree is another red-leafed *dissectum* that holds its garnet color well, particularly in sun. It does develop a greenish cast when in shade. This tree grows vigorously up to about 10 feet.

var. *dissectum* 'Seiryu': This is one of the only, if not the only, upright Japanese maples with dissected leaves. Generally, it grows 10–15 feet by 8–10 feet wide, although my two monstrous ones are wider than tall, with a vase-shaped habit and rich green leaves, which turn brilliant gold, orange, and orange-red in fall.

'Atropurpureum': This is the term used to denote the red characteristic of a Japanese maple, whether *dissectum* or not. A noncultivar Japanese maple with red leaves is simply *Acer palmatum* var. *atropurpureum* or var. *dissectum atropurpureum*, and cultivar names of these varieties are attached to the end of this nomenclature, as we've seen above.

'Viridis': This name is used to refer to any green form of *dissectum*.

We enjoy this Japanese lantern in our backyard. It sits among
several different Japanese maple cultivars.

The slow, determined growth of a Japanese maple creates its elegance. Its maturity may take time, but the observer needs no patience to enjoy its perennial grace. Japanese maples exude the beauty of waiting, the beauty of development, the beauty of the journey.

THE GIST OF JAPANESE GARDENS

A JAPANESE GARDEN IS THE LANDSCAPE, or a part thereof, in miniature. It is planned, just like a Western garden. But its patterns and rhythms attempt to represent and symbolize those in the larger landscape of the world beyond its borders, and disguise the hands of man in the design. Balance and proportion are sought, yet asymmetrical placement of plants and features and odd-numbered groupings suggest the incompleteness and ruggedness of nature. Predominant and permanent browns, grays, and greens are contrasted with the periodic spotted color of fruits, flowers, and leaves, suggesting the cycles of change, the passage of time. Moving water and solid stone display the harmony of oppositions in nature—the fluidity and solidity inherent there. The sounds of wind-blown plants and running water, the dance of shadows and sunlight, and the contrast of empty space and occupied space imitate nature in its wholeness.

Stones, stone groupings, stepping stones, stone pavements, sand, stone lanterns, stone towers, stone Buddhas, signposts, bamboo watering troughs (both *tsukubai* and *shishi odoshi*), streams, waterfalls, stone or wood shore protections and bridges, bamboo fences, sleeve fences, gates, and walls are various elements used to infuse the Japanese garden with the state of nature. They are used to represent and imitate—to develop relationship.

There is no particular vista in a Japanese garden; rather, there are many views, each differing as the traveler passes through. Smaller gardens usually have one focal point and one theme that is developed; larger gardens may have many more. Subtlety prevails, clutter does not, as too much movement, too much color, too many forms give undue attention to the separate parts of the garden. It is the total effect—balance that suggests quietude and repose—that is sought.

When I enter a Japanese garden I see intricacy that is simple, simplicity that is profound. I feel spiritually invigorated, yet soothed in the soul. I feel at peace.

LESSON 51 ❦ September 3–9
Butterflies and Insects

If all mankind were to disappear, the world would regenerate back to the
rich state of equilibrium that existed ten thousand years ago. If insects were
to vanish, the environment would collapse into chaos.
—Edward O. Wilson (b. 1929)

Butterfly Attractors Bring Movement to Your Garden

I DON'T REMEMBER SEEING MANY butterflies when I was a child;
an occasional glimpse and chase were magical and excited anyone
nearby. I do remember thinking them lonesome creatures, finding solace from their solitude in the flowers they perched upon.
But you know, I lived in the city at a time when the norm was
manicured shrubs and lawns with little or no color, other than
spring-flowering trees and azaleas. The butterflies had nowhere to
propagate or eat. We did not invite them and their magnificent
movement into our lives. Furthermore, our neighborhood was
sprayed with DDT, or some such chemical, during the summer to
rid us of mosquitoes and, of course, that didn't help the butterfly
population either.

But things have changed. Rarely do I see a butterfly making a
solo flight. Instead, I witness masses of them, dancing in uncho-
reographed style above and around the tremendous assortment of
flowering plants that we now enjoy in our landscape.

Butterflies don't come to just any flower, yet their needs are
quite simple and specific, and you can create a habitat that will lure
them to your landscape.

- First, select a sunny spot for your butterfly attractors.
  In order to fly, butterflies need sun to keep their bodies
  warm—between 85°F and 100°F. If air temperatures

are cool, they will bask in the sun to warm themselves enough so they can take flight. The longer the sun shines on your plants, the better, since the males will have longer to mate and females longer to feed and lay eggs. Also, warmer habitats encourage more rapid development of eggs and caterpillars, perhaps resulting in more butterflies. Sun also increases the nectar production in flowers, the ultimate attraction for the butterflies, and larval host plants in ample sun produce more fresh leaves for the hungry, maturing caterpillars.

- Select a protected area for your butterfly garden, which will keep cooler winds from the butterflies, encouraging more flight. It will also keep them from having to expend too much energy fighting the wind currents. Warmer, protected areas are particularly beneficial during spring and fall when nighttime temperatures can become quite cool. They also help your flowers from becoming damaged, possibly extending blooming time.
- Introduce some nectaring plants to your garden, massing them together; the more you have, the more inviting they will be. Be sure to include enough variety so you will have something flowering throughout the blooming season. Use plants of varying heights since many smaller butterflies stay low while larger varieties prefer to be higher when they feed.
- Select nectaring plants from the many lists that you can now find in almost every gardening book. A few of my favorites are:
  - Butterfly bushes (large, woody, deciduous bushes)
  - Homestead purple verbena (a perennial in this area)
  - Zinnia (annual)
  - Chives (a tall perennial)
  - Coreopsis (perennial)
  - Pentas (annual)
  - Liatris (perennial)
  - Purple coneflower (perennial)

- Yarrow (perennial)
- Shasta daisy (perennial)
- Queen Anne's lace (perennial)
- Butterfly weed (perennial)
- Lantana (annuals in this area, although 'Miss Huff' and other newer varieties perform as a woody perennial—don't prune them in late fall or winter; otherwise, the hollow stems will collect water that will freeze, harming or killing the plant.)

IT'S A MATTER OF FACT

Some flowers and herbs release fragrances to attract insect and animal pollinators, but violets can't seem to make up their minds whether they want the visitors or not. Their scent (from the chemical ionone) is an intense sweetness that comes and goes from moment to moment.

The list goes on and on and includes annuals, perennials, wildflowers, shrubs, trees, and vines. When choosing butterfly attractors, remember that the brighter the color, the better; although butterflies can see the full spectrum of colors, they like yellows, oranges, purples, and reds the best. Also consider these pointers:

- Include some larval host plants that will support the eggs and caterpillars for the kinds of butterflies that frequent your garden. You'll know which ones because you will have observed them on your nectaring plants or because you will have checked various resources to discover their habitats. (And see the list below.) Scatter the host plants since predator birds will have a harder time searching out and destroying the caterpillars. You may prefer placing the plants in distant bordering areas since many are invasive wildflowers or relatively unattractive weeds and grasses. Also, tattered foliage from feeding caterpillars might be unsightly in the garden proper. Visit the Web site http://butterfliesandmoths.org. It's an excellent source for matching host and feeding plants with various butterflies and moths. You'll find that many ornamental plants do serve a host plants, such as:

- Artemesia
- Common buckeye
- Sunflower
- Pussy willow
- Weeping willow
- Smooth-leaved aster
- Black-eyed Susan
- Bluemist (hardy ageratum)
- Lance-leaved coreopsis (tickseed)
- Sweetbay magnolia
- Tulip poplar
- Lespedeza
- Wisteria
- Various oaks

- Provide water for your visitors at a regular site. Butterflies gather at "puddling places" such as sites along dirt roads where water accumulates and then evaporates, leaving moisture and a concentration of minerals and salts, which are important for mating and egg production. Just as deer and cows are attracted to salt licks, butterflies are attracted to animal scats and urination sites. You can create a puddling place, with added salt and nutrients, by filling a container with sand and aquarium gravel, keeping it very shallow. Add some mushroom compost to the gravel, then periodically sprinkle water over the feeding haven. Butterflies will hasten to the moist, but not wet, area with its flavorful, nutritious waste. Add some rocks on the periphery so your satisfied guests will have a place close by to bask in the sun.

- Do not use pesticides. Butterflies are insects; pesticides kill insects. There are lots of alternatives to chemical controls for pests you truly don't want. And besides, it's not really necessary for you to have a perfect garden. A chewed leaf here or there is part of the scene, a reminder

of the games at play, the balancing act constantly being
waged by Mother Nature. Don't try to destroy that dance.
It has its own beauty and is wrought with messages just
waiting for your attention.

PESTICIDES OR PREDATORS—YOUR PICK

LATE SUMMER EVENINGS IN ATLANTA during the 1950s and early
1960s were too-good-to-be-true times. Bike riding and roller
skating along the sidewalks occupied us until twilight drew over
our neighborhood. As dusk crept along, we played baseball and
kickball, until dark sent us home before the ghosts roamed. But
some of the most sultry evenings were spent languidly in the yard,
wiping sweat and watching for bats, hoping they wouldn't swoop
down and snatch our hair, scratching and giving us rabies.

I have since learned that bats are not the monsters of vampire
fame. They don't want to get tangled in our hair, and they rarely
carry rabies. They do, however, provide superior pesticide services,
pollinate flowers, and disperse seeds. Each bat eats an estimated
1,000–3,000 insects each night.

I still enjoy seeing bats and welcome them to our home, along
with the insect-eating martins that attack the water's surface of
our lake and convulse through the air above our fields. But I'm
concerned about these natural predators just as Rachel Carson was
when she wrote her influential 1962 book, *Silent Spring*. She con-
demned the use of synthetic, nonselective, persistent insecticides
and alerted us to the imminent peril of such use to our environment. But chemicals continue to pose a danger, as do many of
man's activities, particularly those that destroy habitats.

The recent dramatic decline in the honeybee population
(colony collapse disorder), threatening the pollination required
for our food, as well as for our ornamental plants, seems to be, in
the words of the band Spirit on their album *Twelve Dreams of Dr.
Sardonicus* (1970), "nature's way of telling [us] something's wrong."
So rather than using synthetic pesticides—which destroy the pests
along with the natural predators, and bees and butterflies—let
Mother Nature take care of things. It's amazing how good she is at
it. We can rely on bats, martins, and other predators as our natural
pesticides.

LESSON 52 ⌒ September 10–16
Magnolias

[B]ut what appears very extraordinary, is to behold here, depressed and degraded, the glorious pyramidal magnolia grandiflora, associated amongst these vile dwarfs, and even some of them rising above it, though not five feet high; yet still showing large, beautiful and expansive white fragrant blossoms, and great heavy cones, on slender procumbent branches, some even lying on the earth; the ravages of fire keep them down, as is evident from the vast excrescent tuberous roots, covering several feet of ground, from which these slender shoots spring.

—William Bartram (1739–1823)
*Travels through North & South Carolina, Georgia,
East & West Florida*

Magnificent Magnolias: Sweet Summer Smells, Planted in Fall

WE HAD BOTTOMLANDS ALONG one of the creeks at our Logan-ville farm. The area was tangled with flora and housed a bobcat or two, as well as a cougar whose screams I awoke to one morning while living in an RV during the construction of our log home. For nearly twenty-five years I walked around the almost swampy area but never ventured into it. Then its mysteries became so inviting to me, I insisted on some paths, which followed, as did a bench. It was a beautiful place. Tucked among the sweetgums and towering tulip poplars were sweetbay magnolias (*Magnolia virginiana*)—lots of them. They weren't particularly prominent, but their silver-backed leaves brought attention, especially when the wind blew. These magnolias are different from the ones most folks picture when thinking of the South, and which are discussed below, as they are deciduous, semievergreen to evergreen, and tolerate shade and wet areas. But they, and their fragrant flowers, are similarly pleasing.

E. H. "Chinese" Wilson, a renowned plant collector of the nineteenth century, called magnolias "aristocrats of ancient lineage possessed of many superlative qualities." Fossil remains from the Tertiary Period (2–65 million years ago) support the claim that the magnolia is the oldest of all the angiosperms (flowering plants).

Out of over 80 species of the Magnoliaceae family, it's the *Magnolia grandifloras* that grace the old homes of the South and lend their splendor to the Southern image. Also known as evergreen magnolia or bull bay, these giants reach heights of 60–80 feet and spreads of 30–50 feet. Their 5- to 10-inch-long leaves are lustrous, supplying the perfect backdrop for the syrupy sweet, heavenly fragranced, creamy white flowers.

Why on Earth, I can hear you saying, are you talking now about this tree that blooms and perfumes in late spring and summer? I could say that it's because of the fascinating, velvety cones that start rose-red and become shiny bright red as they split and reveal their seeds in the fall, but it's really because the best time to buy and plant *Magnolia grandiflora* is from August through October. Contrary to most literature that touts spring as the best time to plant them, many nurserypeople and landscapers have found that there is less leaf drop upon transplanting at this time of year. Nevertheless, do be prepared for leaf yellowing and drop the first year or so.

There are well over 150 cultivars of *Magnolia grandiflora*. Some have specific characteristics suitable for particular landscapes; a few that have proven to be the best in this area are as follows:

'**Claudia Wannamaker**': This cultivar has a medium-broad pyramidal shape and dark green leaves with medium rusty brown undersides and flowers at an early age.

'**Little Gem**': One of the smallest cultivars, its 4-inch leaves are a lustrous dark green with a bronzy brown underside. Flowers are 3–4 inches and bloom very young and continually throughout spring, summer, and fall. It is a 2000 Georgia Gold Medal winner.

'**D.D. Blanchard**': This variety is pyramidal to 50 feet or more but is more open than 'Claudia Wannamaker'. Its leaves are unique with lustrous dark green faces and rich orangish brown undersides.

'Coco': Also pyramidal, 'Coco' has lustrous dark green leaves as well as heavy flowering over a long period of time.

Greenback™ ('Mgtig'): This fairly recent introduction is dense and tightly branched. Its lustrous, waxy dark green leaves are long and cupped and are highly reflective on a sunny day.

'Brackens Brown Beauty': A very full, relatively compact and dense form, this magnolia has undulating leaves that are small (about 6 inches long), with leathery, lustrous dark green above and rusty brown underneath. Its flowers are 5–6 inches across, with 2- to 3-inch fruits. This is a very cold-hardy cultivar that was introduced at another nursery close to me. I remember going there in the mid-1980s and being struck by the rows upon rows of clonish-looking magnolias that stamped the landscape.

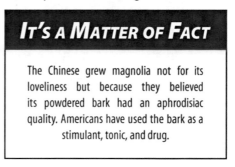

IT'S A MATTER OF FACT

The Chinese grew magnolia not for its loveliness but because they believed its powdered bark had an aphrodisiac quality. Americans have used the bark as a stimulant, tonic, and drug.

Teddy Bear® ('Southern Charm'): A new introduction, this magnolia is superb with its dense, compact, upright, pyramidal form. It is heat, humidity, and drought tolerant and has an eye-catching presence.

These six magnolias are cultivars, *cultivated varieties*, and are different from unimproved, uncultivated "seedlings" in nomenclature, characteristics, and trait reliability. If you buy and plant 'Little Gem' magnolias, you will have trees that are virtually identical in height, breadth, flowering time, leaf color, and habit—refined, but somewhat short on variation. If, on the other hand, you purchase seedling magnolias, you will have more natural looking plants. The trees will all have similar characteristics, but the variations in height, flower production, etc., will be less than uniform. The broad avenues of magnolias of *Gone With the Wind* lore, for example, are seedlings.

Magnolia grandiflora 'Symmes Select' is a cultivar. Cultivars are plants propagated in cultivation that have clear distinctions in some

John planted about 300 Claudia Wannamaker magnolias in the early 1990s. The two rows of them shown on the right had been in the ground about three years when this photo was taken.

traits—physiology, cytology, chemistry, morphology, etc.—from the traits of other varieties of the same genus and that retain these characteristics when reproduced by appropriate means, i.e., sexually (by seed) or asexually (by vegetative propagation). Cultivars receive a name under the *International Code of Nomenclature for Cultivated Plants* from the International Cultivar Registration Authority. (See also Lesson 11 about plant names.)

Although cultivars can be reproduced by seed, the process must take place in a perfect, sterile environment, where pure pollination can occur. Because this situation is difficult to achieve, most nurseries reproduce cultivars of trees, shrubs, and perennials by vegetative means—cuttings, divisions, grafting, or tissue culture—which is the safest way to assure the purity of the offspring. Tissue culture is commonly used for magnolias and is the most perfect form of genetic continuity. One parent is used to produce a host of clones that are identical to it and to each other.

When you purchase a *Magnolia grandiflora* 'Little Gem', you are relying on the integrity of the chain of growers and distributors who have brought that plant to market that it is "true-to-type"—that is has been bred under conditions assuring its genetic purity. When you purchase a plant called simply *Magnolia grandiflora*, you are probably purchasing a seedling—one that is grown from seed under conditions that have not assured genetic purity.

If you're confused, don't be; plantspeople tend to confuse themselves. The terms *variety* and *cultivar* are often used interchangeably in the plant world. (However, a variety is actually a plant that occurs outside of cultivation with unique characteristics. It is designated with the term var. in the botanical name.) So feel free to do the same. Just understand that you should expect consistent characteristics if you purchase a plant that is marked as a cultivar (usually indicated by single quotes around the last part of the botanical name), and you should not if it is called a seedling or lacks the cultivar designation. In any case, if you just use the generic, layman's term "variety" when referring to different kinds of plants in the same species, you'll communicate just fine. And if a specific variety is not available, in many instances there's a substitute—by way of a very close cousin—that will suit you.

In all species of plants, the number of cultivars has proliferated with the introduction of new scientific research and methods, enhancing our landscape and providing uniformity where form and balance suggest the need. More important, they have provided us with improved characteristics—larger flowers, brighter colors, more lustrous leaves, more cold hardiness, more disease resistance, greater drought tolerance, and the like. And just as the seemingly inexhaustible number of flavors of sodas sustains the beverage industry, the continuous creation of new cultivars helps the plant industry.

I think the cultivar magnolias are beautiful, but I still find unique character in the unimproved seedlings. They have a place in our landscape and should not be overlooked. Compare the qualities of a seedling magnolia with those of the many cultivars and decide what suits you and what will best suit your landscape. Decide also what your pocketbook will handle—seedlings are cheaper than cultivars. Perhaps the Scarlet in you will pick Tara after all.

BUT FOR THE PLANT HUNTERS

SOME MAGNOLIAS ARE INDIGENOUS to China. Their native habitat was the destination of many plant hunters in the 1800s. Some returned with the seeds or seedlings of this magnificent specimen. Ernest Henry "Chinese" Wilson, the most prolific of the plant hunters, included several magnolia varieties in his plant introductions.

Wilson first visited China in 1899 at the behest of James Veitch & Sons, part of the Vietch dynasty and predominant force in the British nursery trade. The Veitches dispatched twenty-two plant hunters to search for and collect plants exclusively for their nurseries. The impact on horticulture of the Veitches' forethought is unparalleled, Wilson's contribution supreme.

Wilson, who was sent to find the handkerchief, or dove tree (*Davidia involucrata*), met Augustine Henry, who gave him a crude map covering 20,000 square miles in China with a mark indicating the location of such a tree. Wilson and his entourage journeyed upriver and through the hills near Badong and found their treasure—a stump of the "X'd" tree next to a newly constructed home.

Not to be defeated, Wilson continued his search and later found another handkerchief tree, along with hundreds of other indigenous trees, shrubs, and herbaceous plants. He also found, on his return to England, that another plant hunter, Paul Guillaume Farges, had already brought seed of the treasured tree to France in 1897 and germinated it, earning the right to use the coveted epithet "introduced by."

Wilson returned to China three more times, once for Veitch and twice for Charles Sargent and the Arnold Arboretum of Harvard University. His mission changed from one of commercialism to one of botany and the furtherance of the knowledge of woody plants. Disappointments and hardships continued to plague his journeys, however. He became ill with malaria, and then his boat was disabled, delaying the start of one trip. Another time, over 18,000 lily bulbs packed without a clay coating rotted en route to the United States, necessitating another regal lily hunt, which ended abruptly when Wilson suffered a broken leg from a rock slide and endured a train of mules passing over him as he lay injured. However, his team successfully gathered up the lily bulbs they had found before the accident and shipped them to the United States.

Wilson ended his hunting career with trips to Japan and Korea. He left an incredible legacy of over 1,000 plant introductions, tens of thousands of herbarium specimens, thousands of packets of seeds, botanical writings, and photographs. His introductions include the Kurume azaleas and Kousa dogwood commonly found in our Southern landscape.

They may not have our *Magnolia grandifloras* in Massachusetts, but they do have weeds, grass, and things needing tending in the yard. James and Cat help Gram (John's mother) during a visit in August, 1990. Thus so, the lessons are taught, the generations continue, and the circle of life keeps on, uninterrupted.

CONCLUSION

ACTUALLY, THERE IS NOTHING TO CONCLUDE—we have come full circle, and all simply continues. And that is what I hope you will do—continue through the cycles. Go through this book again; you may get more out of it the second time around since you'll have a better picture of the whole and be able to grow upon what you've learned this past year. Remember, change takes time.

I have given you lots of information to digest, although I have tried to give it to you in small enough bites to allow for better absorption. Several themes emerged that I would like to summarize for you:

- Think ahead and plan before you do.
- Know that there is a mind-boggling array of plants from which to choose.
- Know that in selecting a wide variety of plants, you decrease sameness in the landscape and increase its pleasantness.
- Know if your plant selection needs sun, shade, or something in-between.
- Know the mature size of your plant selection.
- Plant in beds, rather than single holes, if at all possible and practical.
- Always prepare your beds thoroughly.
- Compost and use it.
- Mulch around plantings.
- Minimize your lawn.
- Be mindful of using invasive plants.
- Create an easy-maintenance garden.
- Xeriscape, using water-saving techniques.
- Water more deeply, less often.

- Be proactive and prevent problems before they occur.
- Use chemicals sparingly, if at all.
- Use your local Cooperative Extension Service for information, testing, and diagnosis, when appropriate.
- Use books and the Web to get beyond the basics.
- Talk to plantspeople—neighbors, nurserymen, horticulturists, Cooperative Extensive Service agents, Master Gardeners.
- Be flexible and evolve with your yard.
- Be prudent and do a little at a time, but do it.
- Be patient; growth takes time.
- Be connected; think about the consequences of your activities.
- Breathe. Touch. Smell. Listen. Look. Feel.
- Enjoy the journey.
- Enjoy the moment.
- Embrace your entire landscape.

> *A generation goes, and a generation comes,*
> *But the earth remains forever.*
> *The sun rises and the sun goes down,*
> *And hastens to the place where it rises.*
> *The wind blows to the south,*
> *And goes round to the north;*
> *Round and round goes the wind,*
> *And on its circuits the wind returns.*
> *All streams run to the sea,*
> *But the sea is not full;*
> *To the place where the streams flow,*
> *There they flow again.*
> —Ecclesiastes 1:4-7

BIBLIOGRAPHY

SELECTED WRITINGS AND WEB SITES THAT PROVIDED
INFORMATION OR INSPIRATION FOR THIS BOOK

Ackerman, Diane. *A Natural History of the Senses*. New York: Random House, 1990.

————. *Cultivating Delight: A Natural History of My Garden*. New York: HarperCollins, 2001.

Aden, Paul. *The Hosta Book*. 2d edition. Portland, OR: Timber Press, 1988, 1998.

Alexander, Taylor R., R. Will Burnett, and Herbert S. Zim. *Botany*. New York: Western Publishing Company, 1970.

Altea, Rosemary. *Proud Spirit: Lessons, Insights & Healing from "The Voice of the Spirit World."* New York: William Morrow, 1997.

Armitage, Allan M. *Allan Armitage on Perennials*. New York: Prentice Hall Gardening, 1993.

Armitage, Allan M. *Allan Armitage on Perennials*. New York: Prentice Hall Gardening, 1993.

————. *Armitage's Garden Perennials: A Color Encyclopedia*. Portland, OR: Timber Press, 2000.

————. *Armitage's Native Plants for North American Gardens*. Portland, OR: Timber Press, 2006.

————. *Herbaceous Perennial Plants: A Treatise on Their Identification, Culture, and Garden Attributes*. Athens, GA: Varsity Press, 1989.

Aronovitz, Avis Y., and Brencie Werner. *Gardening 'Round Atlanta: The best plants for Atlanta . . . and more*. Atlanta, GA: Eldorado Publishers, 1996.

Atkinson, Brooks, ed. *The Essential Writings of Ralph Waldo Emerson*. New York: The Modern Library, 2000.

Bales, Suzanne Frutig. *Vines*. New York: Macmillan, 1995.

Bartram, William. *Travels through North & South Carolina, Georgia, East & West Florida*. (New York: Penguin Books, 1988) 1791.

Bender, Steve, ed. *The Southern Living Garden Book*. Birmingham, AL: Oxmoor House, 1998.

Berry, Wendell. *Another Turn of the Crank: Essays by Wendell Berry*. Washington, D.C.: Counterpoint, 1995.

———. *The Gift of Good Land: Further Essays Cultural and Agricultural*. New York: North Point Press, 1982.

———. *Sex, Economy, Freedom & Community: Eight Essays*. New York: Pantheon Books, 1992, 1993.

Botkin, Daniel, et al. *Forces of Change: A New View of Nature*. Washington, D.C.: National Geographic Society, 2000.

Bowman, Daria Price. *For Your Garden: Paths and Walkways*. New York: Friedman/Fairfax Publishers, 1997.

———. *Hydrangeas*. New York: Friedman/Fairfax Publishers, 1999.

Breathnach, Sarah Ban. *Simple Abundance: A Daybook of Comfort and Joy*. New York: Warner Books, 1995.

Capon, Brian. *Botany for Gardeners*. Rev'd ed. Portland, OR: Timber Press, 2005.

Carson, Rachel. *The Sense of Wonder*. Berkeley, CA: The Nature Company, 1956, 1990.

———. *Silent Spring*. New York: Houghton Mifflin Company, 1962.

Copeland, Linda L., and Allan M. Armitage. *Legends in the Garden: Who in the World Is Nellie Stevens?* Atlanta, GA: Wings Publishers, 2001.

Dallmeyer, Dorinda G., ed. *Elemental South: An Anthology of Southern Nature Writers*. Athens: The University of Georgia Press, 2004.

Dean, Bradley P., ed. *Wild Fruits: Thoreau's Rediscovered Last Manuscript*. New York: W. W. Norton, 2000.

DeGraaf, Richard M. *Trees, Shrubs, and Vines for Attracting Birds*. 2d ed. rev. Hanover, NH: University Press of New England, 2002.

Dennis, Jerry. *It's Raining Frogs and Fishes: Four Seasons of Natural Phenomena and Oddities of the Sky*. New York: HarperPerennial Publishers, 1992.

Dirr, Michael A. *Hydrangeas for American Gardens*. Portland, OR: Timber Press, 2004.

———. *Manual of Woody Landscape Plants: Their Identification, Ornamental Characteristics, Culture, Propagation and Uses*. 5th ed. Champaign, IL: Stipes, 1998.

Duncan, David Ewing. *Calendar: Humanity's Epic Struggle to Determine a True and Accurate Year*. New York: Avon Books, 1998.

Elliott, Charles, ed. *The Quotable Gardener*. Guilford, CT: The Lyons Press, 1999, 2002.

Exley, Helen. *Flowers: A Celebration in Words and Paintings*. New York: Exley Giftbooks, 1992.

Farb, Peter. *The Forest*. New York: Time-Life Books, 1970.

Fearnley-Whittingstall, Jane. *Ivies*. New York: Random House, 1992.

Feltwell, John. *A Creative Step-by-Step Guide to Climbers and Trellis Plants*. North Vancouver, Canada: Whitecap Books, 1996.

Ferree, M. E. "Butch," ed. *The Georgia Master Gardener Handbook*. 4th edition. Athens: The University of Georgia and Georgia Cooperative Extension Service, 1993.

Frome, Michael. *Strangers in High Places: The Story of the Great Smoky Mountains*. Garden City, NY: Doubleday, 1966.

Galle, Fred C. *Azaleas*. Portland, OR: Timber Press, 1987, 1995.

———. *Hollies: The Genus* Ilex. Portland, OR: Timber Press, 1997.

Gardiner, James M. *Magnolias*. Chester, CT: The Globe Pequot Press, 1989.

Gardner, Jason. *The Sacred Earth: Writers on Nature & Spirit*. Novato, CA: New World Library, 1998.

Greenlee, John, and Derek Fell. *The Encyclopedia of Ornamental Grasses: How to Grow and Use Over 250 Beautiful and Versatile Plants*. Emmaus, PA: Rodale Press, 1992.

Hall, Charles R., Alan W. Hodges, and John J. Haydu. "Economic Impacts of the Green Industry in the United States." 2005. http://www.utextension.utk.edu/hbin/greenimpact.html.

Hayden, Tom. *The Lost Gospel of the Earth: A Call for Renewing Nature, Spirit, and Politics*. San Francisco, CA: Sierra Club Books, 1996.

Heilmeyer, Marina. *The Language of Flowers: Symbols and Myths*. New York: Prestel Verlag, 2001.

Heinrich, Bernd. *The Trees in My Forest.* New York: HarperCollins, 1998.

Hifler, Joyce Sequichie. *A Cherokee Feast of Days.* Vol. 2. Tulsa, OK: Council Oak Publishing, 1996.

Hill, Lewis, and Nancy Hill. *Daylilies: The Perfect Perennial.* North Adams, MA: Storey Communications, 1991.

Hogan, Linda, and Brenda Peterson, eds. *The Sweet Breathing of Plants: Women Writing on the Green World.* New York: North Point Press, 2001.

Homan, Tim, ed. *A Yearning Toward Wildness: Environmental Quotations from the Writings of Henry David Thoreau.* Atlanta, GA: Peachtree Publishers, 1991.

Howell, Patricia Kyritsi. *Medicinal Plants of the Southern Appalachians.* Mountain City, GA: BotanoLogos Books, 2006.

Hughes, Holly, and Mark Weakley. *Meditations on the Earth: A Book of Quotations, Poetry, and Prose.* Berkeley, CA: The Nature Company, 1994.

Huxley, Anthony. *Green Inheritance: The World Wildlife Fund Book of Plants.* London: Gaia Books, 1992.

Jerome, Kate, Meegan McCarthy-Bilow, and Wanda Supanich. *Indoor Gardening.* New York: Pantheon Books, Knopf, 1995.

Jones, Alison. *Larousse Dictionary of World Folklore: A Remarkable Guide to the Hidden History of Humankind.* New York: Larousse, 1995.

Katz, Cathie. *Nature a Day at a Time: An Uncommon Look at Common Wildlife.* San Francisco, CA: Sierra Club Books, 2000.

Koch, Maryjo. *Seed Leaf Flower Fruit.* San Francisco, CA: Collins Publishers, 1995.

Kunstler, James Howard. *The Geography of Nowhere: The Rise and Decline of America's Man-Made Landscape.* New York: Simon and Schuster, 1993.

Lawson-Hall, Toni, and Brian Rothera. *Hydrangeas: A Gardener's Guide.* Portland, OR: Timber Press, 1995.

Loewer, Peter. *Ornamental Grasses.* Des Moines, IA: Meredith Books, 1995.

Logan, William Bryant. *The Tool Book.* New York: Workman Publishing, 1997.

Long, Kim. *The Moon Book.* Boulder, CO: Johnson Publishing, 1998.

Martin, Deborah L., and Grace Gershuny, eds. *The Rodale Book of Composting.* Emmaus, PA: Rodale Press, 1992.

Matthews, John. *The Winter Solstice: The Sacred Traditions of Christmas.* Wheaton, IL: Theosophical Publishing, 1998.

McDowell, Christopher Forrest, and Clark-McDowell, Tricia. *The Sanctuary Garden: Creating a Place of Refuge in Your Yard or Garden.* New York: Simon and Schuster, 1998.

Musgrave, Toby, et al. *The Plant Hunters: Two Hundred Years of Adventure and Discovery around the World.* London: Ward Lock, 1998.

Odum, Martha, and Eugene P. Odum. *Essence of Place.* Athens: Georgia Museum of Art, University of Georgia, 2000.

Ortho's Guide to Successful Houseplants. San Ramon, CA: Ortho Books, 1994.

Paths and Paving. New York: DK Publishing, 1999.

Perl, Philip et al. *Ferns.* Alexandria, VA: Time-Life Books, 1977.

Pollan, Michael. *The Botany of Desire: A Plant's-Eye View of the World.* New York: Random House, 2001.

———. *The Omnivore's Dilemma: A Natural History of Four Meals.* New York: Penguin, 2006.

———. *Second Nature: A Gardener's Education.* New York: Dell Publishing, 1991.

Quinn, Daniel. *Ishmael: An Adventure of the Mind and Spirit.* New York: Bantam Books, 1992.

Ray, Janisse. *Ecology of a Cracker Childhood.* Minneapolis, MN: Milkweed Editions, 1999.

Reeves, Walter, and Erica Glasener. *Month-by-Month Gardening in Georgia.* Franklin, TN: Cool Springs Press, 2001.

Richards, E. G. *Mapping Time: The Calendar and Its History.* 1998. New York: Oxford University Press, 1998.

Robinson, Peter. *American Horticultural Society Complete Guide to Water Gardening.* New York: DK Publishing, 1997.

Schneider, Peter, ed. *Taylor's Guide to Roses.* Rev'd ed. Boston: Houghton Mifflin Company, 1995.

Schultz, Warren. *For Your Garden: Arbors and Trellises*. New York: Friedman/Fairfax Publishers, 1995.

————. *For Your Garden: Pots and Containers*. New York: Friedman/Fairfax Publishers, 1996.

Seike, Kiyoshi, and Kudo, Masanobu. *A Japanese Touch for Your Garden*. New York: Kodansha International, 1992.

Sheldrake, Rupert. *The Rebirth of Nature: The Greening of Science and God*. Rochester, VT: Park Street Press, 1994.

Solbrig, Otto T., and Dorothy J. Solbrig. *So Shall You Reap: Farming and Crops in Human Affairs*. Washington, D.C.: Island Press, 1994.

Stern, William. *Plant Names Explained: Botanical Terms and their Meaning*. Boston, MA: Horticulture Publications, 2005.

Stokes, Donald, and Lillian Stokes. *The Butterfly Book: An Easy Guide to Butterfly Gardening, Identification, and Behavior*. Boston, MA: Little, Brown and Company, 1991.

————. *The Wildflower Book: East of the Rockies—An Easy Guide To Growing and Identifying Wildflowers*. Boston, MA: Little, Brown and Company, 1992.

Tekiela, Stan. *Birds of Georgia: Field Guide*. Cambridge, MN: Adventure Publications, 2002.

Thoreau, Henry David. *Walden and Other Writings*. ed. Joseph Wood Krutch. New York: Bantam Dell, 1962.

Toogood, Alan, ed. *Plant Propagation*. New York: DK Publishing, 1999.

Vertrees, J. D. *Japanese Maples*. 2d ed. Portland, OR: Timber Press, 1987.

Vitale, Alice Thoms. *Leaves: In Myth, Magic, & Medicine*. New York: Stewart, Tabori and Chang, 1997.

Watson, Lillian Eichler, ed. *Light from Many Lamps*. New York: Stewart, Tabori and Chang, 1951.

Welch, William C., and Grant, Greg. *The Southern Heirloom Garden*. Dallas, TX: Taylor Publishing. 1995.

Wells, Diana. *100 Flowers and How They Got Their Names*. Chapel Hill, NC: Algonquin Books, 1997.

Whitehead, Emma Chloe Adams. *The Adams Family: James Adams Line, 1795–1982*. Franklin Springs, GA: Advocate Press, 1983.

Wilkins, Malcolm. *Plantwatching: How Plants Remember, Tell Time, Form Partnerships and More*. New York: Facts on File Publications, 1988.

Wilson, Charles Reagan, and William Ferris. *Encyclopedia of Southern Culture.* Chapel Hill, NC: The University of North Carolina Press, 1989.

Wilson, Edward O. *The Future of Life.* New York: Alfred A. Knopf, 2002.

Ziff, Larzer, ed. *Ralph Waldo Emerson: Selected Essays.* New York: Penguin Books, 1985.

WEB SITES

Below, I have listed Web sites that were of particular assistance to me or that I think will be sites of interest to you for exploration. Since the Web is replete with sites concerning plants, gardening, the environment, and nature in general, a simple search for whatever word, phrase, idea, or subject you desire will land you a wealth of information. However, remember to exercise caution in your reliance on the information you find, paying careful attention to its source. And, in the plant world, one must always be aware of the varying plant names, cultural requirements, growing habits, climatic factors, and other attributes that depend upon place. Pay attention to the location of the site source, as the information most likely lends itself to that area.

http://www.all-americaselections.org/

For a list of the All American Selections winners—those flowers and vegetables that have been tested and judged to have superior performance—1933 to the present (with images for those from 1989 to present).

http://www.almanac.com/

For *The Old Farmer's Almanac* information that helps keep you attuned to the rhymes and rhythms of nature.

http://www.arborday.org/

For all there is to know about Arbor Day, dates of observation, tree resources, seminars, and essentially all you might want to link to regarding activities on behalf of trees.

http://www.butterfliesandmoths.org/

For a comprehensive listing, picturing, mapping, and detailing of butterfly and moth characteristics, habitats, host and food plants, and conservation status, all of which can be accessed by state.

http://www.caes.uga.edu/departments/hort/extension/goldmedal/
For descriptions and pictures of the Georgia Gold Medal plants from 1994 to date.

http://www.caes.uga.edu/departments/hort/extension/mastergardener/
For information about the Georgia Cooperative Extension Service volunteer program as well as numerous links to botanical gardens and other resources.

http://www.caes.uga.edu/extension/
For general information about and local contacts for the University of Georgia Cooperative Extension Service and a gateway to a wealth of gardening information.

http://www.caes.uga.edu/publications/subject_list.html
For an expansive list of online publications on all facets of agriculture, horticulture, and the environment.

http://www.gainvasives.org/
For a comprehensive site on species (plant, animal, and pathogens) of concern in Georgia. Developed as part of the Georgia Cooperative Agricultural Pest Survey Program.

http://www.gardendigest.com/
For a little of everything—from gardening history to gardening inspiration.

http://www.georgiaencyclopedia.org/nge/Home.jsp
For a vast collection of articles covering every aspect of Georgia, its history, culture, industry, politics, resources, etc.

http://www.georgiaorganics.org/
For information about organic growing in Georgia as well as educational resources and events.

http://www.gfc.state.ga.us/
For a wealth of information about forestry, trees, and environmental issues as well as links to many sites with similar subjects.

http://www.invasive.org/
For detailed information, lists, reports, etc., about invasive species.

http://www.joegardener.com/
For gardening advice of all kinds, with particular attention to eco-friendly ideas.

http://www.PinebushNursery.com/
For a look at our nursery, Pinebush Farm and Nurseries, Inc.,

some gardening tips, pictures, plant descriptions, other useful information, and some recent *The Leaflet* gardening publications.

http://www.plantexplorers.com/
For a marvelous exploration of the history of plant discovery, those involved in it, and numerous wanderings to other plant-related information.

http://www.plants.usda.gov/
For a comprehensive list of plants (with their pictures, characteristics, and classifications) found across the United States, with various search vehicles.

http://www.usna.usda.gov/
For the United States National Arboretum. The site is full of information, with state links. It has a good summary about invasive plants, including examples of the degrees of invasiveness and how one should think about certain plants.

http://www.usna.usda.gov/Hardzone/
For the USDA plant hardiness zone map and helpful information about how the zones are determined and other factors that affect plant hardiness.

http://www.walterreeves.com/
For a little advice on just about everything for your garden, including events, a seasonal calendar, and tons of links.

INDEX

Bolded page numbers indicate a definition.

Cornus florida (flowering dogwood), 114, 179–182
  anthracnose, 180
  destruction of, 181
  grafted, 180
  pruning, 142
Cornus kousa (kousa dogwood), 180, 325
Cortaderia selloana (pampass grass), 131
  'Pumila', 131
Corylus avellana 'Contorta', 178
Cotinus coggygria, 178
cows, 188
crabapple. See *Malus*
crape murder, 144, 289
crapemyrtle. See *Lagerstroemia indica*
  various cultivars. See *Lagerstromia indica*
creeping Jenny, 283
creeping raspberry. See *Rubus pentalobus*
  syn. *R. calycinoides*
crepe myrtle. *See* crapemyrtle
crested iris (*Iris cristata*), 202
'Crimson Queen' Japanese maple, 311
crocus, 52
crop rotation, 212
Crusaders and spice trade, 192
Cryopteris erythrosora (autumn fern), 45, 283
Cryptomeria japonica (Japanese cedar)
  conifer, as, 148
  hedge, 166
  pruning, 143
  'Yoshino', 44, 151
cultivar, **74**, **322**, 321–23
  naming, 74–76
  reproduction of by man, 58–60
cultivating, tools for, 97
cultivation. *See various plants*
cultural requirements. *See various plants*
Cuphea spp., 234
Cupressocyparis leylandii (Leyland cypress), 86
  bot canker, 151
  diseases, 151
  pruning of, 143
  for screening, 151, 166
Cupressus arizonica (Arizona cypress)
  'Carolina Sapphire', 86, 151
  hedge, 166
cutting back, **140**
cutting tools, history of, 141
cuttings
  for indoor plant propagation, 68
  for reproduction, 59, 322
  of UGA privet hedge, 220
cycles of nature
  time and, 106–08
cyme, 182
Dad (Godwin), 70, 72, 147, 214, 217, 284, 285

daffodils, 50–51, 54–55
Davidia involucrata, 324
day, calendar, 107
"day-neutral" plants, 235
daylily. See *Hemerocallis fulva*
daylily chromosomes, 259
deadheading, **16**
  hydrangeas, 144
  lantana, 231
  Lady in Red salvia, 231
  perennials, 250
  roses, 137
  zinnias, 16
deciduous, **89**
deer
  and anise hyssop hybrids, 46
  and Lenten rose, 123
  and pink muhly grass, 132
  salt licks and butterflies, 317
deodar cedar, 86
dianthus, 29,
  and butterflies, 29
  and hummingbirds, 29
  as ground cover, 283
Dianthus barbatus 'Amazon' series, 29, 234
Dianthus gratianopolitans
  'Bath's Pink', 43, 282
  'Firewitch', 282
Dianthus plumarius
  'Mountain Mist', 282
  'Vanilla', 282
dibble, 97, 284
dioecious plants, **182**
Dionysus, 100
diploid, **259**
Dirr, Michael A.
  abelia, 20
  'Alice' hydrangea, 239
  breadth of plant material, 177
  'Chantilly Lace' hydrangea, 239
  on crapemyrtles, 287
  on deodar cedar, 86
  Hightower® Willow Oak, 300
  on hydrangeas, 236, 238
  Hydrangeas for American Gardens, 238
  'Lady in Red' hydrangea, 238
  Manual of Woody Landscape Plants, 177
  Mini Penny™ hydrangea, 238
  Plant Introductions, 238
Discula destructive, 180
dissectum, **309**
dissectum Japanese maples. See *Acer palmatum dissectum*
dividing perennials, 56–58
divisions, **25**, 55, 57, 197, 200, 322
  planting, 204–5
Doctrine of Signatures, 228
Dodd, Tom III, 159

Orahood, Louise, 134, 135, 138
orange, 205–6
organic agriculture, 212
organic gardening, 207, 212
organic matter
  as amendment, 35
  composting, 35–36
  to correct drainage, 37
  decomposition of, 29
  humus, 35, 273
  mulches, 129
  and nitrogen, 40, 57
  and organic agriculture, 212
  to restore balance, 40
  See also mushroom compost
ornamental gardening, 207
ornamental grasses, 48, 130–33
ornamental sweet potato, 232–33
'Oshio Beni' Japanese maple, 311
Osiris, 99
Osmanthus fragrans (fragrant tea olive), 88, 219, 221
  pruning, 143
osmosis, 11, 12, 68
osmotic process, 11, 68
  See also osmosis
overcup oak. See *Quercus lyrata*
own-root roses, 138–39, 296
oxygen
  plant and animal interchange, 12, 228
  and clay soil, 194
  and composting, 36
  and water gardens, 276
oxygenators, 276, 279
Pachysandra terminalis, 282
paean, 216
Paeon, 216
pampas grass. See *Cortaderia selloana*
Pan, 101
panicle hydranges. See *Hydrangea paniculata*
panicle, **131**, 182, **239**
pansies, 28, 219
pantheist, 156
patent. *See* plant patent
paths, 303–7
PPAF, **75**
Paul Ecke Ranch, 83
PDSI, 75
peaches, history of, 266
peat moss, 156
pecan trees, 273
pecans, 73
pectin, 49
pedicle, 182
perfect flower, **182**
Pennisetum alopecuroides (fountain grass), 131–32

Pennisetum setaceum 'Rubrum' (purple fountain grass), 132, 220, 222
pentas, 232, 315
Pentas lanceolata 'Nova', 232
peonies, 216–17
percolation, 37
perennial plumbago. See *Ceratostigma plumbaginoides*
perennials, **18**, 56, **200**–205
  and bulbs, 53–54
  dividing, 56–58
  fall-flowering, 18
  herbaceous, **200**
  planting, 197
  shade-loving, 201–202
  sun-loving, 202–204
  vines, 295–96
periwinkle, 281
pesticides, 318
  and balance, 40
  and bees, 318
  and butterflies, 317–18
  and insects, 318
  and lawns, 187
  and monocultures, 153
  and native plants, 196
  and roses, 137
  and xeriscaping, 129
Peter Pan, 101
petrichor, 128
petunias, 17, 230–31
  and hummingbirds, 118
  Petunia × *hybrida*, 17, 230
  'Purple Wave', 23–31, 230
  Wave® varieties, 17, 230, 231
pH, **37**, 38, 39
  and bed preparation, 194, 195
  and hydrangea color, 236–37
  soil testing, 210
phloem, **302**
phosphorus
  correcting deficiencies, 40, 41
  in soil and fertilizer, 38
  signs of deficiencies, 41
  testing soil, 210
photosynthesis, 11, 182
  and guttation, 67
photosynthetic process, 10
phototropism, **66**
Phytophthora ramorum, 301
picks, 97
pin oak. See *Quercus palustris*
pinching, 140
pine plantations, 147, 150, 151–53
pines, 147, 148
  and ethanol, 152
  needles, 89
  and paper, 152

Printed in the United States
215202BV00002B/2/P